ROYAL MAIL
COACHES

AN ILLUSTRATED HISTORY

ROYAL MAIL
COACHES

AN ILLUSTRATED HISTORY

FREDERICK WILKINSON

TEMPUS

*To my late wife Teresa and daughter Joanna as a token
of my love and admiration*

First published 2007

Tempus Publishing Limited
The Mill, Brimscombe Port,
Stroud, Gloucestershire, GL5 2QG
www.tempus-publishing.com

© Frederick Wilkinson, 2007

The right of Frederick Wilkinson to be identified as the Author
of this work has been asserted in accordance with the
Copyrights, Designs and Patents Act 1988.

British Library Cataloguing in Publication Data.
A catalogue record for this book is available from the British Library.

ISBN 978 0 7524 4212 9

Typesetting and origination by Tempus Publishing Limited
Printed in Great Britain

CONTENTS

	Acknowledgements	6
	Introduction	7
	Notes on the Text	10
1	The Early Post Office	13
2	Palmer and the Post Office	22
3	The Guards	55
4	The Guard's Gear	92
5	Guarding the Horse Mails	130
6	The Journey	144
7	The Roads	178
8	The Coach	200
9	The End of the Road – The Coming of the Railway	234
10	Royal Mail Firearms	245
	End Notes	253
	Appendices	269
	Bibliography	282
	Index	284

ACKNOWLEDGEMENTS

Over the several years spent researching this book I have been most impressed with the staff of the Heritage Archives. They have dealt with a steady stream of requests for documents, maps, books and pictures in a most cheerful, professional and helpful way. They made every effort to point out other sources and contacts and showed a genuine interest in the work. The old cliché is really true in this case, for without their help the book would have been far less extensive. It has been a pleasure and a privilege to work with them, they have now become friends.

Thanks are also due to the staff of the Postal Museum, Green Street, Bath. They were most helpful and were more than ready to provide material for use in the book. Thank you. I would also like to record my sincere appreciation to the many friends and colleagues who have patiently listened and made helpful comments.

Most of the praise and thanks must go to my late wife Teresa. She encouraged the work and despite illness cheerfully suffered my frequent absences whilst researching and, on so many occasions, listened to my latest titbit of postal history or soothed my frustration when an answer could not be found. She read parts of the manuscript and made many practical suggestions. Her unselfish support and encouragement were outstanding, this book is dedicated to her memory with all my love and sincere thanks for everything.

INTRODUCTION

THE ROYAL MAIL COACHES

Although they were operational for little more than sixty years, the Royal Mail coaches left behind an indelible romantic memory. Surely no Christmas would be complete without some cards showing a red mail coach with cheerful, festive passengers, trotting through a snow-covered landscape. In fact, journeys on the coaches were probably seldom the happy-go-lucky events depicted on the cards. The seating inside the coach was hardly luxurious and for the driver, guard and passengers perched outside on the roof, the journey was most likely to be uncomfortable and, on occasion, dangerous.

Leaving aside the sentimental romance, the story of the mail coach period is fascinating. The Post Office of the late eighteenth century was an extensive enterprise employing a large number of people, including many women, for there seems to have been little gender conflict in this particular service. Women were employed as 'Deputy Postmasters' as well as being given contracts to supply materials or services, and in the event of the death of the supplier the widow was usually allowed to continue the contract. However, despite tolerance in some fields, the Postmaster General stoutly upheld the tradition that the Post Office should not employ married women. All attempts to persuade the service otherwise failed, as is demonstrated in correspondence of July 1795 when an ailing Military Officer pleaded that his wife might become Deputy Postmistress as they had no other income.[1] The Postmaster General repeated that their established policy was to not employ married women. There were a few other general restrictions, such as age limits, although these often seem to have been ignored, and in March 1793 it was stipulated that no lame person was to be employed as a letter carrier.[2]

Employees were usually granted pensions upon retirement or redundancy. The senior officials appear to have made an effort to treat their employees fairly, although they did occasionally display some more draconian tendencies. Various indulgences were afforded to the employees, and one item which appears in the eighteenth-century accounts is a payment for the 'feast and drink'. In January 1722 £30 was paid for, '½ years drink money and £20 for ½ years feast money.'[3] The sum of £100 was shared annually among the officers and was paid 'in lieu of small beer.'[4] In 1782 the accounts state that this worked out to about £1 17s per officer, which means that approximately fifty-five people were eligible, but it is not clear on what basis they were chosen.[5] These payments date from 1722 (at the latest) and continue into the 1790s, but the practice then seems to have stopped and there are no further references to the custom.[6] Christmas was not a festive holiday as many letters of the time bear the date of 25 December. However, it was not forgotten, and the account of 1722 lists £16 6s 6d for 'box money to the post boys & other', while on 25 December 1791 there is a reference to wine money for six senior clerks at 5s 5d a quarter.[7]

With a few exceptions the top officials seem to have been hardworking, dedicated professionals, although somewhat set in their ways. The Postmasters General of the eighteenth and nineteenth centuries showed a determination to make the system work and most, apparently, had a genuine concern for the service. On one occasion in February 1793 they rebuked Allen, a surveyor, who had expressed an opinion that differed from theirs and for which he subsequently apologised. They rebuked him not for disagreeing with them but for apologising for that disagreement, they stressed that he must never apologise and always state his true opinion as they respected his experience. This was also to be made clear to the other surveyors.[8]

On rare occasions they were not above rebuking the Comptroller General, as in 1792 when a note was sent to Freeling:

> Please tell the Compel Gal that letters paying an additional postage for going round by London and thereby increasing the revenue is of itself no argument for not making Cross Posts, as it is in effect an additional tax upon the public for unnecessary loss of time.[9]

The coaching network created by William Palmer, a somewhat obstinate businessman, eventually covered most of the United Kingdom, growing from a few routes in 1784 to reach its peak early in the nineteenth century. Surveyors examined and measured the routes while inspectors checked the quality of service and investigated complaints. The volume of letters and newspapers handled by the staff increased steadily and, as the empire grew, the packet service handling overseas mail had to be expanded on an almost continual basis. The birth of the service was not an easy one, and there were quarrels, bickering, obstinacy and pettiness on the way as well as devotion, heroism, dedication and self-sacrifice.

The Mail Coach Office was directly responsible for the livelihood of many coach makers, drivers, guards, letter sorters, leather workers, post boys, innkeepers and their staff. It also created a demand for hundreds of horses and their associated workers: such as blacksmiths, saddlers and ostlers (or horse-keepers.) The officers had to work hard to keep quite a complex organisation running smoothly: they had to cope with poor roads, bad weather, wars, difficult staff, sickness and occasional crimes and accidents. When the railways began to take over the carriage of mail in the 1830s the demand for the coaches and all the associated staff and trades diminished, this had far-reaching effects on local employment and meant great hardship for those made redundant.

Housed in the Heritage Archives at Freeling House in London are thousands of records which set out in great detail the story of the mail coach and its employees. This book is based almost exclusively on those records. From these files it is sometimes possible to follow through a story in detail and get a sense of the satisfaction, the disappointment and, occasionally, the misery of its conclusion. In other cases it is frustrating that not all the records have survived, there are many gaps and consequently no firm conclusion can be reached. Sometimes the information drawn from these records is insufficient to give us a full understanding of the detail, at the time of writing there was usually no need to elaborate as the facts were common knowledge. Despite these *lacunae* there is plenty to interest the reader. The research has taken years, and hundreds of documents, maps, illustrations and associated sources have been scoured but, sadly, there remain several cases where there are still many details lacking.

The majority of books dealing with the mail coaches published in the late nineteenth and early twentieth centuries, with one or two notable exceptions, are largely anecdotal. They are often based on recollections and oral history and make very little or no use of references. This omission means that it is often difficult, if not impossible, to verify some of the statements contained therein. In some instances the primary sources show the statement to be mistaken, in which case full details are given in this text. Sometimes it proved impossible to establish a reliable provenance for a story or statement, when this happened I chose to quote the literary source. Unfortunately, some of the misinformation in these early books has become established 'fact', it is then repeated and given new life by modern information techniques such as websites.

This book is not a history of the Post Office as a complete organisation, rather it is primarily concerned with the coaches and their personnel. Sometimes other events impinge on their story, but matters such as the packet boats, franking concessions and the various penny and two-penny posts fall outside its scope and are not explored in any depth. The author's interest was first sparked by some research into the weapons carried by the guards in the coaches and from there it spread to the guards and finally to the whole coaching system.

NOTES ON THE TEXT

POSTMASTER GENERAL

During long periods of Post Office history this single office was held jointly by two officials but the singular title was used. Orders, letters and instructions were normally approved and initialled by both men.

MONEY

Prior to decimalisation in 1972 English currency was expressed as pounds, shillings and pence. There were 12 pence to a shilling and 20 shillings to a pound and there was also the guinea which was worth 21 shillings. There was a half penny and a farthing which was worth a quarter of a penny. Expressed in figures, three pounds twelve shilling and sixpence halfpenny was £3 12s 6½d. After decimalisation there were 10 pence to a shilling and 20 shillings to a pound

DISTANCE

All coaching distances were measured in the current units of 3ft to a yard, with 220 yards to a furlong, eight furlongs to the mile and 1,760 yards to a mile. A yard is roughly equivalent to nine metres, a furlong to 200 metres, and a mile to 1,600 metres. Since all payment for the coaches was calculated on the number of miles travelled, accurate measurements were important. The office, contractors and surveyors were frequently called on to check the distances.

SPELLING

There are few differences between modern spellings and that of the eighteenth and nineteenth centuries, but where there are these are indicated: e.g. 'cloaths, favor' and others. Grammar differed very slightly and even the educated seem to have had no qualms about the use of a singular verb with a plural subject, 'we was' or 'you was' occurs in several letters.

REFERENCES

Whenever possible the fullest references for all quotations and statements are given, but some records are not paginated and a few ledgers were sub-divided, each section of the volume was separately numbered. In these cases it was difficult to be precise.

1

THE EARLY POST OFFICE

Before the discovery of electricity and its adoption for telegraphs, the great majority of messages, other than oral ones, had to be physically transported. For urgent messages there were semaphores with flags, signal lights and beacons, but their use was limited. If the message was to be written, be it on clay tablets in cuneiform in Ancient Babylon or an order in French from a Norman king, that message had to be physically collected and transported to the recipient. If the journey was short then a carrier could walk or run the distance. If the journey was long or speed was vital then a horse or some other mount would be required.

If the journey was of any distance beyond the endurance of one animal then the tired mount had to be changed for a fresh one. In Europe this meant that for long postal journeys spare horses had to be available as required at certain specified places, hence the development of the stage system. Along routes at set points, spaced usually around ten miles apart, a stage was set up with spare horses and other facilities available to the messenger. The costs involved in setting up and operating such stages were high and their organisation complex, this meant that only a few major routes would be permanently maintained. Other routes would be established for specific purposes (such as war) and then cleared when no longer useful. This system, with variations, was to remain in use for centuries. It was only replaced when mechanical transport and electricity made machines capable of covering enormous distances at speed.

Along the British roads under Roman rule there were stages with horses at intervals of every 5.2 miles (8km). Every third stage was larger and offered a number of amenities for the messengers. Using this system it was reckoned that an important message could cover up to 200 miles (320km) in a day. There were two ways of carrying the message: the first used one hardy rider who would cover the entire distance, changing horses at each stage. The other method was for the message to be passed from one carrier to another as each finished their stage of the journey.[1] The same system was used on the Pony Express in the nineteenth-century Wild West.[2]

When Britain was under Roman Rule the occupying army built good roads radiating from London to some of the main towns: these included Exeter, Chester, York, Lincoln and Wroxeter. When the Emperor Hadrian arrived in England in AD 122 he placed all the English roads under military control and appointed a *Praefectus* in charge of them. Along these roads, at intervals of around 12 miles (19km), there were *mansiones* with facilities for rest, refreshment and overnight accommodation. These were under the control of a *manceps*, who was responsible for a number of horses, oxen and, at some sites, several large buildings. Obviously the main purpose of the roads was to enable rapid and easy movement of the legions and Imperial messengers. Traders were permitted to use them on payment of a custom duty of about 2½ per cent at various custom posts.

Permission for civilians to use the *mansiones* was granted by various warrants that stipulated which particular facilities the holder might use. There was an express service *cursus velox* and a slower *cursus clabularis*: this latter service consisted of mainly heavy four-wheeled wagons pulled by four oxen. The horses reserved for the post, *veredi*, were not available to anybody but officials, although occasional special dispensations were available. The Romans, judging by recent discoveries, wrote many letters using papyrus or wooden tablets with a black wax surface in which the message was scratched. These *tabulae* were roughly rectangular and had a couple of protective boards to serve as a kind of envelope. These were collected by a carrier or *tabularius*, the number of letters recently excavated at various fort sites in Britain suggests that these men must have been kept fairly busy.

This was the basic system that operated in Britain during the centuries of Roman rule, but as the organisation of the Empire deteriorated so did the postal service. When Britain was finally abandoned by the Roman legions early in the fifth century AD the stage system must have collapsed completely; without central control such an organisation cannot exist. As the country gradually split up into separate kingdoms with no central authority, communication between rulers and official bodies such as the Church must have been mainly on a personal messenger basis.

The number of postal systems that survived throughout Europe during this period is unknown, but by the eighth century there is enough Continental evidence to indicate that there was a limited transport of official letters, charters and orders. Charlemagne (AD 771-814) set up some form of post, but it does not appear to have survived his death. Rulers had scribes to whom they, or their officers, dictated the various messages, which were then transcribed and copied. Such orders and commands were then conveyed by the royal messengers, who were often expected to explain or expand upon the details of the communication. Most of the limited amount of correspondence of this early period was legal, royal or clerical.

In Britain during the Middle Ages the King and court were frequently on the move touring the country, which could obviously make it difficult to contact the

King. There was a need for some central body to deal with the more mundane, bureaucratic and routine business that did not require the sovereign's personal attention. This led to the development of the body known as the Exchequer that managed the accounting side of the King's household. There was another section known as the Chancery and this dealt with letters, charters, leases and similar matters. Both departments obviously employed messengers and these were apparently managed by a paid official known as the Usher. He was the wage master of the messengers, but during the thirteenth and fourteenth centuries the part of the Royal Household known as the Wardrobe seems to have taken over control of the royal messengers. After 1342 the Exchequer once again took over responsibility for paying them. The royal messengers were bound by an oath and were generally well treated, with the prospect of a pension and possibly the award of some official position on retiring.

As Government became more complex there was an increasing amount of correspondence and firmer systems of control had to be established. Standard rates of payment were developed based on the distance covered by the messengers. Those journeying to the northern counties of Britain were allowed up to eight days for the journey, in 1135 they were paid 20 pence for such an undertaking.[3] These officials received a travel allowance in addition to their wage and were bound to take an oath of loyalty and confidentiality.

Much of the official correspondence was from the sovereign to his nobles, the sheriffs and mayors who were the King's local representatives. They in turn would often need to pass on instructions, so there was a growing amount of official correspondence. From the early times of the monarchy letters were usually written on parchment and collected and delivered in soft, white, leather bags fitted at the neck with a drawstring and with the destination written on the outside. The use of leather bags of various sizes, materials and colours by the Post Office was to continue well into the nineteenth century. They were in constant need of either repair or replacement and represented a regular heavy cost to the Post Office.[4]

The King's court was not the only official body to maintain some form of courier service and all messengers, either the *nuntii* or *cursors*, had the legal right to demand the use of horses and carriages should the need arise. As can be imagined this practice was not popular with those affected and caused considerable resentment, occasionally even violence. Not all messengers were totally reliable and there was always the danger, admittedly small, of theft or non-delivery. The messengers appear to have been accepted as rather special and there are only a few recorded cases of any being attacked. Later on the supply of horses for the post became yet another duty of the poor, over-worked and unpaid parish constable. Noble households also maintained a number of messengers but the 'royal' network was the largest group.

London, as the capital with its court and thriving commerce, obviously generated a great deal of correspondence. As early as 1528 there is mention of a possible site for a Post Office in Lombard Street in the City of London. It was to remain at this location until the early nineteenth century when the organisation finally outgrew the space available. City innkeepers were also ordered to make four horses ready to be kept at Old Jewry, not far from Lombard Street, ready for the post. Both sites were fairly near the Lord Mayor's residence and he also maintained a small group of messengers for his own service. Other officials also had a need for such men, and there was a steady increase in the amount of mail and the number of messengers.

Town officials were expected to keep horses ready for the royal messengers as well as for duly authorised officials, especially in times of crisis. The costs of such a duty were not cheap and town records show that the totals could soon mount up, much to the annoyance of the local officials. Only two routes were entirely funded by the Government, one was north to Berwick and the other was the road to Dover, the gateway to Europe via Calais. It was along this route that most court officials travelled to Europe carrying with them the appropriate local passports. In addition to the intermittent messengers en-route for Europe there were a number of regular posts to some towns, such as Venice, that had special relationships, political or economic, with England. There were other main routes but these lines of communication were not always permanent, and they were often closed when the circumstances which had led to their development passed.

By the late Middle Ages some commercial interests had set up their own posts to the Continent. The Merchant Adventurers, an association of businessmen primarily dealing with the Netherlands and North Germany, had a Postmaster in London who arranged for weekly deliveries to be dispatched. There was also the Strangers' Post, set up by foreign merchants with its own Postmaster and based in London. This private post annoyed the native London merchants who claimed it gave foreign merchants, the Flemings in particular, an unfair advantage. However, in 1551 there was an internal dispute as to who should be chosen as the Strangers' Postmaster. Unable to settle the matter themselves the merchants unfortunately asked Elizabeth's Council of State to adjudicate. To their dismay they were told that they were not entitled to a separate official and the organisation was taken over by the Master of Posts. The situation cropped up again in April 1591 when Elizabeth I forbade 'all merchants, both strangers and others', indeed anybody, to carry the mail from abroad, except those duly appointed to this task. Anybody found to be handling mail without due authority would be held and the letters sent to the Privy Council. Part of the purpose here was to examine foreign correspondence that might give a hint of the preparation of plots against the sovereign or the country. Elizabeth's officers, including John Stanhope, 'master and comptroller general of all our post, were ordered to be vigilant.'[5] During Elizabeth's reign it was ordered that every post was to have two horses and at least two bags of leather, well lined with baize, a soft woollen or cotton material, to protect the contents.

Increasing bureaucracy and more complex administration put pressure on the monarchy to formalise the postal service and in 1512 there is a record of a payment to Brian Tuke, described as Master of Posts. Under his direction all towns were commanded to keep post horses and guides in readiness to accompany the royal messengers and other authorised travellers on the various stages of their journey. The costs of these measures had to be borne by the towns.

In 1515 Tuke was knighted and held the position of Master of the Posts until his death in 1545 whereupon two men, Sir William Puget and John Mason, were appointed in his place. Whether the doubling-up was down to the demands of the job having become so heavy or if it was merely a way to reward two loyal men is not clear. This practice of appointing two men to the one post was to be continued through much of the later history of the Post Office. When Paget died Mason held the post until he died in 1567. It was during his period in office that, in 1558, an Act of Parliament (4 and 5 Phillip and Mary) was passed. This Act set down that Sir John Mason, Master of the Posts, would see that ordinary posts were laid at Dover, Canterbury, Sittingbourne, Rochester, Dartford and London. Each post was to have six horses at least, two for the packets and four for the 'goers and comers'. No one was to ride post without a guide, who were themselves to have a horn to blow in the towns and places where the post was laid. The horse was supposed to travel at an average speed of 7mph (11.2kph). This proclamation also states that ordinary posts are to be marked out by hanging a horn at the door or with some painted sign to show that it was a post.[6] This use of horns by the post was to continue until well into the nineteenth century. The Postmaster was also to record details of correspondence received by him together with the details of its disposal.

When Sir John Mason died Thomas Randolph was made Comptroller of all Her Majesty's Posts, with Robert Parminter as his deputy. In official correspondence the title of Master of the Messengers and Runners was also applied to Parminter. In 1583 he issued a proclamation laying out the conditions for the various posts and they were to set the pattern for many years. Each post was to have three horses, three good and strong leather bags lined with baize or cotton and finally three horns. Each missive was to be sent on its way within a quarter of an hour of its receipt. Details of all the letters were to be entered in a book which were then to be forwarded to the Master of the Posts at the end of each month. In addition, various instructions were set out listing penalties for non-observance.

In 1603 the newly crowned King, James I (1603–1625), was advised that the system was being misused, and in 1604 a decree was issued stressing the orders to be followed by his officers. Only riders holding special permission would be allowed the use of the post horses, and payment for their use was to be made before starting the journey. To conserve the health and stamina of the post horses, a top speed of 7mph (11.2kph) was set for summer, April to September, and 6mph (9.6kph) in winter. Each mount was to be used for one stage only, unless special arrangements had been made. A maximum of 30lbs (13.6 kilos) was set as the load to be carried by the horse in addition to the rider. A guide was to accompany the rider and he was to receive a groat (4 pence) and there was a charge of 2½ pence a mile for those riding on special commissions. All charges to be paid in advance and for all other users the charges were to be agreed before setting out. Mounts could only be hired from those authorised to keep post horses.[7]

This proclamation was soon followed by another in 1609 that forbade any who were not fully authorised from collecting, delivering or in any way handling mail, while the posts were made a royal monopoly. These prohibitions applied only to the post roads, thus letters travelling between other destinations, known as bye-posts, were unaffected. There were only four main posts, one to Ireland, one to Scotland, one to Plymouth and the most important one to Dover.

The Master of the Post in this period was Lord Stanhope with Matthew De Quester as his deputy. De Quester would later be responsible for great improvements in communications with the Continent. In 1619 the King, in recognition of his services, created for him his own department and granted to him and his son the title Postmaster of England for Foreign Parts out of the King's Dominions. The appointment pleased neither the foreign merchants nor Lord Stanhope, whose letters patent had granted him sole rights to the post. His department was now more or less halved and he also suffered financially from the loss of certain benefits from the foreign mail. Despite appeals by Stanhope and his son, the Privy Council rejected their claims.

The Stanhopes fought back by causing as much trouble as possible for De Quester. There was no settling the dispute on a simple basis for, when the Council finally accepted the Stanhope case, they did not revoke De Quester's patent. Confusion reigned, and in 1632 De Quester passed his patent to Thomas Witherings and William Frizell. Witherings, the more industrious of the pair, found the post in a parlous state with Postmasters' salaries heavily in arrears – some were owed seven years' money. Many had given up keeping the post horses while mail, more often than not, was carried on foot with inevitable delays.

After carefully considering matters, Witherings produced a comprehensive plan in 1635 which involved setting up a central office in the City of London to receive all letters. From there they would be dispatched along set routes to the main towns and even along branch lines to the smaller towns. The letters would be carried by horse or foot depending on the distance. He promised travel of 120 miles (192km) in twenty-four hours, as well as a timetable of collection and dispatch. On arrival at a Post Office the bag would be passed to a courier bearing on his arm a badge of the royal arms,[8] who would distribute the letters to nearby destinations. The use of the royal arms was a reversion to the reign of Henry III (1216-1272) when messengers wore the royal arms.

For this service Witherings planned to make a charge, in this he was no doubt influenced by a scheme that had been set up in 1633: the inhabitants of

Barnstaple and Exeter had created a system whereby their letters were collected and would then be picked up by the King's post from Exeter. A charge was levied for this local service of 6 pence for a single letter and 8 pence for a double one, Witherings advocated a similar arrangement for letters all over the country. This income would boost the royal coffers, which until then had maintained the posts – usually at a loss. A set scale of prices depending on size or weight was agreed. This was a great step, for in effect anybody could now make use of the posts and send letters anywhere in the country. In addition to their basic duties of carrying the mail, the riders also played a part in spreading news and gossip for they were often the peoples' only contact with the wider world.

In 1635 Witherings was ready to implement his scheme which proved to work very well. When Stanhope died two years later Witherings was appointed as Master of the Posts. He set out various regulations for the smooth running of his post and strictly ordered that carriers kept to their set journeys with no diversions to collect or deliver other letters. Unfortunately his success turned sour, for uncertain reasons he was charged with various offences and was sacked in 1640.

In his place was appointed a merchant of London, Philip Burlamachi, who was to fill the post but only under the control of the Secretary of State. Witherings did not submit meekly to his discharge and fought his case with vigour, but in 1642 he assigned his patent to the Earl of Warwick. Urged on by a powerful friend, Edmund Prideaux, Burlamachi retained his possession of the letter office and the conflict eventually involved both Houses of Parliament. The confusing controversy was finally resolved in 1644 when the House of Commons appointed Prideaux to the office of Master of the Posts, Couriers and Messengers.

Prideaux had great plans for a regular post all across the country, but his grand ideas were not matched by basic planning. The City of London set up its own post to Edinburgh in 1649, much to the displeasure of Prideaux who lodged an official complaint. Eventually Parliament stepped in and the City post was closed, but as a result of a review by Parliament it was decided that Prideaux would have to pay a fixed charge of £5,000 per annum for the right to claim the money paid for the carriage of letters. This system, or farming, whereby a sum was paid to the Government and any income above that was kept by the person holding the farm, was to continue in the Post Office for many years.

Prideaux left his post after 1653 and Captain Manley paid £10,000 per annum for the privilege of holding the office. After two years his contract expired and Oliver Cromwell gave the position to the Secretary Thurloe (1616-1668) at the same rent. In 1657 an important piece of legislation was passed: the Act for Settling the Postage of England, Scotland and Ireland. It established the Post Office of England under the control of a Postmaster General and Comptroller of the Post Office, who together would have the sole rights to collect and despatch letters and the supply of post horses. Nobody else had the right to set up any form of postal service on foot, by horse or by way of packet boats. The two universities of Oxford and Cambridge were exempted and allowed to continue with their long-established post. As this Act had been enacted during the Commonwealth and there was some fear that it might be challenged in law, it was later re-enacted after the Restoration of Charles II in 1660, (12 Carl II *c.*35).

There were minor differences between the two Acts but they were basically the same. Prices were set with a rate of 2 pence a mile for distances up to eighty miles (50km). For those towns not located on a post route the price of postage was considerably increased, for there was no arrangement for mail to go direct from one town to another unless they were on the main route. The cross post: i.e. direct links between towns not on post routes, did not exist and this situation was to continue for many years. The letter had to go via London which obviously greatly increased the distance it travelled. The price of hiring post horses was set at 3 pence a mile plus 4 pence for the guide that was officially required for each stage. The power to seize a horse without the owner's consent was removed from the messengers, but if they were delayed for any length of time they could hire a mount.

Following the Restoration in 1660 a new Postmaster was appointed and Henry Bishop had to pay £21,500 rent for his seven years in the post. For various reasons Bishop surrendered his lease, which was taken over by Daniel O'Neile in 1663, but only under the direct control of the Secretary of State. In 1663 the Duke of York was granted the revenues from the mail but they were later transferred back to King James II. When the lease expired in 1667 the new master was Lord Arlington.

One of the factors which limited the use of mail was the lack of public awareness about just what facilities were available. There seems to have been no approved list showing which towns had posts and, if they had, where they were situated. The citizens of London, with their mercantile connections, were probably more in need of some sort of postal system than most other people, yet their needs were ill-met. Communication was mostly on a personal basis but on 1 April 1680 there was a serious attempt to improve matters. William Dockwra, a London merchant, produced a scheme that was comprehensive, simple and effective. London was divided into seven districts and several hundred Post Offices were opened up to receive letters. Just as importantly their locations were publicised. There was an hourly collection and letters for the country were taken to the main Post Office. Those letters for local delivery were sorted and then sent out. The system also handled parcels up to a maximum weight of 1lb (4.5 kilos) and there was even an insurance scheme providing cover up to a maximum figure of ten pounds. The cost of a letter was one penny, except for those destined for some of the more outlying areas, these were charged at 2 pence. In 1708 Charles Povey established a halfpenny post with his men touring the streets ringing a hand bell to collect the letters. The Post Office objected and the collection was stopped, but the Post Office kept the idea of the bell ringing by the collectors.

In order to keep some sort of check on whether the postage due had been paid, Dockwra introduced the postmark. This was a device that showed at which office the communication was received and at what time. The new, efficient system generated more post and although Dockwra gained little profit at first, there was obvious moneymaking potential. The Duke of York, who held the royal monopoly on the post, soon saw the scheme as a good earner and claimed that his monopoly was being infringed. The law backed his claim and in 1683 the penny post was made part of the main Post Office. Dockwra lost his scheme and was liable for damages as well. It was not until 1690 that he received any recognition of his great contribution when he was granted a pension. Later he was appointed as Comptroller of the Penny Post at a salary of £200. However, in 1700, charged with several rather vague offences, he was dismissed. However, the changes he had initiated were to be continued in the eighteenth century, which was to see the start of the transformation of the British mail system.

2

PALMER AND THE POST OFFICE

The eighteenth-century Post Office was archaic, muddled, vulnerable and, in many respects, very inefficient. Many of the problems were nobody's fault but, like so many other institutions, the system had expanded and developed gradually, so that few people noticed the growing problems. It was accepted as being the normal state of affairs and one which few people thought to query. Social changes had created a need for much more correspondence and the increased demand exacerbated the basic weaknesses. The delivery time for a letter was often quite long. This was a big problem, but it must be pointed out that it was in keeping with the standards of the time. It was annoying for both recipient and sender, but it was also normal. Cost was another problem, especially if the letter was not travelling directly between one of the main towns and London. This mail would be sent to London and then redirected on to the original destination. When charges were based on the distance covered by the item this obviously pushed up the cost of the letter and extended the delivery time. There were a certain number of cross posts developed under Allen's plan where letters went directly from town to town, but they were very few indeed.

Postal security was weak and was to remain so for much of the century. The letters were collected together at the various offices and sent to Lombard Street. From there the letters were sorted and put into labelled leather bags which were then handed to the post boys to be taken on to their next destination. The majority of post boys were literally boys, their ages ranged from twelve to sixteen and they were mixed in with older and apparently sometimes semi-disabled men. These 'boys' loaded their leather bags into small carts or strung them across the back of a usually poor-quality horse and rode off to deliver them to the next office. Until the 1780s the offices did not close until late in the evening, and by the time the letters had been sorted it was night or early morning before they set out on their journeys. They were very obviously vulnerable and, despite the risk of severe punishment if caught, robbing the post boys was an attractive option for villains. In addition to the risk of theft there was also a temptation for the post boys to handle mail which was not part of the official system and pocket the postage themselves.

One of the commemorative medals struck to honour John Palmer for his setting up of the mail coaches. This was but one of the tributes paid to Palmer.

Ralph Allen was one of the first to appreciate the potential benefits of some basic changes in the system. He saw that not only could he improve the service but that there was the prospect of ensuring himself a good income. He was born in Cornwall in 1693, his father owned an inn in the county but legend has it that at an early age he went to live with his grandmother. She was the postmistress of the small town of Saint Columb, located on the main post road from Launcester to Falmouth, a packet boat station. It is said that his work in managing his grandmother's records was so impressive that a Post Office surveyor thought him worthy of a more important job. Early in the eighteenth century he was transferred to Bath where he was made a clerk. The town had been made a stage post around 1675 and was on a main road leading to the busy port of Bristol. The Roman baths made it a popular place for the 'quality' to spend a holiday sampling the waters and socialising. The quantity of mail passing along this route was considerable, Allen was no doubt kept busy and gained useful experience and understanding of the postal system.

In August 1714 Queen Anne died and the crown passed to the House of Hanover. George I acceded to the throne but there was some opposition to this new King and his German court. There was a muddled Scottish Jacobite rebellion in 1715 in support of the Stuart succession and some talk of armed opposition in England. A body of troops under the command of General Wade was sent to the West Country to maintain order. He set up his base at Bath and it seems that Allen played some small part in supplying information concerning the alleged conspiracy. Possibly as a result of this, he seems to have become friendly with General Wade and, perhaps through his influence, was made Postmaster of Bath.

John Palmer, 1742–1818, the pioneer of the Royal Mail coach system.

His experience as clerk and Postmaster gave him a good understanding of how the Post Office worked and he must have seen very plainly that there were serious flaws in the system. In 1719, having worked out his plan to improve the post, he came to London with a proposition to put to the Postmaster General. Considering the novelty of his scheme it is reasonable to suppose that he must have had some considerable backing, either implied or open, from his friends in Bath. Allen had pinpointed one of the major causes of delay and increased costs in the system. Letters intended for London were not a problem for they simply went directly there. There was another group of letters known as bye mail, which were letters going to addresses situated somewhere along an established London route which did not need to reach the capital, being delivered en route. The third group were letters addressed to anywhere that was not on a postal route, for these there was a double journey, going first to London and then being redirected to their intended destination. The smallest group were the cross-post letters and these avoided the redirected London route and travelled directly from town to town. This last system was obviously much more efficient, cheaper and quicker, but sadly there were only two such routes in the entire country. One, started in 1696, went from Exeter to Bristol and was later extended to Chester, the other was from Bath to Oxford.

Allen proposed that he take over the running of the few cross posts in the West Country as well as all the bye mail for England and Wales. For this privilege he was offering the Post Office a farm, as the fee was called, of £6,000 a year for a period of seven years. Any income that he made above this figure was his to keep as profit. The sum of money involved was considerable and suggests that Allen had done extremely well to rise from a country clerk to somebody dealing with this level of finance. He promised at least three services a week, moving at a speed of 5mph, as well as having post horses available at half an hour's notice. He must have put up a pretty convincing case for, in April 1720, the Post Office officials agreed to this venture and the contract was signed. He was free to choose and appoint all the Deputy Postmasters and would pay their salaries.

His first action was to stop the carriage of the large number of letters that were never part of the official postal system but were carried privately by post boys and Postmasters who kept the postage paid. He instituted a system of checks and introduced a voucher system. The vouchers were sent to him at Bath where he carefully checked and cross-checked, any discrepancies were investigated by his surveyors. For a time it was a battle between those who were reluctant to lose an illegal income and Allen, who was determined to stop it. It took time, and in the first year he made a loss but was allowed to continue with the contract. He also developed a number of cross posts directly linking many towns and thus generating more business. Gradually he succeeded in gaining firmer and firmer control of the system. He now ensured that all letters were handled by the official system and were duly charged at the correct rate.

When his original contract expired he had been so successful that he had no problem in getting an extension and his income correspondingly increased. He was also fortunate in that Bath was expanding and there was extensive building going on, large amounts of the stone used came from quarries on his land. He retained the postal contract for life and made a name for himself in many fields, he died in 1764 a much respected and very wealthy man.[1] On his death the Postmaster General took over the running of the system and moved the main office to London. There is little doubt that Allen's scheme brought about many improvements in the postal service but it remained an inefficient system. The amount of checking and planning that Allen had to introduce in order to tighten and improve the post may be appreciated when his instructions are studied. Refer to the end notes for further details.[2]

The second and more innovative reformer was John Palmer, born in Bath in 1742 and a native of that city. He was the son of a brewer and theatrical impresario who managed a theatre in Orchard Street, Bath. A headstrong youth, he resisted his father's plan to put him into the church and for a while worked as a labourer in the family brewery. As a result his health suffered and he left the brewery and became involved in the family's theatrical venture. After the passing of the Licensing Act of 1727 the Lord Chamberlain had the right to censor all plays as well as the power to license theatres: only two in London were so licensed. In order to establish a theatre in Bath a royal licence or patent was required. Young Palmer was entrusted with the task of obtaining the licence and consequently was obliged to undertake trips to and from London. His time spent in London organising the grant of the Royal Patent seems to have enabled him to make friends with many quite well-placed people, including politicians and actors. He was successful in his application and obtained the much valued Royal Patent in 1768. John then became the manager of the Bath Theatre Royal and later ran another theatre in Bristol until 1785 when, because of his connection with the Post Office, the demands on his time led to his resignation.

His theatrical duties still involved a certain amount of travelling which contributed to his growing awareness of the situation as far as coaches were concerned. The road between Bath and London was reckoned to be one of the best maintained roads in the country, and it soon became very obvious to Palmer that stagecoaches made the journey far quicker than the mail carts. A letter leaving London on the Monday night would not reach Bath until the following Wednesday, but Palmer knew from experience that the faster stagecoaches completed the journey in a day. Exactly why this was the case is not entirely clear, but Palmer became seriously interested in the system of mail delivery and general travel. He claimed that he undertook some practical research by travelling in various coaches and on different routes. As a result of his observations he came to the conclusion that one reason for the slowness of the mail deliveries lay in the use of poor quality post horses, many of which were incapable of maintaining a good, steady pace. Another contributory cause was the time taken by the Deputy Postmasters to effect the mail changeover. This involved taking charge of their bags arriving from London and handing over those destined for other offices. He was also well aware that security of the mail was, to say the least, weak, as the post boys were such easy prey. The stagecoaches were far less vulnerable but were forbidden by law from carrying letters.

He became convinced that all the problems of poor horses, slow changeovers and general inefficiency could be overcome. As far as the transport of mail was concerned, why not use the much faster coaches instead of the slow and cumbersome carts? He claimed that the speed of a coach could be maintained at 8 or 9mph and, even allowing for the various stoppages, the journey to Bath from London could be made in sixteen hours, rather than the thirty-eight to forty that it needed. He argued that if the Deputy Postmasters were ready and waiting for the coaches to arrive then the time taken to collect the incoming post and hand over the outgoing post would be greatly reduced, thus the changeover could be accomplished very quickly. Whilst this was being done the ostler would be changing the team of horses, replacing the tired ones with fresh steeds.

However, if this plan was to succeed then the Postmaster would have to know the time at which the coach was due to arrive at the inn. This in turn meant that the coaches would have to run to a set timetable to achieve the necessary reliability. This regularity of delivery would be wholeheartedly welcomed by the public, especially by those in commerce. Uncertainty about the timing of the mails arrivals and departures was high on the list of grumbles about the postal service, as is evidenced by a typical letter written on 12 December 1782 on behalf of the Liverpool Chamber of Commerce. It was addressed to Anthony Todd, the Secretary to the Post Office, and stated:

> The many and great inconveniences arising from the uncertainty of the arrival of the posts from London at this place which has been long a subject of complaint is now become so serious a business that the associated body of merchants assembled in their Chamber of Commerce have directed me to lay the matter before you & to request in their joint names that you will endeavour to procure it proper attension (sic).[3]

Palmer also suggested that if the scheduled timetable idea was used and a coach was late then a rider could be sent to track back along the route to find out why. Although not unreasonable, this backtracking was one idea that was not pursued when Palmer's plan was adopted.

In between the time he spent managing the Theatre Royal in Bath he put together a carefully considered plan. By 1782 it was sufficiently formed for him to contact his local Member of Parliament, the Hon. J.J. Pratt, who approached William Pitt the Younger, Chancellor of the Exchequer. Pitt evidently saw virtue in Palmer's plan and encouraged him to develop the idea, he then passed the plan to the senior Post Office officials and sought their opinions. Their reaction was less than enthusiastic and they unanimously condemned the whole scheme as a potential disaster. It was not surprising that the reception for his plan was so antagonistic, for it indirectly condemned the system in use at the time as slow, inefficient and poorly organised. Not unnaturally they resented the implied criticism from an outsider. Their animosity intensified when Palmer's scheme was officially adopted, and whilst sabotage is perhaps too strong a word to use some actions by the officials came very close to it.

The acceptance by Pitt of Palmer's proposals was beset with problems and he had to overcome hostility, ignorance and prejudice to make them reality. He sets out his version of events in a *Memorial of John Palmer Surveyor and Comptroller-General of the Post Office*,[4] which he placed before the Lord Commissioners of His Majesty's Treasury in 1797. In this document he gives his version of how the scheme was greeted by the officials. He says that in 1782, after undertaking research, he left his home in Bath and communicated his plan to Mr Pitt. He was encouraged to do some further work on the scheme and returned the expanded plan to Pitt in January 1783. Pitt was sufficiently impressed to plan an early trial. Unfortunately for Palmer, Pitt's party was voted out of office so progress was halted. In his Memorial Palmer goes on to list all the details of his problems with the Post Office, and delivers an, at times, withering condemnation of his critics. Palmer's plan had been passed to the three chief surveyors of the General Post Office for their observations. In Palmer's words:

Thomas Telford (1757-1834), one of the leading road builders and largely responsible for opening up the Scottish Highlands.

...in July 1783 the Post Office furnished three volumes of objections, declaring the plan absolutely impracticable and prejudicial to the revenue and commerce (*ibid*).

(The three volumes to which he refers are presumably the sets of comments put forward by the Surveyors Draper, Hodgson and Allen.)

In the meantime the plan to reform the post, and it must be remembered that Palmer's proposals covered far more than just the coaching system, was subjected to very hostile analysis. A handwritten list of all of Palmer's proposals, which from its context indicates a date of about June 1783, is bound in with the observations of the surveyors on the practicality of the scheme.[5] A similar handwritten copy of the plan can be found in another part of the archive,[6] it reads as follows:

Plan for the Reform and Improvement in the Management of the Business of the General Post Office

1. The post at present instead of being the swiftest is almost the slowest, conveyance in this country; and though from the great improvement in our roads other carriers have proportionally mended their speed, the post is as slow as ever.
2. It is likewise very unsafe, as the frequent robberies of it testify, to avoid a loss from this people generally cut bank bills or bills at sight, in two, and send the parts by different posts.
3. The Postmaster lately advertised directions to the public of the best method he could devise of dividing a bill in such a manner as to prevent it's being of any use to the robber. Rewards too have been frequently offered by him for the

best-constructed mail cart on some plan to prevent the frequent robbery of the mail, but without effect.

4. It is at present so little taken care of that it is generally trusted to some idle boy without character, mounted on a worn out hack, who is so far from being able to defend himself, or escape from a robber, that he is more likely to be in league with him.

5. The post should certainly be as safe and expeditious as any other regular stage, for till it is so, whatever penalties are held out to coachmen, for carrying parcells (sic), the public, as their convenience (sic) directs will send by the safest and most expeditious conveyance, to the very great loss of the revenue of the post office.

6. A comparison between the post and a diligence[7] from Bath to London, may pretty near serve for the whole kingdom:

The diligence that sets out from Bath, at 4 or 5, on Monday afternoon will deliver a letter about ten on Tuesday morning; the post that leaves Bath at ten or eleven on Monday night does not deliver a letter until two or three Wednesday afternoon frequently much later, nothing therefore prevents the post being the conveyance of many more letters than it does at present but the cheapness of the carriage by post over that of the diligence.

By the first a single letter is four pence by the latter booking carriage and porterage about two shillings, yet many persons both at Bath and Bristol send by the latter, and indeed throughout the kingdom, all letters to which expedition is necessary are so sent, where diligences are established though even by those there often is great delay in the delivery by the London porters to prevent which it is often thought worthwhile in letters of consequence, to write on the back 'an extra sum will be given the porter, if he delivers this letter immediately.'

7. To remedy this it is advised to contract with the masters of this diligences to carry the mail and a guard to protect it and this it is insured may be done by him not only better (but as cheap as the present method) to the office which in general is three pence a mile for the boy and horse.

8. They should go at the rate of eight or nine mph, this, allowing a quarter of an hour stoppage to change horses and for each postmaster to change the bags (which, at most places is full enough) will take the mail from Bath to London at most in sixteen hours.

9. The mail diligences would have accommodation above all others for passengers and parcells (sic) as it would be always punctual to time and protected by the guard, which must prove an additional motive for the masters to contract the cheaper with government.

Diligences are now established from almost every town in the kingdom to London and in many cities.

And capital towns where the cross post communicates as from Bath and Bristol to Exeter, Plymouth, Portsmouth, Birmingham, Liverpool, Oxford, Chester, which would be a great benefit to the cross post, and in many places where they are not yet established a contract for the mail might induce people to do it.

The delay at the different post offices on the road cannot be worse than it is now; perhaps too if the offices were enlarged the General Post Office and more sorters and runners employed the letters might be delivered much sooner after the mail arrives than at present.

10. The guard should by no means be left either to the postmaster, or master of machines to provide, as those they could procure could be little relied on in any respect. A soldier is accustomed to the discharge of firearms, to keeping them clean, and to watch and fatigue in late hours; a sufficient number of them, well recommended by their officers should be distributed over the kingdom, and one quartered at the inn of every stage or every other stage where the diligences stops to change, he might be seated on the top of the coach, with the mail behind him, here he could best command the road and observe suspicious persons, he might have two short guns or blunderbusses, and the coachman might have pistols to use if necessary, they should have some extraordinary pay and be liable to military punishment for neglect of duty, the swiftness and punctuality of the post would be almost as great a security as the guard for if at any time it did not arrive to its hour a man and horse should be dispatched to seek the cause of the delay, and if robbed pursuit immediately made, so that it would scarce possible for the robber to escape at present the post is so very uncertain in time that many hours may elapse ere information can be given of the robbery.

No outside passengers to be allowed.

11. If the diligence was free of turnpikes it would be a great saving to government and a very trifling loss on the tolls which for a carriage and pair from Bath to London is about nine shillings, and a carriage and four about eighteen, this would be so much towards payment of the carriage of the mail and taken all through the kingdom must amount to a very large sum annually.

12. It is requested to know what the provisoes are respecting the two universities as they are exempted in some respects in the Post Acts but it is not mentioned what.

13. It is certainly a hardship on individuals being liable to a heavy penalty on sending letters by diligence and in this respect they may go out at an hour when the post does not and at a time when a letter requires dispatch yet two or three guineas must be paid for an express or a servant sent post to do what may be done much better for half a crown by the coach.

All that government wants is to secure the postage of any letters not sent with parcels of goods, or by private hands, oblige every person therefore sending a letter by any other conveyance than the post to take the letter to the post office and pay the postage to the place where it is directed, let it be stamped with the post-mark and signed by the postmaster, then suffered to be carried as directed, and the sender and carrier freed from any penalty if the letter is of such consequence that the post cannot be waited for it is worth paying the extra postage for, and but few people would hazard the payment of a heavy penalty which they could easily avoid but the great aim must be to carry cheaper, safer and swifter than any other carrier and that will secure the business better than any penalties.

14. The postmaster of every town must know the exact time the mail should arrive, and either himself or servant be ready at the inn where they change horses with his packet of letters to put in the general bag and take out those brought for him, he must be very inexpert, if he cannot(as most places) change his packets as soon as the ostler does his horses if he is not ready the diligence by no means to wait, the letters for this town going on to London and none from it will point out to the secretary at the post office the negligent officer and the inhabitants not receiving the letters they expected and finding their own not forwarded will of course complain of his neglect – If on inquiry the salaries of officers are not proportional to the trust and duty government will undoubtedly advance them but no more keep a negligent servant in a department of the post office than in the excise, something more should be allowed to those officers where the mail stops in the night and the letters are received and made up late.

15. As the hours of sending the mail from every office in the kingdom are set-tled to accommodate the general office, by the proposed alterations they must be changed in most places to some, perhaps the alteration may prove more con-venient to others inconvenient, yet at the very worst, the consideration that the letters which may be sent on the morrow will arrive at the place it is intended for as soon as one now sent today will over balance it.

No constant good regulation can take place whilst they are obliged to wait at the general post office for the letters from the different offices of government and as the post on this plan will be so much more expeditious the indulgence may certainly be dispensed with, they may always be in time for common business and if the let-ter be of great importance it would be much better to pay the expense of a special messenger than to stop the whole post business of one part of the kingdom.

16. A committee of gentlemen merchants etc might perhaps suggest a bet-ter method of regulating the post for their own district than persons always employed in the office in London and they would undoubtedly be pleased with the compliment of being consulted. Intelligent outriders who travel for orders in the different parts of the kingdom and have experienced inconveniences in their correspondence would be likely to furnish very useful information which the office should encourage from every quarter.

17. Where new roads are continually making and villages growing into great manufacturing towns the post of such a country must be open to continual transition and improvement.

18. It may be advisable to consult with the merchants etc in London how far it may be proper for the general office to shut at seven or eight in the evening the Change closing at three and the bankers at six the business could be much better done than at twelve at night or one or two in the morning and cheaper to government it must be better too for all clerks and servants etc for let the hour be ever so late many persons will delay writing to the last on examination perhaps it may be so regulated that the letters may be delivered so much earlier than they are at present as to leave full as much time after the receipt of the letter to answer it as there is now though the post will go out earlier the increased expedition of the post too would well allow for the missing one an earlier hour as the office would occasion earlier hours for the dispatch of business that is to be communicated by it.

19. It is presumed that by these and other improvements which may be made letters might be delivered in nearly half the time they are now from many parts of the kingdom in perfect safety and as the public pay any additional tax with less ill humour when it is grounded on great improvements and convenience suppose the postage was to be advanced in proportion of two pence to six pence but double and treble letters in a smaller degree for as the diligences can carry any weight of letters every encouragement should be given to send small packets by the post and as government would pay but about three halfpence lb for one hundred miles the public should not be charged one shilling and four pence oz.

20. By the Act of 1765 the postage of a single letter which used to be three pence for any distance under eighty miles was altered to a penny for one stage and two pence for two stages under the idea that by so doing it so cheap government would have the great number of letters sent by carriers etc in preference to them not considering that they were sent for expedition not for cheapness as the carriage and porterage of a letter to ever so small a distance generally exceeds three pence.

21. By the present regulation of the prices of postage from the general post office a single letter is a penny for one stage twopence for two stages any distance beyond that and not exceeding eighty miles threepence from eighty miles to any part of England be the distance what it may to Berwick upon Tweed which is three hundred miles only four pence so that beyond eighty miles there is no sort of proportion kept up betwixt the distance and the charge, to Edinburgh indeed it is sixpence. Letters which pass through London to any part are charged the postage to London and then the charge to the places of destination is added.

The post charge from Edinburgh differs from that to it for any distance not beyond fifty miles twopence not beyond eighty miles three pence and beyond eighty even to London but fourpence double letters all over the kingdom is charged double treble quadruple or an ounce weight one shilling and four pence which should be well considered and moderated and be in a less proportion than according to the rate of single letters. The American charge seems to be on a better plan than that in England they pay for single letter not above sixty miles four pence not above one hundred sixpence not above two hundred eight pence not above three hundred tenpence.

Suppose the charge here in future was at the following rates for a single letter:

Not exceeding

20 miles	2d
40 miles	3d
60 miles	4d
80 miles	5d
100 miles	6d

…and after that an additional halfpenny on every twenty miles to and from any part of the kingdom whether it went through London or not or suppose no letter was charged less than threepence as before the Act 1765 perhaps too, a much less charge in proportion to the distance beyond a hundred miles than proposed would be better.

22. The gross receipts at the post office annually from the time Charles 2nd first installed it, to the Act passed by Queen Anne for its improvement, gradually increased to one hundred and eleven thousand four hundred and sixty one pounds, seventeen shillings and tenpence and is now understood to be about five hundred thousand pounds. From the proposed and other improvements some reform in the conduct and expense of the Packets, the increased price of postage, the tolls for the mail machines etc the revenue would not only be increased to a very considerable amount but the public be much better accommodated.

Postage is really not a tax but a fair and reasonable price for so much labour which government by its monopoly is enabled to do cheaper than any individual and should do quicker and safer or lay its account to the public employing other carriers in preference to theirs.

(N.B. This plan is incomplete, the regulation of Franks[8] and several other matters intended to be introduced into it had not been fully digested. The last check on Franks, I think, would be the members writing the day of the month and year the letter is sent to the office which should be charged if not sent on the day it is dated.)

In the bound volume of Treasury Letters these objections are set together with the handwritten copy of the plan interleaved with a letter from Todd to the Treasury:

I enclose you the copies of two of our Surveyors Observation upon Mr Palmers plan respecting this office and hope to send you in a week or ten days the observations of another now in Yorkshire upon a survey to whom it has been referred.[9]

The Surveyors' responses deal with each point of Palmer's plan in turn and frequently repeat each other's comments. The first reply is by Nathan Draper, Resident Surveyor, who goes through the plan pointing out why it would not work. He doubts if the proposed diligences or mail coaches could match the chaises in their journey time, as there was business that had to be done at the offices along the way. He regrets the robberies but says the best protection would be a guard on horseback. However, he gives no reason to justify this claim and says that the expense would be great. In any case he is convinced that cutting the notes in half is a much better safety measure than the provision of guards. This cutting of bank drafts and bills was the official security policy of the Post Office (see below). The idea was that if the notes were cut and the two halves sent by different posts then, in the event of a theft, only half the note would be lost. The stolen piece would thus be useless and could not be cashed. This policy was advocated in the newspapers but it did mean that transactions were delayed and the cost of postage increased.

Draper stresses, quite rightly, that the determined villain could eventually overcome any security measure. He quotes the example of a mail cart, specially reinforced with iron, that was stopped and ripped open on the North Road. He also claims that the stages were robbed more than the mail. Palmer answered this by pointing out that there were far more stages than mails, so obviously more were robbed. He stressed that armed guards would solve this problem, claiming that he did not know of a single stage with a guard ever being robbed, even when the guards were 'such people as the proprietors furnish.' This claim is perhaps a little too optimistic, for there are several recorded cases of guarded coaches being attacked.

Draper makes a relevant point by stressing that the London Bath Road was one of the best in the country and that the speeds possible on it might not be matched on other roads. Another of his claims was that all those involved in dealing with the mail should be under the direction of the Post Office. He suggested that if they were not confusion would inevitably result. There was some foundation to this criticism. Later on there were problems with those coachmen or drivers who were never directly employed by the Post Office and were only responsible to the contractors. There were occasions when the action of the driver was in doubt but the Post Office could only ask the contractor to take action. In the early days the guards were presumably also supplied by the contractors, only later did they become employees of the Post Office.

Draper did not believe that any diligence travelled at 8 or 9mph, and he was convinced that the time taken for the bags to be opened and the contents sorted would vary so much that the time allowed under Palmer's plan would be insufficient. Another point that Draper made, and one which may have influenced Palmer's final plan, was that if regular troops were used as guards, and he accepted that 'a soldier is certainly the properest guard and the most likely to answer the end proposed,' then an order from the King as Commander-in-Chief or an Act of Parliament would be needed to authorise their use.[10]

Draper was sure that changes in timing would lead to muddle, and Palmer's suggestion of a committee that might help in the local planning of the system was contemptuously dismissed with the comment:

> No committee of gentleman can be so proper judges of a general regulation for correspondence as the Postmaster General and the officers under them.

Draper was sure that Post Office officials were the only ones to have an overall picture and understanding of the postal system. He was convinced that the then system, founded on experience, was the very best possible. He agreed that the public have a right to expect quick and efficient service, but was convinced that Palmer's plan would not provide it.

The second list of comments was supplied by Mr Philip Allen, a Riding Surveyor. He supported Draper's comments about the time allowed for business and then claimed that the stages were robbed more than the post. He makes a further point about the speed of coaches to Bath, saying that in the case of journeys to that city diligences stayed on the one road for most of the time, which was not the case on many other routes. He declines to comment on the virtues of a contractor and guard and considers any estimate of their cost to be 'too speculative'. However, he rightly points out that if each coach was to have one guard then the total number required would be quite high. Palmer had also suggested stationing a soldier at each stage and this system would certainly have needed a very large number of troops. In fact, as was seen when the scheme was operating, no more than 150 would have been required. He made the further point that, if soldiers were used, it would be more proper for them to be under the control of the 'Chief of the Land Forces than the Postmaster General'. Allen was fair in that he thought Palmer's ideas about costs were worth considering. He suggested that a trial would be the only fair way to assess the practical aspects of the scheme. However, he added the qualification that if it was only carried out on the Bath road then the result should not be taken as vindicating the scheme as a whole. A postscript says that some additional observations were left with Mr Pitt for the conference to be held at the Treasury on 21 June 1784.

A similar set of objections is given in *Observations on Mr Palmer's Plan for Reform and Improvement in the management of the business of the General Post Office.*[11] There are three copies, marked *A*, *B* and *C*. These documents, finely written in copperplate script, appear to be a summary of the objections and are set out in two columns. On the left there is the column of objections and on the right is Palmer's response.

Objection number two:

> It is granted that the post of late years has been but too frequently robbed but it
> is apprehended not so often as stagecoaches.

Palmer's reply:

> The proportion of stagecoaches to the post are out of all comparison, therefore
> the former are more frequently robbed but I propose a guard, and the guard to
> be a regular soldier of character though I believe scarce a single instance can be
> produced of a machine being robbed that was guarded even by such people as
> the proprietors furnish.

Objection number four:

> An idle post boy or as idle a machine driver are equally unfit for the care and
> protection of the mail.

Palmer responded that he:

> …relied on the guard more than the driver whose honesty I do not vouch for
> tho' few instances can be produced of their robbing the coach instructed to
> their care.

The Riding Surveyor George Hodgson, who had been in Yorkshire, was probably
the most hostile critic. His comments are neatly listed in Folder C of Post 92/20
pt 2, he obviously needled Palmer because his answers to the objections are pref-
aced by a paragraph:

> Before I proceed to answer this report, I must beg to observe that however
> contemptuously some of the remarks in it are expressed, I have nonetheless
> considered them with the utmost care and most impartial attention, and chiefly
> concern'd to find the habits of office seem to create a sort of confirm'd opinion
> of its perfection and resistance to all improvement.

The writer, almost certainly Hodgson, starts by saying, 'I do not see why the Post
should not be the swiftest conveyance in England.' He also thinks that considering the number of mails on the move the number of robberies was relatively small
and that the public did not suffer unduly. He supported the cut bill system and
refers to the case of the iron-bound cart. He then makes the (very suspect) claim
that coaches and diligences, 'which are robbed almost every night in the week,'
are then, 'through the influence of the proprietors with the printer of newspapers

information thereof often kept from the public.' He goes on at length about the time required by Postmasters to sort the mail and does not see how Palmer's plan could possibly allow for this. He also expresses doubts about whether the guard would improve security and thinks that in fact they might well delay the coach – how he does not indicate – but it seems to suggest that he thought the guard would do nothing except guard the coach.

Hodgson was also very scathing about Palmer's suggestion of a committee to help plan the post:

> It is not probable that any set of gentlemen merchants or our riders can instruct officers brought up in the business of the Post Office, and it is particularly to be hoped if not presumed that the surveyors need no such information.

However, the section that probably irked Palmer most was that which dealt with security, section 14:

> The safety or security of the letters seems also here to [have] escaped attention, no provision being made to guard the bags and mails in the absence of the post master against the number of idle people who generally crowd the yards and doors of inns.
>
> Indeed it is a pity that the author of the plan should not first have been informed of the nature of the business in question to make him understand how very differently the present Post Offices are conducted to what he apprehends and that the constant eye that has long been kept towards their improvement in all situations and under all circumstances have made them now as perfect as can be without exhausting the revenue arising therefrom.

Aside from the pomposity of the paragraph, the writer's ignorance of Palmer's work in researching the whole procedure and the existence of the guard must have been galling.

If it is possible to sum up the general objections then the majority were refusals to accept that any change could be good. There was much to say about times and collections, but these fears were eventually shown to be groundless when the scheme was implemented. There were occasional hitches, but in general Palmer's plan worked and the post was made more efficient, its scope was extended and the service generally improved.

Pitt's party was voted back into office, and on 21 June 1784 he took the bold step of calling the interested parties together for a conference. Evidently he was not won over by the objectors and directed Palmer to run a trial on the Bath and Bristol road. Palmer hired a coach from a supplier, Fromont of Thatcham, and made arrangements to change horses with five innkeepers on the route. The service was advertised in the newspapers and the fare was to be £1-8-0 (£1.40) each passenger. The coach, with driver, guard and four inside passengers left the Rummer Inn in Bristol at 4 p.m. on Monday 2 August. The run went well and the coach arrived at the Swan with Two Necks inn, Lad Lane, London around 9 a.m. the next day. The coach ran exactly to schedule, thus cutting the normal post run time in half and Palmer's claim was vindicated. A similar run from London to Bristol was equally successful. There is some discrepancy between the illustration purporting to show the first coach and the newspaper account which says the coach was drawn by a team of two, the illustration portrays a team of four.[12] Since the coach was a light one and carried only four passengers it seems likely that a two horse team would have sufficed. As Palmer had no official position in the Post Office he was held to be responsible for all the arrangements and costs and this situation continued for some time.

As a result of this success he was encouraged by many to organise other runs and Pitt ordered the officials to assist him. Next it was intended to set up a route to Norwich, but this was delayed largely as a result of obstruction or near sabotage by some members of staff. Not only were they prejudiced about an outsider trying to tell experienced postal workers how to do their job, but the new system would lead to some loss of income to them. Although the Norwich route was planned to start late in 1784 it was not until March 1785 that it first ran, to be followed by other runs to some of the main towns.

In the issue of the *London Gazette* dated 15-18 October 1785 the following routes were recorded:

Bath and Bristol from The Swan with two Necks and Gloucester Coffee House Piccadilly (commenced May).
Norwich and Yarmouth from the White Horse, Fetter Lane.
Nottingham and Leeds from the Bull and Mouth, Bull and Mouth Street.
Manchester from Swan with two Necks (commenced July).
Liverpool, again from the Swan with two Necks (commenced July).
Portsmouth from the Angel behind St. Clements Church.
Southampton and Poole from the Bell and Crown, Holborn and Gloucester Coffee House.
Gloucester from the Angel.
Birmingham from the Swan with two Necks.
Worcester and Ludlow from the George and Blue Boar, Holborn and Gloucester Coffee House.
Bath and Bristol via Andover and Devizes from the Swan with two Necks and Gloucester Coffee House.
Shrewsbury from the Bull and Mouth.
Cirencester and Stroud from The George and Blue Boar.
Windsor from the Three Cups, Broad Street and Gloucester Coffee House.
Chester and Holyhead from the Swan with two Necks.
Carlisle via Manchester from the Swan with two Necks.

A similar list published in the *General Evening Post* of January 1786 includes six extra routes: including Dover, Exeter and Hereford as well as divergent routes to previously named destinations.

Opposition within the Post Office was not stifled, and in the early days some officials took any and every opportunity to denigrate the scheme. Comparative tables of cost were drawn up for the periods before and after the adoption of Palmer's scheme, proving it to be far more expensive.[13] Despite these and other complaints the public took to the new system, and although postal charges[14] were increased about the same time, business still increased. During this time Palmer still had no official position and indeed was still subsidising the scheme with his own money, much as he had done with the trial run. When the time came to give him some official standing there were legal problems and the lawyers had to examine all the various Acts of Parliament dealing with the mail right back to 9 Anne *c*.10. The main problem seems to have been the question of the royal monopoly on the mail and where the money to pay Palmer should come from.

A letter from Palmer dated 21 May 1788 states that after Bristol & Portsmouth mail started on 5 May 1785 Pitt told him to extend the service to as many principal towns in the kingdom as he thought fit.[15] Pitt was delighted at the success of the scheme, but Palmer's agreement was yet to be confirmed and Pitt would consider the situation. Palmer received an offer of £1,500 a year and 2½ per cent of profits on increased revenue, on 22 October 1785 he agreed with the added request that the appointment be made by the Treasury and not the Post Office. However, terms in the Queen Anne Act made this impossible and clearly stipulated that he had to be appointed by the Postmaster General and could not be appointed for life.

During the early days, not surprisingly, there were teething problems. There was some trouble with late deliveries, mostly caused by the winter weather and poor sorting, which were seized upon by Palmer's opponents in the Post Office. Comments, rumours and gossip suggested that the scheme would probably not be continued. On 11 March 1786 Palmer wrote to Pitt rebutting the various complaints and Pitt apparently accepted his comments. However, Palmer was having difficulties and his health, weakened by his spell in the brewery, was suffering. On 8 April 1786, with typical bravado (or arrogance, depending upon your point of view) he inserted an advert in the London newspapers declaring that these early problems were largely due to the bad conduct of officials in the Post office, but that he would soon be in a position to guarantee that the letters would be delivered on time. He had expected a public reaction but was still gratified by the public response, he was even forgiven by Pitt and his appointment was confirmed. Probably realising that he had gone a little too far he attempted to mend matters. He entered another notice saying that the first advert did not imply that the Postmaster General was in any way personally responsible and he apologised for any misunderstanding.

PAUL CLIFFORD

A nineteenth-century romantic concept of a highwayman. In fact they were usually very crude and brutal, but fiction has created a false aura of dashing heroism.

His appointment was now confirmed: Carteret, one of the Postmasters General, signed the agreement but the other, Tankerville, agreed to sign but then resigned as he felt that he had been ill-treated by Pitt. Lord Clarendon was appointed as the new Postmaster General and he approved but did not sign, as he felt that the offer of a percentage of the increased revenue was possibly illegal. After much discussion it was agreed that Palmer would relinquish the percentage and ask Pitt for £3,000 per annum instead. Pitt was not happy, for he had felt that the percentage agreement would encourage Palmer to work harder in order to improve business and so raise his income. In the end the Warrant for his salary was granted from January 1784.[16]

The Treasury Letter book for March 1786 - June 1789[17] has the official agreement dated 1 August 1786 and is signed by Pitt and others. The entry says that as Palmer's plan has been in operation it has been agreed that it will be implemented throughout Great Britain and that the Postmaster General should appoint Palmer as Comptroller General of the Mails and Surveyor. He was to get a salary of £1,500 per annum plus 2½ per cent of Post Office income generated above a total of £300,000, subject to certain conditions. On 1 August it was agreed that this could be done legally and he was duly appointed from 5 August 1786.[18]

The terms of the official approval stated that he had sufficient authority over all those involved with letters in the Kingdom: surveyors, comptrollers, postmasters, contractors, deputies, clerks, sorters, window men, letter receivers, letter carriers, messengers and other officers and servants. He was given the power to suspend or dismiss officers for neglect and he was to be paid from 5 August 1786. It will be noted that he was not given the authority to appoint officers, an omission (whether accidental or deliberate) that was to lead to problems later. On 15 April 1789 George Rose wrote to the Treasury Chambers saying that he had mentioned to Mr Pitt that Palmer had made several appointments in office. William Pitt then stated that it was not his intention that any such thing should happen and that these people should be reappointed by the Postmaster General as Palmer was only given authority to suspend and not to appoint. It was decided that in future Palmer would have to go to the Postmaster General to get his approval, but as events show he seems not to have heeded this instruction.[19]

At the same time he was given permission to establish his office staff. However, by 5 December 1788 Palmer was already asking for an increase in his staff numbers (already large), to be taken-on when the new system was established. On 23 December 1786 the size of his establishment had been queried by the Treasury. On 29 December the Postmaster General replied that he had checked the situation and the number of staff was appropriate for the new system.[19A]

Palmer was either very lucky or a very shrewd judge of character, for among those appointed was Thomas Hasker, who was made Superintendent of Mails and Mail Coaches at a salary of £100 a year. He had joined Palmer in October 1785:

> …in consequence of the innumerable blunders and mischief that were continually arising from the stupidity or the perverseness of the deputies in the management of the new constructed Bye Bags and the impossibility of its being attended to by any of the people then in the service. His business has been to instruct the guards also in that part of the duty and as occasion required he has been stationed on different parts of the roads to correct irregularity in the conduct of the contractors, the guards and the coachmen and contributed greatly to the good order which authority alone is now wanting permanently to establish. When at home he is of great assistance in preparing the Post Time Bills and similar letters that are periodically sent to the several contractors and is otherwise very useful in the office.[20]

Hasker was hard-working, dedicated and apparently indefatigable. He travelled the country dealing with problems and he was, judging by some letters, a compassionate man who was prepared to give most people the benefit of the doubt, a trait which would cause him some problems. In one notice he points out that some guards are ferrying quite large quantities of meat in their boxes – presumably to sell to friends. Some were carrying up to 150lbs of meat and Hasker thought this was excessive. Superintendents were instructed to check, but Hasker said that he would have no objection if they limited themselves to just an odd joint of meat or some fish for their family.[21]

He petitioned the Postmaster General late in the 1780s, the letter is undated, making out his case for an increase in salary. Hasker gives an outline of his responsibilities in town and on the road in a statement.[22] He rightly stresses that when the mail coaches started there was no existing structure or office procedure to build on and that he had to do everything and create the administrative system. He lists the many records that he had to keep: including schedules, uniforms, black books that list guards' errors, guards' bondsmen and many others. There was a time book of guard's duty and a directory, a contractor's register for each road. He pointed out that, in addition to all the administrative work, he also had to travel the country checking routes and guards. Unlike some other officers neither was he provided with any official living accommodation in London, which involved him in extra expense. He points out that he had to set up many operational procedures as well as physically supervise the routes.[23] There are sound reasons for granting Hasker far more credit in the successful setting-up of the system and running of the mail coaches than his current reputation reflects. Little is known of his personal history, but the archives supply plenty of evidence of his importance and the great part he played in creating the system. Palmer may have produced the plan but it was Hasker who worked out the details and did so much to make it work. He served the Mail Coach Office well for thirty-two years before he retired in 1817.

Another man who played an important part in the day of the mail coach was Francis Freeling, although he was perhaps not as directly involved in everyday matters as Hasker. He had distinguished himself as chief clerk at Bristol Post Office and had a wide knowledge of all postal matters. Palmer employed him from the beginning of April 1785 with the permission of the Bristol Deputy Postmaster. However, his efficiency and reorganisation skills persuaded Palmer to ask for his release from Bristol and he joined the mail coach staff in London as a full-time surveyor on 23 July 1785. For some time in the early days of his service he received no regular salary but was paid expenses as he travelled over the county. He was one of three surveyors who applied for a salary increase for their riding work on 15 October 1788.[24]

Later on, Freeling dealt more directly with the Postmaster General and became, in effect, a kind of managing director whose main job was keeping an eye on the overall picture. He gradually took on more responsibility and when Palmer left virtually became head of the department, he rose to the post of assistant to Post Office Secretary Anthony Todd in 1797. The Postmaster General informed the Treasury that if Todd died or retired (he was then aged eighty), Freeling was to be appointed as Secretary at a salary of £500 in addition to his existing income.[25] Todd died in 1798 and Freeling became Secretary. He remained with the Post Office, was made a Baron in 1828 and died in 1836. There is nothing to suggest anything other than a reasonably good working relationship between Freeling and the Postmaster General although there is perhaps just a hint of exasperation on occasion. On 5 June 1814 the Postmaster General comments rather acidly:

I almost inclined to doubt the sanity of the writer who proposes to convey at the rate of 30-60 mph letters, passengers and heavy goods thro a tube laid underground by strong and continued blast of air. Can it be necessary to answer this letter? I regret only that you have thought it necessary to write anything on the subject.[26]

Freeling did incur the Postmaster General's displeasure over some plans he made in Scotland, but as they were done on instructions from Palmer he was relatively blameless (see below).

Another of the early pioneers was Charles Bonnor of Bristol, an actor, and in this instance Palmer's character judgment appears to have let him down, for this man was later to bring about the suspension and dismissal of Palmer. Bonnor had at one time been apprenticed to a coach maker before turning to the stage in 1777 and appearing in the Bath and Bristol theatres:

Chas. Bonnor First engaged in the mail coach plan in July 1784 (when he quitted his theatrical situation for the remainder of that summer at Brighthelmstone.) and has devoted his attention to it ever since. He retained his engagement at Covent Garden Theatre the next winter but the leisure a theatrical life affords and the application of all the time he could command to this object rendered his business at the theatre no impediment to the proper discharge of his duty to the post plan. At the close of Covent Garden Theatre in May 1785 he declined engaging in any other employ and dedicated all his time and attention to the Post Plan. The permanence of the plan not being thoroughly established when Covent Garden Theatre opened in September 1785 he waited upon Mr Rose in order to ascertain whether the terms upon which his services were intended to be retained would warrant his final relinquishment of his theatrical situation, at the same time intimating to Mr Rose it would not be worth his while to do it for less than a salary of £500 p ann. exclusive of house rent, coals and candles. These points acceded to he gave up his engagement at Covent Garden Theatre entirely.[27]

When Palmer set up the coaching staff Bonnor was made Resident Surveyor and Deputy Comptroller, he officially commenced his duties on 9 November 1786. In fact he was working for the office from 5 July 1784 and was duly paid the back salary.[28] He was appointed as it was believed that, 'Palmer will often be absent on duty.'[29] He became, as of 29 November 1786, the Surveyor and Comptroller General at the agreed salary of £500 pa with a house and allowances of candles and coals. Some nine years later, on 30 June 1795, the Treasury agreed to his retirement. However, in the intervening period he had played a chequered role in the story of the mail coach.[30]

According to a fifteen and a half page letter written by him on 30 July 1784, Bonner had a meeting with Todd the Secretary together with Allen the Surveyor.

Model of a post boy.
(Permission of Bath Postal Museum)

The meeting began in a very unfriendly spirit as Bonnor was representing Palmer. However Bonnor, no doubt using his acting skills, convinced them that despite appearances he was not keen on the planned mail coaches, which in his view were not going to work. He was only supporting Palmer because they had been friends for a very long time. Since Todd and his officers predicted disaster and were anxious to stop the scheme why did they not let the trial run go ahead? It would surely fail and their opposition would then be justified. Their antipathy towards Bonnor was immediately modified and henceforward they treated him as an ally. They even gave him permission to talk to the various Postmasters. Bonnor later claimed that some of those Post Office staff that he spoke to gave him information on examples of direct intervention undertaken by Todd which were obviously intended to upset the mail coach runs.[31] The outcome was that the trial run was permitted to proceed, and of course it proved a success.

Bonnor then was no longer seen as a friend of the critics, and in a letter to Todd on 8 April 1785 he states that most of the complaints about the coaches were caused by a lack of co-operation by Post Office personnel. He added that Todd had always opposed the plan and had made little effort to remedy matters.[32] Palmer had wanted an official poster pointing out that there was an office to deal with the mail coaches at 87 Lombard Street, but Todd was unco-operative. The underlying tension is clear in a letter written by Todd on 30 August 1785 in which he says that

Palmer has been complaining that some Postmasters are ignoring his instructions. He says that if any Postmaster is ignoring any instruction given by the Postmaster General regarding Palmer's plan then he will be punished. This was actually a rather sly way of suggesting that really Palmer was not directly in charge.[33]

Bonnor himself admitted to his lack of administrative skill. He was involved in the payment of the guards' wages and when the Deputy Postmasters were instructed to pay them there was confusion. The Postmaster General frequently complained about the wages and pressed Bonnor to sort out the problem. Bonnor was apparently rather conscious of his position and the need to assert his authority, in September 1785 he sent a letter to Todd demanding the sacking of one member of staff for refusing to accept that he had the right to give orders or speak to the Liverpool guard. The member of staff had abused both Palmer and Bonnor and refused to take any action.[34]

Palmer's relationship with his Postmaster General was, at best, frosty, and it may be that the stubbornness he displayed in his youth had developed into arrogance as his powers grew. It seems that he considered himself to be above dealing with mere routine details. As in the case of the firearms (see below), it would seem that he had a habit of making all manner of arrangements without consulting or informing his masters. Not surprisingly, they resented his high-handed approach and thus conflicts were inevitable.

In the early days no chance to denigrate Palmer's plan was missed by the Old Guard staff. This is clearly shown by the notice put out by Todd on 5 February 1785 stating that, 'it has been resolved to make a further trial of Mr Palmer's plan for conveying His Majesty's Mails.' The implication was that there was still some uncertainty about the scheme. The new runs were just another experiment which, by inference, belittled the scheme and suggested that it had still not proved satisfactory, which it most certainly had. Palmer protested but the advert for a proposed Norwich run appeared as quoted.

The changes in the running of the Post Office introduced under Palmer's control were considerable, on 15 February 1788 a 'before and after' chart was drawn up under the headings of Old and New.[35] It goes into detail about how the carriers' walks were adjusted, how timing was improved and how discipline, morale and general attitude were developed and the whole system of accounting tightened. Special arrangements were made for the delivery of late arrivals of mail. Security was increased and the loss rate of valuable mail was cut dramatically. As this comparison was presumably drawn up under Palmer's guidance it may be, perhaps, a little over stated, but even so the changes were undoubtedly beneficial. It was claimed that the bag man had been claiming for new and repaired bags without any checks being made. Now bags were checked for condition as they arrived and a list made of numbers requiring attention resulting in a reduction of costs. The outlay on prosecutions was put at £4,000 per annum but now:

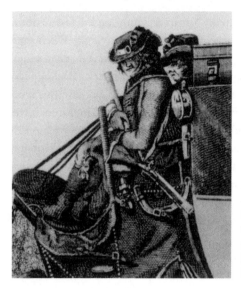

A detail from the engraving of the
original London-Bristol coach. It shows
Carter – the guard – who was later
to be dismissed for drunkenness. He
carries what is probably a blunderbuss
in addition to that which is slung across
his shoulder.

All the mails conveyed upon the new plan are protected by a guard who is provided with a blunderbuss, a brace of pistols and proper ammunition for the use
of the same. Each guard is sworn to his duty and finds two responsible bond-
men as sureties for his good behaviour.
(The document is undated but comments, in particular about the guards, would
indicate a post-1788 date.)

The Postmasters found dealing with Palmer difficult, and he seems to have made
little, if any, attempt to accommodate their wishes. On 8 May 1790 the Postmaster
General together wrote to the Treasury sending details of the mail coach expenditure. In the letter they said:

We wish to observe to your Lordships that it has been the practice ever since the
Mail Coaches were adopted for the Comptroller General to make and execute
the contracts without our ever having seen or signed them or been parties to
them as to the covenants they contained in any manner whatever, at present we
understand all contracts are discontinued and the agreements are verbal only.

They were unhappy that the contractors were free to make all manner of claims
while they had never cut any of Palmer's accounts. They were particularly upset
that they had not been receiving the Riding Journals from the surveyors, a
requirement set down by Lord Carteret when the system first started.[36]
    Palmer was either a stubborn and arrogant man or just plain unimaginative, but
he certainly adopted a rather cavalier attitude to the Postmaster General. In one
letter he told them that he would not obey any order which he thought to be

wrong or damaging.[37] He was undoubtedly a man of vision and determination and had to deal with a wide range of postal matters. In August 1787 he was deeply involved in organising a post between London and Paris. He stayed at the Hotel de l'Europe in Paris and argued the case for a number of posts from Boulogne to Dover and Dover to Calais. The matter was not simple, there was discussion on the number of posts a week, whether French boats should carry English mail, the costs involved and whether a port tax should be charged by the French.[38] A full English translation of the treaty was given on 11 March 1793.[39]

Despite his undoubted ability, tact and tolerance seem not to have been Palmer's strong points. Relations with the Postmaster General were frequently strained and on 19 October 1790 they sent another long letter to Pitt at the Treasury detailing the situation with Palmer.[40] The request was for a meeting as:

> …we cannot help feeling anxious in the present moment; until we shall be able to convince you that the appeal which the Comptroller General has made to you is unnecessary and the assertions which his letter to us contains have not the smallest foundation.

It was only their sense of duty and desire to act correctly that made them trouble Pitt:

> …otherwise we should have found it very easy to retort upon Mr Palmer (and to prove our assertions) that the charge of unhandsome and unprovoked behaviour, but as in his letter which we have sent to you Mr Palmer has thought proper to accuse us of an endeavour to undermine his authority, and of the commission of many acts tending to clog and impede him in the discharge and exercise of his duty.
> (They have no doubt Pitt will demand that Palmer prove his allegations.)

One point they stress is that Palmer had appointed officers, promoted them and granted them salaries; a function that was not authorised by his commission and which created costs that the Postmaster General did not have the authority to pay. Palmer's accusation was that measures to improve the service were stopped because 'he did not choose to submit it to our judgment.' He had to attend Board meetings but he also had the responsibility to place on record all instructions and proposals, which would then be entered in the Journals of the officers and signed by him. This was one of the conditions that Lord Carteret had promised the Treasury he would implement, and the concept of providing details of the duties was an important condition of the Treasury's consent to the appointment of the Comptroller. The Postmaster General could not possibly sign warrants for sums of money which were not clearly specified. Accounts presented by Palmer were poorly kept and inaccurate. Indeed they only just managed to get the accounts of guards' wages – amounting to £7,000 – completed, and even that is muddled, some guards have been overpaid and others underpaid. Palmer demands that any blame should be clearly apportioned, but it was not their intention to blame anybody. Indeed, some of Palmer's own past faults were discreetly sorted by them, these actions certainly weren't consistent with people making, 'an unprovoked and wanton insult upon himself and upon the officers of his department.' They had no records in their possession of Palmer's proceedings since his appointment and so they came to the inevitable conclusion that, 'we can neither approve nor disapprove that of which we have no knowledge.'

The Postmaster General details the question of the guards' wages and how money was kept back to build a fund to pay for their clothing, sick pay, supernumerary and substitute guards as well as:

> …for other articles of which no account whatever was laid before us; a great part of the taylor's (sic) demand for the furnishing of the cloathes (sic) for the guards is still unpaid; the bill is now produced without either the patterns or prices of any of the articles of which the total consists, which are charged at £3-19-6 pr suit for coat and waistcoat only so that we have not the usual and necessary means to check which is required by every regiment in England before the public money can be issued for its cloathing (sic).

They went on to state that the appointing of the guards, 'amounting to 150 in number', would normally be, and later was, in their hands. They had not seen the contracts with the mail coach masters, although contracts were signed by Palmer and they had signed warrants for the payment of above:

> …£700 for firearms which by the printed terms of the original contract the contractors themselves were obliged to furnish. We now understand that all contracts with them are abolished and that the whole carriage of the mails is carried on by verbal agreement.

Much is made of the fact that a Letter carrier, Mr Johnson, appeared to have been given a free hand to make far-reaching changes in the organisation. This had been done without him acquiring any official responsibility and he went on to modify the entire 110 walks of the Carriers. Whilst in general the changes were approved, they should still have been placed before the relevant authorities for approval. They also disputed claims made by Palmer that his plan had been responsible for a great increase in revenue for the Post Office. The letter was accompanied by copies of Palmer's commission and extracts of minutes which they claimed backed their case.[41]

On 4 April 1791 Palmer sent a minute that was, by any standards, extremely blunt. It concerned the payment of the Port Patrick and Dumfries costs which

Palmer had agreed, however the Postmaster General had then decided it should be approved by the Treasury. This was the start of a number of minutes from Palmer blaming their Lordships for interference with corresponding threats from the contractors to stop working; eventually Hasker and Woolmer had to be sent on several long trips to sort out the matter. Palmer also demanded answers to three questions regarding the Postmaster General's intentions. The Postmaster General replied the next day stating that Palmer did not answer their queries and took action without any approval from them. They were unable to answer his first question because they had no information over its substance, the second question was no more than an insult and the third was something that had been raised before and Palmer had not responded to.

Matters did not improve, and on 16 April the Postmaster General sent a minute to William Pitt saying matters were so bad that business was at a standstill. Palmer responded with his usual claim that in reality he was responsible to the Treasury and not the Post Office. The scarcely concealed hostility between Palmer and the Postmaster General was inevitably going to lead to serious problems. In 1787 Lord Walsingham had been appointed as one of the Postmasters, he was a stickler for correct procedure, attention to detail and delighted in minutes, records and above all checking accounts. In 1788 a report on the working of the Post Office was presented by a Commission and its presentation led to much manoeuvring by Palmer and Walsingham, each of who was trying to get his views adopted. In September Palmer had been confirmed as Surveyor and Comptroller General, he was subsequently granted a fixed salary with a commission of profits. His control over all staff was confirmed, he had the authority to suspend but not dismiss. It was emphasised by Walsingham that all plans would have to be seen by the Postmaster General.

Bonnor, as Palmer's deputy, was heavily involved in the finances. However, his accounting was not always as precise as it should have been. He even admitted that at one time in the past he had been obliged to stay in France to escape creditors. He was not well organised and his problems were made even worse by a highly suspicious 'fire' in his office which destroyed some of his vouchers (or receipts) in January 1788. No suspect was caught and no explanation of how it started was confirmed. To make matters worse there was an 'attack' on his office at Lombard Street, in which cupboards and drawers were broken into and papers and a box stolen. Despite intensive inquiries no thief was found, indeed there seemed to be no clues at all. Unfortunate as these events might have been, they certainly eased the pressure on Bonnor. As many of his records, warrants and accounts were missing he now had an excuse for not being able to justify the accounts which others queried.

In 1789 Bonnor presented some accounts and Walsingham's checking called much of the accounting into question, in fact some irregular payments were found. By June 1791 he was in such a financial mess that he had to confess to Palmer and seek his help. He wrote of how pressure of business and heavy demands on his time were responsible for a breakdown in his health, he was also upset by the unjust insinuations which were being made by staff. He begged Palmer's help and admitted a deficit of around £1,200. Palmer, to his credit, did settle some of the deficit with his own money. To make matters worse one of Bonnor's clerks submitted a false account for his travelling expenses and an attempt was made to cover this up. Palmer's misgivings about Bonnor were strengthened when it was found that Bonnor had, in contravention of the rules, been financially involved with the manufacturer of the coaches used by the Post Office. Bonnor eventually managed to wriggle his way out of the situation, he even made some money from Vidler (the coach maker).

The final event which was to lead to Palmer's eventual dismissal happened in July 1788. Palmer was invited to Dublin to receive the Freedom of the City while King George III was staying at Cheltenham after an illness. Walsingham thought it proper that the royal mail should be sent to the King daily by two special coaches. Thus Bonnor was ordered, in Palmer's absence, to arrange this without worrying about the cost. When Palmer discovered what had been done he was upset, claiming that Walsingham was not in a position to make such arrangements. He also condemned his readiness to pay more than the standard rate, for this would lead to other contractors demanding higher rates just when Palmer had managed to get a general agreement with them to accept something more reasonable.

Matters were not helped when Wilson, the contractor involved, submitted an enormous bill. Palmer blamed Walsingham for the great expense incurred and said it should not be paid. Walsingham insisted it should be paid and that if there was no other way of settling the matter he would let the matter go to law. At this point Palmer changed his mind and told Walsingham to arrange arbitration. This was done and Wilson was paid, but at a very high figure. Palmer claimed this was all down to Walsingham's incompetence and interference.

Bad feeling was exacerbated in 1790 when Palmer sent Freeling to Scotland to set up various routes and make arrangements to extend the post. Freeling performed this task with great skill and received a letter of appreciation from a Scottish lord, which he then forwarded to Walsingham with a covering letter. Unbeknown to Freeling, or Palmer for that matter, Walsingham had been working on plans for Scotland and was not best pleased to find out that he had been bypassed. Taking apparent umbrage, Walsingham ordered that Freeling's plans be put on hold. He then wrote to Freeling, telling him – in effect – that he had no business reporting directly to him and that correspondence should only be sent via the Comptroller. On 12 October 1790 Palmer wrote a stinging letter to the Postmaster General complaining of their, 'attempt to supersede my commission and your further interference with my regulations.' He said that he was appealing to the Treasury, 'to whom I consider myself responsible for my conduct for though I am nominally under the Postmaster General I am virtually under the Treasury.'

It may well be that Palmer made this claim, for it was the Treasury that gave final financial approval to his employment and the scheme, but the claim itself is surely no more than an attempt to justify his actions. He berates the Postmaster General for daring to interfere with the situation and then goes on to assure them of his great respect, despite the, 'very unhandsome and unprovoked conduct you have used towards me.' Palmer defies the Postmaster General to point out a single blot on his working record, therefore why, he wondered, 'this wanton interference, threatening me, and insulting and disgracing valuable officers.' He later stated that he had met a lot of opposition at the beginning of his tenure of office, but that with perseverance he overcame it and succeeded in his plan.

Palmer goes on to promise total disobedience to any orders from the Postmaster General if he considers them dangerous or ill conceived. He then warns them that, 'you know not how delicate and dangerous an engine you are playing with.' He points out that he would suffer financially if he mismanaged the mail coaches and goes on to tell them how nasty they have been to Mr Freeling, he even suggests that they should grant him some reward for the anguish they have caused him.[42] It is difficult to know how much of this was Palmer's outrage and how much was rhetoric, but the language he used was hardly diplomatic, or even sensible considering the Postmaster General's place in the hierarchy. Although both parties approached Pitt seeking his backing in the squabble, he managed to avoid any involvement.

As if matters were not bad enough, in the following year, 1791, there was trouble over rates paid to the contractors for the Port Patrick – Dumfries run. These rates were more than normal to compensate for the small amount of business in that area. Walsingham refused to approve them as he considered them to be too high, to which Palmer retaliated by withdrawing four routes. A year later this was followed by Walsingham discovering problems with some of the accounts submitted by the Inland Revenue. He found there were some discrepancies in the Post Office returns and, not unreasonably, instituted stringent checks to see if the results produced were the same as those given by the Post. These cross-checks took time and inevitably led to some delays in the service, but Walsingham foresaw this and had already sent the Deputy Accountant to explain matters to Palmer who seemed most understanding.

There matters stood until 9 February 1792 when the *Public Advertiser* carried an advert announcing a meeting to be held on 15 February. This meeting was to protest about the delays in the mail. Palmer now made a serious error of judgment. He instructed Bonnor to make it quite clear to one of the leading members of the meeting that the delays were caused by the extra checks instituted by Walsingham. Bonnor actually went even further and hinted that Palmer had opposed these steps only to be frustrated by Walsingham. He was also to indicate that matters could be helped if a group of merchants were to appeal to Pitt so as to ensure that Palmer was supported in his opposition. Bonnor was also told to supply them with official papers backing Palmer's claims.

The church of Saint Mary
Woolnorth, situated next door to the
Lombard Street Post Office.

Bonnor then panicked, according to one of his later accounts he then told
Palmer that his conscience was greatly troubled. He feared that he might be
caught in the middle of this affair and at worst could lose his job. He wrote
to Palmer declaring that he was unhappy about matters and could no longer
take part in the plot. Palmer now made a second error of judgment and offered
Bonnor a kind of bribe: if Bonnor handed back the papers given to him by
Palmer and resigned from his position then he and his wife would receive an
'annuity'. Bonnor declined the offer, the planned meeting then collapsed and
failed to generate any of the backing that Palmer was hoping for.

Palmer then compounded his errors by trying to dispose of Bonnor. This he
did by indirectly informing him that he was no longer his deputy, in effect sacking him, he also threatened that if he did not return the papers, action would
be taken against him. Furthermore he would not pay Bonnor 'one shilling'. On
28 February 1792 the Postmaster General asked Palmer to send a copy of the
warrant from the Treasury authorising Bonnor's suspension.[43] With no response
forthcoming from Palmer, the Postmaster General lifted Bonnor's suspension and
heightened the crisis even further. Bonnor's reply was to publish a pamphlet setting out his version of events and blaming Palmer for double-dealing. It seems
likely that he had already made sure Walsingham was in possession of the details
of the plot.

Support for Bonnor and Palmer was split, but obviously the matter had to be tackled by the Postmaster General. Letters were exchanged which implicitly told Palmer to reinstate Bonnor as Palmer had not, as requested, supplied the reason for his suspension. Bonnor wrote to the Postmaster General saying that Palmer had refused to give him the key to his office and had threatened that if he turned up at Lombard Street he would be thrown out by constables. This blatant disobedience to the Postmaster General's instructions called for one response: on 7 March 1792 Palmer was suspensed from office and a direct order to surrender Bonnor's key was given.

Both sides of the quarrel attempted to involve Pitt who, perhaps from a sense of loyalty, had supported Palmer from the beginning. However, Pitt was not inclined to do anything more than set up an official inquiry. At this point Bonnor delivered the *coup de grace*: he sent the Postmaster General sworn statements from postal officers stating that Walsingham's checks were not the real reason for the postal delays and that Palmer himself had not helped matters. Worst of all were some of the letters in Palmer's handwriting that he sent to Bonnor in confidence. One dealt with the Cheltenham coach episode and clearly shows how Palmer was doing his best to make capital out of Walsingham's action. These six letters all indicate that Palmer was prepared to use any means necessary to discredit The Postmaster General, and Walsingham in particular.[44] In the face of such dishonesty Pitt had no alternative but to dismiss Palmer, this was done on 5 April 1793, however, Palmer was granted a pension of £3,000 per annum. Bonnor was now appointed Comptroller of the Inland Office, but his powers were restricted and were in fact less than he had previously held as Deputy. Francis Freeling was given more powers as Resident Surveyor, while responsibility was also further delegated to other officials.

Bonnor's victory, such as it was, was empty: he was seen as a traitor at worst and a bad friend at best. Palmer was certainly viewed by much of the media as having been betrayed and ill-used. Subsequent financial inconsistencies, such as that concerning payment for obtaining a post for a John Hepburn, further undermined Bonnor. By now he had lost almost all his support, in an attempt to protect his own position he lashed out with a variety of accusations, but these were widely dismissed as having no substance. He gave evidence to a committee considering irregularities in franking, the committee then decided that the affairs of the Post Office were not 'being conducted as they ought to be.' It thought matters could be improved if Bonnor were removed; he was then 'retired' with a pension of £460 p.a. on 30 June 1795 by the Treasury.[45]

Bonner did not give up easily, he claimed there were all manner of problems in the Post Office, threatened legal action and named Freeling as being responsible for mismanagement. He published yet another pamphlet putting his side of the case, but by this time he had lost all credibility and was eventually imprisoned in the King's Bench prison for debt. He died in November 1831 and his pension reverted to the Revenue.[46]

Freeling was made joint Secretary in 1796 and became full Secretary in 1798, he remained in this position until his death in 1836. Now responsible for the overall planning and ably assisted by Hasker, he ensured a successful continuation of the mail coaches.

Palmer meanwhile went from strength to strength; he was honoured by cities and boroughs, was twice Mayor of Bath and was also a Member of Parliament. He was not entirely satisfied with his financial rewards from the Treasury and it was only with the support of his son, Major-General Charles Palmer, that in 1808[47] Parliament was persuaded to grant him the payment of many thousands of pounds, as well as the 2½ per cent commission of Post Office revenue promised in the original agreement. He died in 1818 aged seventy-six and was buried in Bath.

Palmer was a visionary with the determination to pursue his ideas, credit is due to him for his refusal to be deterred by the conservatism of the Post Office hierarchy. He pressed on with the coach system and, aided by stalwarts like Hasker and Freeling, made it work. In general his work was appreciated by the public to whom he gave a reasonably reliable postal system. He was duly honoured for this by being elected to various offices and even having a coin minted in his honour, but on the other hand he was also largely responsible for his own downfall. He only held a Post Office position between 1784 and 1793, and was in effect sacked as the result of his own stubbornness. A little more flexibility in his dealings with the Postmasters might well have meant many more years in office, but his stubbornness was the very quality that enabled him to bring his scheme to fruition.

3

THE GUARDS

In order to understand the dangers and problems facing the eighteenth-century Post Office with respect to its security and the safety of the mail, it is important to look at the levels of policing at the time. Prior to the nineteenth century, policing, at least in the modern sense, did not exist in Britain; law enforcement was essentially a local affair and was generally quite inefficient. In most of the country the only law enforcement officers were the parish constables; they were known by a variety of titles like head boroughs or tythingmen. In larger communities there was often a head constable who supervised them. These constables were elected by the local court or vestry and normally served for one year, they were unpaid and could, if they wished, pay a fine to be excused from the office, or hire a deputy to serve in their place. In some cases this meant that only the poorer people served in this office. They were usually under the control of the local Justices of the Peace. Their powers were restricted to their parish, a felon might escape them simply by crossing over the parish boundary. The parish constable was a relic of rural life, for with small communities the system worked reasonably well; neighbours knew one another, there was a sense of involvement and strangers or unusual behaviour were immediately spotted. With their larger populations towns lacked the necessary sense of community, neighbours were often strangers and the population was transient.

There was little co-operation between these local officers, and consequently information about crime and criminals was seldom circulated. Many constables, not surprisingly, did their best to keep out of trouble and simply waited for their term of office to end. After all they still had to live in the community and some people had long memories. This does not mean that all of them were useless, there is plenty of evidence to suggest that many tried to do the job with both honesty and a sense of duty. In many towns there were also official bodies, such as the Watch, which were supposed to patrol the streets at night. These, too, often lacked resources, initiative and enthusiasm. Ralph Wilson, a self-confessed highwayman, writing his life story in 1720, tells how, in London, he and his accomplices robbed a coach but the alarm was raised. He writes, 'the Watch poured in upon us from all parts, yet at the fire of a pistol over their heads they retired as fast.'[1]

It is difficult to assess just how dangerous civic life was in Britain during the eighteenth and nineteenth centuries. Contemporary newspapers that emphasise the dangers, perhaps sensationally, can create a somewhat unbalanced impression. Certainly in the towns, London in particular, there can be little doubt that there was much crime and people were well advised to be ready and able to defend themselves and their property. Travellers were particularly at risk, and from the seventeenth century onwards highway robbery was common. However, it should be stated that the romantic vision of a well-mounted, gallant, considerate highwayman is a myth. Coaches and riders were stopped by mounted thieves interested only in the booty and a quick get-away, they were certainly not inclined to indulge in pleasantries with their victims. The majority of cases of highway robbery were attacks by violent men and the crime was almost invariably crude, brief and rooted in harsh reality. Many travellers reported that, as a pistol was waved under their nose, the challenge was far more likely to be 'Give me your valuables or I'll blow your brains out', rather than the traditional 'Your money or your life'. This was the very phrase quoted by one post boy who had been robbed in December 1798.[2]

The Government policy for controlling crime was in essence one of deterrence. Make the punishment severe enough and people will be too frightened to commit the crime. Public hangings at Tyburn in London and elsewhere around the country were intended to horrify and impress the public. In fact, hanging days became virtual public holidays, often with the condemned playing to the crowd and aiming to be 'turned off' in style. A large number of offences were designated as capital crimes so that a guilty verdict automatically meant the death penalty. The theft of anything worth more than 12 pence was a capital offence, and on occasions juries would commit only for 11½ pence in order to avoid the ultimate penalty. Generally the deterrent policy was ineffective and, despite the prospect of possible execution, hanging in chains[3] and subsequent dissection by the surgeons, there were plenty of people, some driven by poverty, others by greed, prepared to risk all these horrors. Such was the lack of fear that there are recorded instances of pockets being picked at Tyburn whilst hangings were in progress. On 30 March 1802 Parkin, the Post Office solicitor, reported that John Nutcher, convicted at Lancaster for robbing the Wigan mail, was to be hanged and his body hung in chains.[4] In addition to the deterrent policy the Government offered various inducements to encourage the public to take action against the highwaymen. Rewards were offered and informers were invited to betray their criminal colleagues. Dotted around the countryside, by the side of many roads – often at crossing points – were gallows from which the felons were hanged, and in some places where their corpses were left to rot as a stark warning to any who might be tempted to turn to crime.

Despite the fact that robbing the mail was a capital offence,[5] attacks on the post boys were common. It was not until the late eighteenth century and the early nineteenth century that the number of attacks began to diminish. Indeed, only in 1835 did stealing documents from the Post Office cease to be a capital crime, sacrilege was also removed from the list by the same Act, (52 Geo III *c*.143).[6] On 13 February 1832 John Barrett, a sorter of franked and paid letters, was hanged at Newgate after pleading guilty to secreting a letter from the Inland Office.[7] He was the last to suffer death for this crime.

Villains knew that their chances of being captured were not very high, especially if they quickly left the scene of the crime. Even if a full description of the suspect was available and carried in the newspapers, the fact that there was no real, national press meant circulation was likely to be rather limited. In any case, a verbal description was not always sufficient to lead to recognition. The *General Evening Post* of January 1787 carried an account of a robbery from a post boy. A suspect, one James Elliott of Padstow, Cornwall, was described as being:

> ...about 30 years of age, 5 feet 9 inches tall, of a sallow complexion, wears a black tye wig, his natural hair which is beginning to grow out is also black; he walks ill owing to having corns or tender feet.

Apart from his tender feet there is little in this description to distinguish the robber from hundreds of other men. Literacy was also a limiting factor, considering that much of the population were unable to read. Despite all these limitations, it was not impossible for the thief to be captured, tried and sentenced, indeed the archives carry details of a number of such events.

Theft and robbery were serious problems for the Post Office; from the seventeenth century onwards the records contain numerous reports of post boys being robbed, beaten and, on occasions, killed. The Post Office made some provision if the worst happened, and on 4 January 1792 the Treasury agreed to pay an allowance of £12 per annum to the widow of John Hayworth, a post boy murdered when carrying mail between Warrington and Manchester.[8]

To add insult to injury it was not unknown for the thief to make off with the post horse as well as the bags of mail. Brief details of the robberies[9] were listed in the *London Gazette* and other newspapers. However, some earlier writers did exaggerate the danger, J. Wilson Hyde claimed that, 'it was an almost everyday occurrence for the mail-bags to be robbed on the night journeys, when the principal mails were carried.'[10] According to listings in the *London Gazette*, the worst period for mail robberies was between 1720 and 1800, a time when the numbers recorded ranged between only eleven and thirty-seven a year. These totals included theft from the offices as well as those involving post boys.

To the Mail Guards.

———

GENERAL POST-OFFICE,
June 14th, 1800.

HALF my Time is employed in receiving and answering Letters of Complaint from Passengers respecting the improper Conduct and impertinent Language of Guards. I am very sorry to dismiss sober honest Men, but I must have Civility also, and when you behave impertinently to Passengers, they find out some other Error to couple the Complaint with, that nothing less than Dismission can succeed. This plainly shews how circumspect Guards should be in their Behaviour, and I must insist that you conduct yourself so properly in all your Words and Actions as to prevent Complaints.

Your's, &c.

T. HASKER.

Printed by Marsh & Teape, Tower-Hill, for His Majesty's Stationery-Office.

Hasker appears to have been a kind-hearted man, but as this circular suggests his patience was sometimes sorely tried. (PO 10/5, no.14)

When a robbery was reported the common practice of the Post Office was to offer a reward for information leading to the apprehension and conviction of the offenders. A considerable sum of money, in contemporary terms £200, was the usual amount offered, and sometimes this system produced results. The Post Office accounts list several such payments:

Paid Mr Joseph Godman as a reward for apprehending and convicting John Hawkins who robbed the Bristol Mail on 11 April 1722 £100.[11]

May 31st 1722 paid Mr Godman a reward for the apprehending of Bon Child for robbing the mail.[12]

July 1795 Mrs Ann Osbaldston, Mr Jas. Nicholson, James Reckwick, Thos. Dennison, John Lucas, Nathaniel Woods, Wm. Horrocks qualified for the Reward of £200 for apprehending the persons, two men, possibly Irish, who robbed the mail and murdered the post boy James Hogworth on 15th Sep 1790 at 5 am, about a mile from Warrington, Edward Miles having been convicted thereof.[13]

A similar procedure was followed in Ireland, for example a notice in the *Dublin Chronicle* of Saturday 4 August 1787 offered a £100 reward with the usual conditions for information about the robbery from a post boy near Gormanstown. Three bags of mail were taken on 1 August and there was an extra inducement for the Lord Lieutenant offered a free pardon to any accomplice who betrayed the robber.[14]

When robbers were captured and convicted the reward was shared among those involved in that particular case, however, the distribution could cause problems. In April 1801 two brothers, John and James Austin, were convicted of two robberies; in August Mr Parkin, the Post Office solicitor, informed the Postmaster General that he had shared the reward of £200 among seven people. The amounts awarded ranged from £50 down to £5, but this division did not please a Mr William Anderson who wrote in protesting vigorously that the share-out was unfair and that he was entitled to more. The surviving correspondence does not disclose the outcome of the objection.[15]

Over the years the payment of these rewards constituted a steady drain on the Post Office's budget. The costs of dealing with robberies were increased even more when it became necessary, as it did on many occasions, to hire police officers to investigate cases and track down the offenders. The Post Office normally employed members from a select group of constables attached to Bow Street, London's main police office, this group was known as the Bow Street Runners. They were founded by Henry Fielding early in the century and acquired a great reputation for solving crimes and catching offenders, frequent references to the Runners are made in the media of the time, including the most famous of all: John Townshend. He was to be seen at royal functions and was known personally to many of the aristocracy. These men were considered to be the best police officers in the country, but their fees were high, as is shown by these examples, which are but a few of the many listed in the records:

> July 1791: James Walsh, Thomas Carpmeal (both Runners) for their trouble and expenses in a journey to Boulogne and other parts of France to apprehend James Oxon charged with robbing a mail and who escaped out of the House of Correction at Clerkenwell £100.[16]

(At today's values that equates to thousands of pounds.)

> April 1817 Mr Vickery Bow Street Officer for expenses and loss of time on services under the direction of our solicitor to 30 Jan last £17-19-4d.[17]

In addition to the cash rewards and the investigator's fees, there were other legal and travelling expenses to be met, the whole amounting to a considerable sum per annum. These costs steadily increased as the years passed and the *Treasury Letter Book*[18] lists the following:

> An Account of the Annual Expenses Attending Mail Robberies for ten years from 5th April 1775 to June 1784:

Caution to Mail Coachmen.

WHEREAS on Monday the 18th Day of July, 1814, Thomas Williams the Driver of the Carmarthen Mail Coach, in obedience to Summons appeared before Sackville Gwynne, Esq. one of His Majesty's Justices of the Peace for the Counties of Breco and Carmarthen, and on the Evidence of Thomas Hart, Guard to the said Mail, was fined in the Penalty of FIVE POUNDS, for Negligence in losing Time between Abergavenny and Landovery, agreeable to the Act of Parliament passed in the 50th Year of the Reign of His Majesty George the Third,—Authorizing any Magistrate to punish the Driver of any Mail Coach with Fine or Imprisonment, if he shall not, in all possible Cases, convey such Mail at the speed of such a number of Miles an Hour, as are fixed by the Postmaster-General for the conveyance thereof.

Lapses on the part of the coachmen, who were not Post Office employees, were often severe. The resulting fine of £5 was a substantial sum of money to them. (PO 10/6, no.98)

1775	£66-18-2	1780	£395-3-7
1776	£21-16-0	1781	£895-10-5
1777	£20-16-4	1782	£1477-16-10
1778	£110-3-8	1783	£3777-10-0
1779	£511-8-4	1784	£1189-15-1

By the 1790s the total costs were exceeding £2,000 per annum and they continued to rise annually.

On rare occasions the local population took direct action against the lawbreakers, as at Farnborough, Hampshire, in September 1798. The Postmaster General was told that two suspicious horsemen were spotted lurking in the lanes. A posse of the inhabitants armed themselves and, when the strangers began to follow the mail coach, they challenged the suspects, who immediately galloped off. Shots were fired at them, some blood was later found on the road and it was thought that one of the horses was wounded. The Postmaster General penned a note on the report, expressing the hope that 'this spirited prosecution' would receive publicity and 'tend to deter offences of the kind described.'[19]

As the post boys mostly travelled at night, as soon as they left the town they were more or less in total darkness and consequently at greater risk. During the seventeenth and eighteenth centuries, street lighting was, even in the towns, somewhat minimal, although town regulations increasingly demanded that street lamps be lit at night. The boys could be just as vulnerable in town as in the open country. In February 1730 the Bristol post boy was robbed between Knightsbridge and

Kensington, part of the fashionable outskirts of London. There were highway robberies in central London, victims included senior Government officials and even the King.

Most robberies were straightforward affairs, but occasionally there was one which threw up something out of the ordinary. Such a case is recorded in the trial of Thomas Baker Hopkins, held at the Old Bailey in London on 10 April 1782. He was accused of highway robbery with violence on 16 January 1782. The post boy, John Gladman, left the Lombard Street office at 3.15 a.m. on the first stage of his journey to Barnet with the Chester mail. After covering some five of six miles he was stopped by three men who knocked him down and dragged him and his cart off the road. The robbers took 'two leathern portmanteaus, value 5s and thirty leather bags value 10s, the goods and chattels of our Lord the King.' Gladman was guarded by a man armed with a cutlass who refused to kill him, despite being urged to do so by the other thieves. Eventually the post boy managed to free himself from his bonds and raise the alarm. Some of the bags were later found, apparently unopened, in a chaise in London. Hopkins was identified as the man who had guarded the post boy. He was arrested and found to have on him 'a loaded horse pistol with twelve bits of lead or slugs in it and powder.' Despite a number of witnesses who sought to provide an alibi for him, Hopkins was found guilty and sentenced to death.[20]

With so many thefts from the mail it was not surprising that people fearing robbery were often reluctant to hand over their letters and packages to the care of the Post Office. The chances of them safely reaching their destinations were greatly improved if they were carried on a commercial stagecoach. Passengers on private stagecoaches might well be armed and would be able to defend themselves, making them less attractive targets for the robbers. John Wilson (*ibid*) reports how, in one robbery, he and his companion stopped a coach and the occupants fired at them out of the windows. One robber was wounded by three slugs in his shoulder and Wilson thought that had the occupants held their fire just a little longer they could well have killed both highwaymen. Ordinary solitary travellers such as the post boys were obviously much more vulnerable and consequently at far greater risk.

There was, however, one major problem with using the stagecoaches to carry mail; it had been against the law since the mail was made a royal monopoly in 1638. Only Post Office personnel were allowed to handle letters and it was an offence for anybody else to do so.[21] However, there was nothing in law to prevent stagecoaches carrying parcels, this proved to be a useful loophole, soon letters were being converted into parcels. This subterfuge was commonly used and the scheme was well known to the Post Office officials, who had to admit it was difficult to stop. On 30 March 1798 Freeling commented on the difficulty of prosecuting people who carry letters, as nobody likes to be an informer.[22]

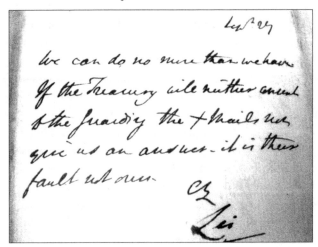

Exasperation over the delay in implementing plans to arm the post riders shows in this note by the two Postmasters, written in August 1796. (PO 10/8, vol 1)

A handwritten notice of 5 June 1798 cautioned 'masters and drivers of stage-coaches and waggons (sic) masters and commanders of vessels, watermen carriers and newsmen' about the offence of handling the mail by giving the details of one case tried in London. It was pointed out that anybody carrying letters contrary to the law would incur a £5 penalty for each letter plus a further fine of £100 a week. This note warned that a recent case had established the fact that, in an attempt to escape this ban, letters tied round with pack thread or enclosed in a piece of brown paper were not turned into parcels.[23] The only alternatives to using a stagecoach or the mail were sending the letter by express or using a personal messenger, however both systems were expensive.

By the 1780s public opinion of the Post Office was pretty low and complaints were commonplace. On 12 December 1782 the merchants of Liverpool addressed a petition to the Secretary, Anthony Todd. They complained of late deliveries, inconvenient office opening times and problems in getting replies away quickly.[24] They pointed out that theirs was a long-standing complaint and they begged him to take action. Palmer was well aware of this disapproval and dissatisfaction and his proposals made many references to the poor service. Writing in his *Plan for the Reform and Improvement of The General Post Office*[25] of 1783, he comments on the post:

> It is at present so little taken care of that it is generally trusted to some idle boy without character, mounted on a worn out hack, who so far from able to defend himself or escape from a robber, that he is likely to be in league with him.

Threatened by a footpad or a highwayman the boys' usual procedure was, very sensibly, to hand over the bags of mail without protest. Any resistance would only result in a beating or, on rare occasions, even death. It was suspected, as suggested by Palmer, that in some cases thief and victim were working together.

CIRCULAR TO MAIL-COACHMEN.

November 14, 1825.

A Circular has this day been issued by the General Post Office to Mail Guards, acquainting them that they are entitled to no Profit or Perquisite whatever, except their Weekly Wages and the Gratuities given to them by Passengers; that the Inspecting Officers are directed to make strict search for Packages or Parcels; and that if any be found in or about the Coach unentered on the Way-bill, the same are to be taken away; and also that, if any Guard presumes to disobey the instructions contained in the said Circular, he will be suspended, and the case reported to the Postmaster-General. It is likewise stated therein, that if any Guard connives at a Coachman putting an outside Passenger inside the Mail without accounting for the inside Fare, he will be seriously punished.

This, therefore, is to acquaint you, that you are entitled to no Profit or Perquisite except your Weekly Wages and such Gratuities as may be given you by Passengers; and that, if you carry a Passenger or Parcel, or put an outside Passenger inside, without entering the same on the Way-bill, you will be suspended or dismissed; and punished further by your Employers, as the case may seem to them to require, and the law will allow.

(Signed)

Towards the end of the mail coach era the number of passengers greatly diminished, in consequence the drivers and guards suffered a loss of tips. Some possibly became a little too pushy in soliciting tips from the remaining passengers. (PO 10/6 127)

The post boys had no means of defence, for until the early nineteenth century they were unarmed. However, from then on the riders on those routes considered to be the most dangerous were supplied with firearms.

One of the primary claims of Palmer's plan for reforming the Post Office was that security would be greatly increased by the presence of an armed guard on every coach. Writing in 1783 he very clearly favoured the use of soldiers for this task. In paragraph ten of his proposals he stated that:

> The guard should by no means be left either to the postmaster or master of machines to provide, as those they could procure could be little relied on in any respect.[26]

In his original plan Palmer stated that he would employ regular soldiers as the mail guards,[27] but the use of soldiers was decried by several of his critics. It was suggested that the number of soldiers needed would be quite large, to which Palmer replied:

> A guard may be thought necessary only to the great roads and principal cross-roads, but if it should appear to be equally proper for the others there is certainly a sufficient number of soldiers who can be spared for the purpose.[28]

One of the Post Office Resident Surveyors, Mr Nathan Draper, had suggested that if regular troops were employed then an order from the King, as Commander-in-Chief of the Army, or an Act of Parliament would be required to make it legal. Another critic pointed out that if soldiers were used then there was a potential problem over their command and control. They would, strictly speaking, only respond to the orders of their officers and not the Postmasters. Palmer must have taken due note of the criticism aimed his way about the potential use of soldiers, it came not only from the surveyors but also from the Treasury. Palmer had written to Mr Rose of the Treasury who replied:

WITH RESPECT TO THE GUARD, THERE ARE MANY OBJECTIONS TO EMPLOYING SOL-
DIERS, AND DIFFICULTIES IN THE WAY OF DOING IT; THAT CAN HOWEVER, MAKE BUT
LITTLE DIFFERENCE IN THE POINT OF EXPENSE OR SAFETY.[29]

Whether Palmer wholeheartedly accepted these points or acted merely out of expediency is a moot point. Nevertheless, by the time the first mail coaches ran in 1784 the idea of using soldiers as guards had been abandoned.

The records of the system's first operation in 1784 make no mention of soldiers being employed, in fact there are very few direct references to the guards at all. There is a common misconception that the Post Office preferred to employ ex-soldiers as guards. This may well be due to Palmer's original plan, but throughout the history of the coaches at no time is there any question of the guards being required to have had any military experience. The Post Office wanted men of good character, and the main requirements demanded of a guard were reliability and respectability. The character reference required by the Office had to be given by a person who had known the applicant for at least one year, and this alone could well have excluded military personnel. There is one case recorded where a sergeant was appointed as a guard by the Postmaster General on the recommendation of a friend, but this seems to be in recognition of some special service.

The Appointment Ledger Post 58/53 lists the details of guards appointed between 1801 and May 1840. It records the birthplace, previous trade, who recommended him, who appointed him, date of appointment, age, which route he was given and in many cases what happened to him. The occupations of newly appointed guards were very diverse and included plumber, footman, policemen, student, veterinary surgeon, druggist, stage guard, surgeon, ironmonger, chemist and druggist, cow keeper, gamekeeper, potboy and schoolmaster among many more. It is also very clear that the chances of being appointed as a guard were greatly enhanced if the proposer was titled. There are one or two nominations by un-titled people, but these are very few in number. The other remarkable feature is that the rule about an oft-quoted age limit of thirty seems to have been somewhat elastic. Although the majority of appointees are in their twenties, there are several well past that figure:

BELL AND CROWN,
HOLBORN.

ROYAL MAILS AND COACHES
TO

ANDOVER, BATH, BRISTOL, BOSTON, BRIGHTON, BRIDGEWATER, CAMBRIDGE, CHARD, CANTERBURY, DOVOR, EXETER, EGHAM, GLASTONBURY, HONITON, HERTFORD, LOUTH, LYNN, MILBOURN PORT, OXFORD, POOLE, STAMFORD, SHAFTESBURY, SUNNING HILL, STAINES, SHERBORNE, SALISBURY, SHEPTON MALLETT, UXBRIDGE, WARE, WELLS, WATFORD, WENDOVER, YEOVIL, &c. &c.

ROBERT FAGG & Co. Proprietors.

Carriage ....

Porterage ....

JEREMIAH WALTER DAVIES, Porter.

Passengers and Parcels Booked at Fagg's City Office, No. 11, GRACECHURCH STREET, and their Western Office, WHITE BEAR, PICCADILLY.

10,000—March 25, 1841.

Advert for the Holborn Bell and Crown Inn listing mail and stagecoaches. The date is 1841, a time when the number of coaches on Britain's roads was falling due to the growing number of railway lines. (Permission of Bath Postal Museum)

Joseph Challis, born Westminster, coachman, recommended by two plain misters, appointed by Marquis of Coningham, on 19 November 1834, aged thirty-nine, to London to Dover coach, resigned July 1838.

John Powell, born Bishop Auckland, mason, recommended George Hodgson, appointed 27 October 1807 aged forty-nine to Newcastle to Carlisle coach, pensioned 1836.

Lott Vickers, born Wellington, Derbyshire, locksmith and gpo, appointed 6 February 1807, aged fifty-one to York Hull coach, retired 1847.

It is possible that the clerk entering details got the dates wrong, for Powell would have been seventy-eight when he retired and Vickers would have been ninety-one!

The precise origins of the Post Office guards are rather obscure, the available evidence indicates that in the early days of the coaches the contractors were responsible for the arming and employing of the guards. Writing in 1893, Joyce[30] states that the early guards were supplied by the contractors but were 'of poor quality'. Unfortunately he offers no evidence to support the claim. As will be seen there is evidence to suggest a decision was reached that the guards would be employed by the Post Office. The archives have, so far, not supplied a firm date of when such a decision was taken. There is some evidence in the archives that at least one employee of the Post Office was almost certainly used as a guard on one of the early coaches.

In September 1793 Hasker was corresponding with the Postmaster General over the fate of a dismissed guard named J. Carter. The man's wife had written in saying that her husband was no longer fit for service, largely due to drink. Agreeing that Carter was indeed in poor condition, Hasker's good nature was such that he wanted to do whatever he could for the man. He forwarded an extract from the record of Carter's service, saying that it made pretty depressing reading, but Carter kept promising to improve. So many people spoke in his defence that Hasker was prepared to give him another chance. He had also been persuaded to do this since Carter had been, 'the first mail guard that started and a post boy for many years before.'[31] He wrote that he:

> …was the first guard that started with the Bristol mail before which he had been the driver of a mail cart into Marlboro' I believe near twenty years also I fear he has no way of giving the least support to his family.[32]

Hasker had previously thought of asking for superannuation to be granted but now that Carter had been dismissed for misconduct there was no possibility of any such payment.

Whereas **WALTER PRICE,** the driver of the Chester and Manchester Mail Coach, on Thursday night, the 22d of November, 1810, on arriving in Chester, incautiously left his horses without any person at their heads, to give out a passenger's luggage, (while the Guard was gone to the Post-office with the mail bags,) when they ran off with the Mail Coach through the city of Chester, taking the road for Holywell, but fortunatel without doing any injury; in consequence of which neglect, the driver wa: on the Saturday following, brougl up before the Magistrates, and fined i the full penalty of **Five Pounds,** accor ing to the late Act of Parliament.

November 26, 1810.

Teape, Printer, Tower-hill, London, for His Majesty's Stationery-Office.

Either the guard or the coachman was supposed to stand by the head of the horses whilst teams were being changed at the inn. Failure to do so could lead to accidents, such as that recorded here. (PO 10/6/70)

On 10 May 1794 Hasker received a letter from the Postmaster General referring to Carter. Presumably the missive showed his sympathy, suggested that he be
reinstated and offered the poor man some help. Hasker replied that although he
felt sympathy for Carter's family, deepened by the Postmaster's show of humanity,
he could not employ Carter without greater authority. He offered to find him
a job but the contractors on the Bath – Bristol route did not want him, as he
was considered to be too slow on changeovers. If Carter would move to Bath
or Bristol he could have a job on the Exeter and Birmingham coaches, which
would perhaps separate him from his drinking companions, Hasker later wrote
that, 'if his wife will let me know where he is I will send to him and if he should
reform his salvation will be due to his lordships.' That Carter was in a bad way
is very obvious, and on 25 September 1793 Hasker said that when Carter was
suspended he had intended to take back his uniform, but as he had no other
clothes, I could not act so very rigid to a man who has been so long in the
service.[33]

Carter tried hard to get sympathy and public support, and the Postmaster
General wrote to Freeling saying that Carter had written to Lord Walsingham.
It soon became clear that Carter had been seen begging in the street wearing an
'almost new guard's uniform and a dismissed guard should leave his uniform for
his successor.'[34]

The case of Carter took up quite a space in correspondence, and it would seem
that the Postmaster General became a little impatient, for he wrote to Mr Hasker
asking him to:

> …do as he pleases about restarting him or not he certainly has the appearance
> of a drunken man. The P M Genl would not attend to the personal applications
> of Members of Parliament in such cases. They must apply if their constituents
> desire it. Tho in many cases they would be sorry if their applications were suc-
> cessful.

(This reference seems to suggest that there had been some pressure from
Members of Parliament.)

> It is not that the PM Genl wants to act rigidly by taking away the uniform of a
> dismissed guard, but that a worthless man should not impose upon the world by
> wearing the office uniform and that the office may not be put to the expense
> of furnishing a new coat hat & C to a new man. Better is such a case give him
> something to buy a coat not a uniform tho that would be a payment to a man
> who does not deserve it.[35]

(The end of this unfortunate man is not recorded in the archives.)

Several other entries suggest that Hasker and Freeling were caring employers. On 10 November 1808 Freeling was in touch with his masters, seeking ways to help John Williams, a Welsh guard, who had been injured when a drunken driver overturned the coach. A petition, signed by Admiral Sir Charles Morgan, had been forwarded by Hasker. Freeling now asked the Postmaster General's permission to seek the admiral's support in applying pressure on the contractor, after all it was their driver who was responsible for the accident. Approval was given but one intriguing point is made in the Postmaster General's answer, it is not clear whether the reply was instituted by Sandwich or Lichfield, but the writer says that the admiral is a 'gallant naval officer. He has an estate in the neighbourhood of Huntingdonshire and was formerly a friend of mine.'[36]

There is another reference to some guards being directly employed by the office from the beginning of the service. It is included in a note to the Treasury, probably made out by Post Office staff in an attempt to discredit Palmer's plan:

> A Comparative state of the postage of letters upon the Bath and Bristol Road for twenty days viz from the 1st to the 20th of August 1783 from the 12th to the 31st of July 1784 during the 20 days preceding the commencement of the plan for conveying the mail by stagecoaches and from the 1st to the 20th August 1784.

It efficiently summarises the costs, and delights in claiming that under Palmer's plan the cost per annum would be much higher than under the old system, £967-4-0 as against £691-10-0. This document includes the statement, 'the guard as at present four men at half a guinea each per week £109-4-0.'[37] It could well be that two of these men acted as escort for the coach to Bristol and two more escorted it to London.

With various sources corroborating each other, it seems likely that the guards on the early coaches were mostly, if not entirely, supplied by the contractors as part of their agreement. At some point a decision was taken that the guards should become Post Office employees. Although no positive statement of this has (so far) been found in the archives, there is a certain amount of supporting evidence.

In the Incident Payments for the quarter ending 5 July 1788 there is an entry:

> Mr John Palmer Esq;
> A qtr wages to the mail guards £757-5
> Another £910-7-6
> Another £836-11.[38]

If these are payments for three distinct quarters it may be assumed that the first payment was probably for the quarter ending 5 January 1788, as such these guards were probably working during the last quarter of 1787.

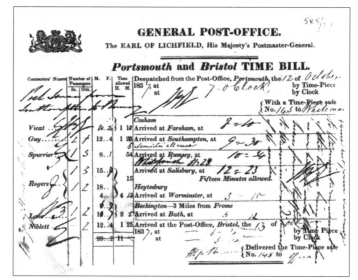

Time bill for the Portsmouth run which shows the number – 145 – of the timepiece carried, a detail often omitted. The timepiece was at one time carried on the Yarmouth run. (PO 10/7)

There is another indication that guards were being directly employed by the Post Office in the wording of a petition from an old guard, William Roberts, applying for a pension. He claimed that as a result of exposure to inclement weather he had fallen ill, was unable to work and that a substitute guard had been employed in his place. He could no longer support his wife and five children. In the petition he states that he was appointed as a guard in Chester on 14 October 1786.[39] The Postmaster General sought permission to pay him £20 a year, but on 11 April 1791 the Treasury refused.[40]

Corroborating evidence is to be found in the wording of the early entries. Listing of payments to the contractors for these pieces of work seem to indicate that they were being paid to do two jobs. The entries refer to 'guarding' and 'conveying' the mail, this wording is standard until early in 1787.

Sept 1785; Messrs Wilson, Fromont, Porter, Williams & Dover for carrying and guarding the Bristol mail £621.[41]

Dec 1785; Messers Humphrey Repton, John Carouse for carrying and guarding the Norwich mail for six months £ 744-16.[42]

March 1786; do do for 3 months £372-8

April 1787; for carrying and guarding.[43]

In the entries for June 1787 the wording has changed and states that the payments were for the conveying or conveyance of mail. The term 'guarding' is omitted, which surely indicates that this was no longer the contractors' responsibility.

Taken together these references seem to indicate that late in 1786, or early in 1787, there was a change in Post Office policy. Thenceforward the Post Office apparently assumed direct responsibility for guarding the mail and now the guards were hired, armed and equipped by the Post Office. Presumably the purpose of the change was to ensure more control over the guards since, as employees of the contractors, they were not directly answerable to the office. Whether the new, official, Post Office staff were the same men as those previously employed by the contractors as guards, or whether new people were recruited is unclear.

It was almost certainly during this period that the first regulations for the guards were formalised, probably by Hasker, and each guard was issued with a copy. The earliest copy of the guards' instructions so far located in the records dates only from 1812 (see Appendix 4). There is another example dated 1829 which differs slightly (Appendix 5). A third set of details seems more a job description than a set of rules (Appendix 6). As evidenced below, for some time the Postmaster Generals seemed unaware of the new status of the guards (see page 94).

The guard's job was a demanding one and his duties were numerous. The position required considerable stamina and applicants were warned that they would be expected to be capable of 'standing great fatigue'.[44] If proof were needed, an example is offered by a paragraph in the *London Evening Mail* of 5 February to 28 February 1795:

> It is reported that there is at this moment a third of the mail guards ill; either from the intenseness of the severe weather or from colds they have caught in the flood; their exertions were in general very great and meritorious in saving the mail.

The guard was exposed to all weathers as he sat on his seat by the mailbox at the rear of the coach but, despite all the dangers and hardships, it still seems to have been a desirable occupation. He was frequently the subject of complaints and Hasker had to deal with these angry passengers. However, he was prepared to defend the guards. In 1792 he replied to a Mrs Clarke that he would speak to the guard about his impertinence, but he also defended him by pointing out that guards suffered continual complaints. The passengers complained about the bad light in the coaches and the smell of stinking oil, which Hasker suggests they may often have used as an excuse for not tipping the guard.[45] This letter is of interest in that it details two minor, but nevertheless disturbing aspects of coach travel:

Like all public servants the guards were vulnerable and could be accused of anything, with or without reason. In July 1810 the guard, Richard Bosworth, was accused of assaulting Sarah Norris on the coach between Bath and Chippenham. He was suspended pending prosecution but the local parish officers questioned her and expressed doubts about the case, in consequence the suspension was lifted.[46] Some guards were undoubtedly unreliable, and on 8 July 1796 there was an unfortunate incident concerning a Miss Manning and the guard Thomas Nobles. His behaviour was said to be worse than he admitted, and he had already been transferred from the Norwich run because of his violent behaviour. He had apparently threatened to shoot the Deputy Postmaster who was reluctant to do anything 'in case his temper should again get the better of his reason.'[47]

No advert of the time calling for applicants has been traced, but other sources suggest that the mail coach guard was then regarded as a person of some standing in society. The archives list numerous people writing to Hasker, Freeling and the Postmaster General, many soliciting employment as a guard and asking that, if no vacancy existed, their name be added to a waiting list. Equally it is clear that the turnover of guards in a year was fairly small and the wait for a vacancy was likely to be a long one. One letter, written by Hasker in 1796[48], says that he will see an applicant if he is under thirty and fit, but that it can take twelve months for a vacancy to become open. The Postmaster General wrote to a hopeful applicant in 1807 saying that his name would be added to the list but that, 'he fears Mr Hasker's list is heavily loaded.'[49] As late as 1813, when the list was temporarily closed, there were still forty names on it and the waiting period then seems to have been around two years. This information is to be found in a letter written by Chichester in response to a request for a job.[50]

A note to the Postmaster General on 10 October 1818[51] says that following their order of some months ago the list of applicants for guards was now closed on account of the great number on record. It was now down to eight names, six for England and two for Scotland, and it was suggested that the Postmaster General rescind his order. The number could be increased to twelve or fifteen and this would allow a name, such as John Lord (nominated by Lord Charles Spencer), to be inserted. To this they agreed, the nominee was approved, and this can only be interpreted as nepotism.

Over the years requests to be added to the list increased and by the 1820s Freeling was reporting that he had had, in the last year, at least sixty applications[52] and there was still a two to three year wait for a chance of a job (*ibid.* p 68). The number of applicants continued to rise and by July 1823 there were some 200 applications (*ibid.* p268).

One possible explanation for this desire to become a guard may be the income they were believed to make from 'tips'. One writer in the late nineteenth century suggested that the wages given to the guards were really only a retainer, and that they could make up to £300 a year from tips. A statement of the duties of a guard, written in 1832, says:

The actual pay of a mail guard is 10/6 (52.5p) per week. The emoluments are from the gratuities received from passengers and in some cases for the con- veyance of private pouches from gentlemen residing on the high road. These emoluments must of course vary according to the profits of the coach from the number of passengers – on a coach that is not very prosperous the guard may get 30s a week including his salary on some of the most successful coaches the guard may receive 40s a week in addition to the ½ guinea from the office making £2-10-8 a week. The guard succeeds to the best coaches with some attention to seniority chiefly by merit and good conduct. The same list gives the figures of 195 English guards, 69 Irish guards and 44 Scottish Guards.[53]

The same writer also states that there were 365 guards in 1841 (see Nobbs).

There was understandable resentment among the guards over inequality in tips and routes. In August 1796 there was discussion as to how the Norwich run might be slightly amended to ensure that the various guards got a more equitable share of passengers' generosity.[54] Those on the first part of the journey did quite well for gratuities, but those on the later section fared rather worse.

There was obviously a certain job satisfaction and public status to be had in being a guard, for he was virtually a travelling newspaper: his arrival and the attendant gossip he could provide from neighbouring towns would make him the centre of attention at the Post Office or inn. He would offer the locals the first chance to hear the latest news from London and abroad. It appears that occasionally they not only retold the news but invented it as well which could, as will be seen later, have serious consequences.

There is also to be found in this archive a list of six Marine Guards, all appointed in 1832/33, who received six pounds a lunar month. They had to take charge of any mail and travel with it to its foreign destination or bring it back to England. They were strictly forbidden to interfere with the running of the steam vessels, but it would appear from their instructions that the job was quite demanding.

THE GUARD.

Left: Nineteenth-century engraving of a guard. He wears a red coat and has a narrow shoulder belt. This could be for his timepiece, but the hat is not black so it is unclear as whether he is a stage or a mail guard.

Opposite: Turnpike keeper's cottage of the early nineteenth century. Originally from Beeding in Sussex, it is now preserved at the Weald and Downland Open Air Museum.

Each applicant seeking employment as a guard had to supply a character recommendation from a person of some standing, and the higher up the social scale
the writer was the better. However, it was recognised that these character references were not always reliable. Commenting on the case of James Williams, a
dismissed guard who pleaded for re-instatement, Hasker writes that the man was
a 'habitual drinker'. Letters recommending him for a position were apparently
from respectable people, but Hasker went on to write that, 'I fear it is easy to
obtain such testimonials.'[55]

Each application for a position as a guard was passed from the office to the
Postmaster General for permission to add the name to the waiting list. It is apparent
from the records that patronage played some part in the process, for every now and
then, despite the length of the waiting list, the Postmaster General would approve
an applicant for an immediate vacancy. In such cases the person recommending the
applicant often seems to have been either a member of the aristocracy or a friend
of the Postmaster General. However, they did not always oblige, even when the
applicant was recommended by distinguished supporters. In 1818 both Chichester
and Salisbury regretted that they could not support an applicant proposed by the
Earl of Westmoreland, as the list was too full.[56] Another request was referred to the
Postmaster General in October 1826 and passed on by Mr Wilson. The minute asks:

Can Your Lordships with 22 names now on the list and many applications from
friends of your own can now encourage this application from a gentleman who,
however respectable he may be, is, I presume a stranger to your Lordships.

Chichester and Salisbury signed the reply to Freeling, stating that:

I have no knowledge of this gentleman & under the circumstances would be deceiving the young man to hold out any hope.[57]

They could certainly apply pressure when they wanted to, as is shown in a letter written by Hasker to the Postmaster General on 27 March 1795.[58] In it he refers to a letter, presumably sent to the Postmaster General by Lord Exeter, asking that Anthony Sturdy be made a guard on the Carlisle mail coach. Evidently the Postmaster was agreeable and wrote their instructions on the back of the letter when they returned it to Hasker.[59] From the context it seems that Sturdy may have distinguished himself a spell of bad weather, for Hasker wrote that, 'he begs leave yr. Ldsh that some of those who assisted during the hard weather all that are necessary have been fixed some time & their cloaths (sic) made it being only a week to the starting.' The Postmaster General must have been less than subtle, for Hasker says in his reply that 'as you are so very desirous of his being appointed', their instructions would be followed and that he would do the necessary to appoint Mr Sturdy on the first vacancy and oblige by 'some means'.

He also stresses that Mr Sturdy would still have to meet the statutory age conditions before he could be appointed. The age limit was still thirty, and in July 1837 Lichfield curtly dismissed an application from a thirty-two year old with the comment that, 'This man is too old.'[60] Hasker says that as he would shortly be in Stamford, presumably the home town of Mr Sturdy, he would arrange to see him to confirm this. If he proved to be satisfactory then Hasker would send Sturdy to a coach manufacturer for as long as it took for him to gain the necessary knowledge of repairs, which would take him approximately ten days to a fortnight. Mr Sturdy would then be taken on as an extra guard – but Hasker stressed the job was tough and the discipline severe. He enclosed a copy of the guard's instructions for the information of the Postmaster General.[61]

If it suited the office then exceptions to normal practice could be made, and in March 1793 they sought to reward a post boy who had suffered in a robbery between Chudleigh and Exeter. Apparently the office solicitor, Parkin, had written to them suggesting that this boy be made a guard if he was fit enough, they supported the idea with a contingency plan (in the event of a rejection) for a 'pecuniary temporary compensation'.[62] A similar case was mentioned in August 1817, saying that in November 1816 the Postmaster General had granted 10s 6d (52.5p) a week to a post boy wounded during a robbery between Exeter and Teignmouth. It had continued until 2 January 1817 when he was discharged from hospital, but in May 1817 his wounds 'broke out', and he became an outpatient of the hospital. He also suffered from epilepsy, had a wife and two children, and was now unable to work. The Postmaster General was asked to approve a grant of £20, which he subsequently did.[63]

A Liverpool coach clearly showing details like the sword box, guard's seat and folding steps.

A document of 1836,[64] signed by the Superintendent George Louis, outlines the qualifications required of a guard (Appendix VI). He was to be less than thirty years of age, stand 5ft 6in (1m 68cm) tall, be of robust constitution and be 'capable of undergoing great fatigue.' In 1839 there appears to have been a query about the stipulated height, but the Postmaster General was firm that it remained at 5ft 6in.[65] It repeats these details and says, 'it is desirable also that they should be accustomed to horses and carriages', surely an obvious requirement. The applicant also had to be able to read and write plainly. A letter dated 12 May 1836,[66] signed by J. Cumming, states that Daniel Whelan and James Barry had both proved unfit to be guards and so had been paid-off as not being able to read or write. In 1827 the Postmaster General apparently ruled that the candidates for guards should be examined, they were then told by the office that this was very much the established practice.[67] A nice point arose in January 1829 when the Duchess of Leeds proposed a Christopher Dandy for a position. However, he was a Roman Catholic and there were still legal restrictions on the rights of Catholics. The Duke of Manchester said that so long as he took the Oath of Allegiance there was no problem.[68]

Applicants for a position as guard had to produce a 'satisfactory character from his last employer or from some respectable person to whom he has been known for the previous year.' He was to obtain, 'two householders to be bound for him, the penalty of the Bond is £50', and he had to swear an oath (Appendix IV). There is evidence that a Deputy Postmaster was sometimes present at these swearing-in sessions, since in July 1787 the Bath Postmaster was paid four shillings 'for swearing in guards', and another from Salisbury was paid eight shillings.[69] These payments, and the presence of the Deputy Postmaster on this date, could well be another indication that the Post Office was preparing to take over the employment of the guards.

Even if all the applicant's references were satisfactory, before he could be appointed he had to be in possession of money to the value of £5 to cover various expenses. He had to supply his own box of tools, at a cost of £1 7s (£1.35), a small lamp priced at 3s 8d (18p), locks and bars at 12s (60p) as well as paying 1s (5p) for the oath.[70]

In the early days, once accepted as a guard the new man would soon meet Walter Knight, engaged in January 1786 in the capacity of Superintendent of Guards. He was expected to:

> ...go down the several roads – see into the conduct, travel a journey or two with such as require instruction, teach new guards their duty-report their behaviour and inspect into the condition & see to the repair and proper working of the Bye Bags and straps-examine the firearms and in all respects to correct the guards conduct or act as guard himself if necessary at any time till a vacancy is filled up.

For this impressive job description Knight was paid fifteen shillings per week with an extra 6d per day and 1s per night when work took him out of town. At this time he was applying for a rise in salary to eighteen shillings a week.[71]

Another member of staff that the guards knew well was Robert White, who was first engaged on 8 November 1785 as an under clerk. His job was to attend to the arrival of the guards every morning as well as to receive and examine the time bills and timepieces. He was to report any discrepancies or irregularities and note the details on the time bills. He was also to wind the timepieces in the evening, a job later given to another employee. He was responsible for preparing the time bills and delivering them to the guards, issuing any specific instructions or reprimands. He was described as, 'very attentive, diligent and deserving encouragement', and for all this he was paid £40 per annum.[72]

Other documents contain specific extra 'Instructions to Mail Guards', but one of the most complete listings of his duties is a printed form, 'Instructions to Mail Guards', dating from 1812.[73] The first clause stresses that the bags of mail were the primary responsibility and that the guard was threatened with imprisonment with hard labour if he failed in his duty or failed to report any problems. He was to help the driver but never let the mail out of his sight. He would be dismissed if he was drunk or neglected his duty, and on no account was he to allow anybody, other than certain officials, to sit on the mailbox. There were many more instructions detailed below.[74] Whilst these were his official duties, the archives show that many were also well capable of driving the coach if the need arose, on occasion they would indeed take control, often just for the fun of it. A good example is a complaint about coachman Robert Briscow, he was accused of ill-treating a lady in the coach after telling the guard he did not feel well at Northampton. The guard subsequently drove the rest of the journey. Hasker took the view that this solution was preferable to delaying the mail. The guard reported that he had no idea of any problem until he got to Newport, where he stopped to water the horses.

Engraving of the early Liverpool & Manchester Railway, it clearly shows the mail coach at the rear with the guard on his seat who is exposed to the elements. (PO P7272)

The guard was unaware of what had happened inside the coach, nevertheless Hasker thought that the driver deserved to be dismissed and that all contractors should be warned not to employ him.[75]

When the applicant was accepted he attended a swearing-in, and after he had read the instructions he was to take an oath which he was then obliged to sign. This same form included a section which listed the guard's personal details, place of birth, age, physical appearance, previous occupation and the name of the person who was recommending him for the job as well as the date of his signature.

The guard's conduct was not only set down in Post Office instruction but also defined by an Act of Parliament passed in the fiftieth year of King George III and circulated by Hasker, it was 'intended as a caution to Mail Guards and coachmen.' The Act warns about endangering the passengers, loitering on the road, being abusive to passengers and threatens various dire penalties for any transgression of these rules. One very important clause was that:

> ...if any guard or person travelling as such, shall fire off the arms either while the coach is going along the road, or going through or standing in any town, otherwise than for the defence of such coach, or property, or passengers there in, shall for every such offence, forfeit and pay the penalty of five pounds.[76]

One criticism levelled at the guards by some writers in the early days was that they used to fire off their weapons at any target that took their fancy. There is a contradiction here, for the guards were supposed to have their firearms checked at frequent intervals. Since firing a black powder firearm tends to be a messy business, it seems likely that the inspecting Deputy Postmaster might well have queried matters. No doubt there were occasions when the firearms were misused, but the threat of a fine and queries from Postmasters suggest that it was not as common as some of the accounts suggest.

During his service with the Post Office, the guard's conduct was monitored and any transgression was recorded in a *Black Book*.[77] Some offences, such as sleeping on duty or drunkenness, were so serious that they were followed by instant dismissal. In April 1795 four guards were dismissed for various offences, including allowing a passenger to sit in their seat by the mailbox, leaving the box unlocked, misusing it or leaving London without firearms.[78] In November 1804 a further six were dismissed for various similar offences.[79] Some guards were certainly tempted by the chance to do a little 'side trading' and carry letters or small parcels for friends. Hasker was often driven to publish warnings against such practices and regularly asked the contractors to check on the guards. On 5 April 1805 he sent a circular to the contractors asking them to check the guards' boxes and dispose of any unofficial items as they saw fit.[80] On 10 May 1816 he again circulated the contractors:

General Post Office May 10 1816.[81]

Sir,

I am desired by my Lords the Postmaster General to represent their Commands that you will examine the Mail Box as often as possible to see that the guards do not carry any parcels, packages or goods on their own account; And any article in their possession that they do not properly account for take away and dispose of it as you think best by giving it to any workhouse hospital or other charitable institution afterwards informing me of the particulars.

I am Sir, Your obedient servant,

Thomas Hasker

Despite all these warnings and reminders it will be seen below that not all the guards were as punctilious as they should have been. In fact they were frequently very lax, often with unfortunate results.

If the guard broke any of the more important rules then suspension or dismissal followed, but it was not unusual for such dismissed persons to write in pleading to be reinstated. On 27 July 1796 a guard named Hancock, already having been in trouble over the December 1792 rumours (see below), was accused of trying to extort two shillings and sixpence, half a crown (12½p), from a passenger in a dispute over a trunk carried in a coach. Hancock wrote to Hasker protesting that he was innocent and within his rights. On 6 August Hasker replied, pointing out that Hancock's account was incorrect and that the trunk had nothing to do with him, as the contractor had agreed to carry it and it was put in the coachman's box. Hasker went on to tell Hancock that his 'general character along the road is that of being a drunk impudent fellow', who could not do his job properly. In his letter the guard pleaded that as he had no wages his family of five children

One of the many illustrations of the lion attack on the coach near Salisbury.
(PO PE 003)

was suffering; although Hasker sympathised he pointed out that it was Hancock's fault they were in need.

Hancock was nothing if not persistent, for he got a Mr Forward of Exeter to write to Hasker in his defence. Hasker answered Mr Forward by telling him how Hancock had lied, abused and threatened the owner of the trunk, and said that in any case Hancock was a bad character. Nevertheless, despite his misgivings, by 19 August Hasker had relented and reappointed the offender to his position. He did warn him and said that if there were any more complaints he would discharge Hancock without compunction, 'even if you have a hundred children.' He also wrote to the Exeter Postmaster, saying that Hancock seemed to think that because he had five children he did not have to do the job properly. Hasker wrote that he would always consider him 'a bad man'.[82] As can be seen from this story, Hasker seems to have been a kind-hearted person, often against his better judgement. In a similar case he wrote on 1 April 1793 that Mr Palmer had ordered him never to employ a certain guard again, 'but foolish pity got the better of me and when I had an opportunity near two years ago I put him on a second time.'[83]

In December 1792 a very curious incident caused a great deal of consternation. Many letters of complaint were sent to Freeling and Hasker demanding action. It seems that on the morning of Sunday, 2 December 1792, the Leeds coach was forty-five minutes late arriving at the Leeds Post Office. When the guard was questioned as to the reason for the delay, he told a hair-raising story of riots in London, the town on fire, thousands dead and the King beheaded. The same story, with variations, was also reported by the guards in Cambridge, Oxford,

Lewes and Newcastle. Not surprisingly the story gave rise to great panic and a worried population.[84]

The various guards were examined, some were called to London, and the one from Leeds claimed that he had only 'done it for fun'! The Newcastle guard, Beardsley, questioned by Freeling in London, admitted that he had 'been incautious', but claimed he had been told the details by two passengers on the coach. He expressed regret and was firmly rebuked. His claim was backed by a letter from the York contractor, and Freeling stated that he knew the guard well and was astonished at the report of his conduct. Freeling gave him a glowing character reference in the hope that the Postmaster General would give him his job back. At one point the Postmaster General and one or two of the writers feared a conspiracy, but Hasker was unconvinced and thought the whole business was misguided and done, 'for the sake of fun'. On the face of it there were some grounds for viewing it as a conspiracy as it was odd that the guards all told the same story, but equally the guards may have been joking together before they set out, and the mysterious two passengers may have said something at that time.

On 10 December 1792 Freeling wrote to the Post Office solicitor asking him to check over an advert he wanted to issue. It read:

The Postmr Gel. having been informed that reports were spread in various parts of the kingdom on the 1st and 2nd of this month by many of the mail coachmen and guards, asserting that there were riots in the town of London, that the town was in many places on fire, and that the lateness of the departure of the coaches was owing to their having been searched and detained by a mob, and the Postm Genl. being duly sensible of the evil consequences of these reports and of their having the effect of calumniating the inhabitants of this Metropolis at a time when they have been shewing in every part of it so laudable a spirit of loyalty to the King and attachment to the free and happy constitution.

And as from the generality of these reports there may be reason to suppose some person or persons have wickedly and industriously instigated such coachmen and guards to propagate the same therefore all such person or persons may be brought to justice and punished in such manner as the law directs. The PMG hereby promises a handsome reward to whoever shall discover such person or persons so as they may be brought to conviction.

And if any such false and dangerous reports shall again be spread by any mail coachmen or guards Postmasters, Post Boys or by any of the servants subject to the PostMr Genl authority whoever shall give information against them to this office shall be entitled to a similar reward upon their convictions.[85]

On 7 December, in immediate reaction to this distressing story, Hasker apparently drew up a document which all the guards were asked to sign. The context would seem to indicate that it was a statement declaring that the signer had not told any such story. Freeling wrote on 12 December that he was not happy about this declaration but would not censure Hasker for producing it.[86] The Postmaster General was concerned, he felt that many of those who signed would be lying and that those who refused to sign would be condemning themselves. Instead the Postmaster General suggested pointing out to the offenders the damage that they had done and offering a reward to anyone who picked-out the ringleaders.[87] On 14 December 1792 the Postmaster General issued an appeal offering a reward for information, however it was not immediately successful. Despite all their enquiries neither Hasker nor Freeling were able to establish the firm facts, and on 27 December a further notice was issued:

> As the end of all punishment is to prevent a repetition of offences and as the notice that has already been taken of the reports spread by the guards and mail coachmen and this notice to be taken by the advertisement intended to be issued will probably prevent any complaints of the like sort in future the Pmgs would be inclined to give a general amnesty for what is passed for there will be great inconsistency in dismissing the Leeds guard and forgiving others but as the treasury seem to think it requires such serious notice which they have pressed so much in the case of Trowbridge and others the PMG would wish Mr Freeling to desire Mr Rose or Mr Long to take Mr Pitts pleasure upon it as a general measure stating distinctly this to be the principle viz the impossibility of tracing it in many instances, the inconsistency of punishing some and letting others escape the impossibility of dismissing all who charged with it and the detriment the service would derive from losing so many good guards who are equally tho' incautiously involved with many bad ones till this is decided let Beardsley the Newcastle guard return to his duty.[88]

The Postmaster General informed Freeling that his letter of 7 January 1793 should be sent to Hasker, who in turn was to write to the Mayor of Leeds saying reports suggested that all the mail guards were implicated, to varying degrees, in the spreading of damaging rumours. This statement would seem to indicate that the whole business was more widespread than earlier reports suggested. It was impossible to pin down specific culprits, the greater failure was in that steps taken to prevent it happening again had been so effectual that the Treasury offered a general amnesty. In this case it would have been unfair if only the Leeds guard suffered dismissal and others escaped. This being so, if the Mayor of Leeds gave his agreement it was decided that the Leeds guard would be included in the amnesty.[89]

Apparently three guards; John Handcock (sic) from Exeter, Samuel Beardsley from Newcastle and Edward Stretton from Chester were, on 25 December 1792, ordered to travel to London to answer accusations that they had spread these rumours. The guards were detained in London briefly and, on 21 February 1793, a note appears which states that:

> …the three guards were ordered to London on charge of having circulated false reports when his Majesty's Proclamation was issued to call his Parliament and embody the Militiary, extra expenses were:
>
> 25 Dec – 31 1792 £4-13-6 John Handcock 10-31, £4-4 Edward Stratton 15-31 £ 1-15 – they deny the accusation and say they were rumours spread by passengers from London.

This appears to have been the end of the curious business.

Once a year in London there was a procession of the mail coaches in honour of the King's birthday, a special effort was made to impress the spectators and new uniforms were issued to the guards and some others in time for the event. Apparently the first such procession was held in 1791 and the last in 1837, with the only exceptions to it being an annual event were 1829 and 1830.[90] A minute of June 1792[91] sets out the sequence of coaches in the procession. In the lead was the Dover coach, followed consecutively by Portsmouth, Pool, Exeter, Taunton, Bristol, Worcester, Shrewsbury, Holyhead or Chester, Liverpool, Manchester, Leeds, York, Wisbech, Norwich with the last being Ipswich. The sixteen coach sequence was arranged on a geographic basis, starting with those from the towns south of the river Thames, curving southwest, and then north.

It is clear that the programme was not always the same. There is an entry in April 1821 which says that the procession was to start at 5 p.m., pass by Carlton House (home of the Prince Regent) then to Lord Salisbury's, on to Stratton Street and Hyde Park Corner, back to Waterloo Place, down to Pall Mall and Charing Cross and thence to the General Post Office.[92] Malet (*op. cit.*) claims that in 1834 the procession started from Vidler's factory at Milbank with the Bristol coach in the lead, followed by twenty-six others. He states that it made its way to St Martin's-le-Grand via St James Palace, where the King and Queen were watching.

The route was varied from year to year, a letter of 11 May 1837 from Louis the Secretary details that year's route, with a start from Lincolns Inn Field wending its way through central London and finishing up in the yard at St Martin's-le-Grand.[93] This route is mentioned as that for the parade of 17 May 1838 by Harris[94], issued by Lord Lichfield it says that the coaches will assemble at Lincolns Inn Field. The procession was to be led by the Liverpool and Manchester coaches with twenty-two more following on. This list is interesting, for it gives the names of the contractors and the inn at which they were based. Apparently it was a popular London spectacle, and Hone in his *Everyday Book* gives a graphic description of one such occasion.[95] Accounts for 5 April 1835 show a payment of '£18-14 for the gloves for mail guards, saddle horses and riders in the procession', which were paid by Mr Wedderburn, a

Post Office official.[96] In 1836 the July quarterly accounts again list the same amount for the same purpose.[97] By October 1838 this cost had risen to £24-18-2.[98]

Although it may have been a popular public event, it did involve some dislocation of business and incurred additional expenses. In May 1799 Vidler, the prime coach manufacturer, asked the Postmaster General if the procession could be discontinued in view of the cost. The Postmaster General replied that it would be:

> …a very delicate circumstance to discontinue a practice which may have been faulty in its original principles but which has connected itself with the general display of loyalty on His Majesty's Birthday.

He went on to agree with Mr Hasker that the procession should go ahead in that year, at a forthcoming meeting they would consider the situation. In the meantime Vidler would be compensated for the expenses he incurred as a direct result of the procession.[99] Although there is no record of a formal decision, it was obviously thought politic to continue the procession.

Aside from the celebratory parade, the guard's job was tough and dangerous: it involved long journeys, physical risks and heavy responsibility. For this the guard was originally granted a wage of 13s (65p) a week. That was the sum set down formally, but in reality he never seems to have received more than 10s 6d (52½p) a week. The difference of two shillings and sixpence, roughly 20 per cent, was deducted to subsidise the cost of uniforms and other articles, a sum which seems rather excessive. The full allowance of thirteen shillings was credited to Palmer's department and the deduction appears to have been decided by him without reference to anybody else. When this system became known, unsurprisingly the finance departments were not at all happy with the arbitrary nature of the arrangements, in that Palmer held back a considerable sum without any proper accounting. The Postmaster General were not at all happy either, for they claimed they were regularly expected to sign warrants for several hundred pounds, some of which was being retained without any real authority, or proper records being kept. With his usual stubbornness, Palmer resisted all demands to alter the system.

On 25 October 1789, presumably after all efforts to resolve the matter had failed, the whole business was passed to William Pitt for his comments:

Minute of 25th Oct 1789 referred to Mr Pitt for his consideration.

Guards

The mode of paying the mail guards wages has hitherto been this 13s per week has been issued by the Postmaster General for every quarter on a warrant stating that sum to be the amount of guards wages. Which upon the present number of guards employed would come to about £4000 p annum. The fact is however,

The mail coach guard was seen by the public as a man of stature and was honoured by a popular ballad or recitation. In the illustration his top hat has become somewhat distorted, but he still has his timepiece in its pouch. (PO PE 001)

that 10s only of the 13s are applied to the payment of the wages, the other 3s amounting to about £900 pa are retained in Mr Palmers hands to pay for the uniforms and other articles of which the Postmaster General knows nothing, and the amount or appropriation of which they have never seen, no such account having ever been in their possession. They have reason to believe the Commissioners of Enquiry strongly objected to the mode of payment hitherto in practice, that is by issuing the full sum of £4,000 p annum to Mr Palmer or his deputy, thinking it better that whatever was due to the guards should be paid by the deputy postmasters and allowed in their amounts. The Postmaster General therefore ordered the account to be thus made out, but Mr Palmer objects to it unless a warrant is at the same time granted to him or his deputy for the uniform fund, as he calls it. That is for about £230 per quarter which the Postmaster Generals refused to grant, as they conceive they are not authorised to issue money to any person whatever by way of imprest without a warrant from the Lords of the Treasury for so doing and without knowing at the time they issue it what is to be the appropriation of it, of which in the present instance they know nothing either by any account of the actual appropriation this or the past appropriations of any of the sums already issued for this purpose and for which there is no warrant from the Lords of the Treasury. Still less should they, in their opinion, issue it to the person who is to pay the money, because without applying the question personally to Mr Palmer it is directly contrary to the principles upon which they perceive any office of accounts should proceed and directly in the teeth of a position so often laid down in the printed reports to the Commissioners of Accounts: viz, that the same officer who incurs the expense shall benefit by the management of it, and by having a large sum always in his hands to be issued him when, where and to whom he pleases, and without accounts the Postmaster General therefore proposed that the bills for the uniforms and other articles should be presented for his control and his signature as arose, and then the warrant would specify both the sum required and the immediate service for which it is to be applied.

Mr Pitt is therefore desired to give his orders whether this money so claimed by Mr Palmer is to be issued to him or not in the manner he proposes, for till it is settled the accounts of about 40 postmasters who have advanced out of the postage in their hands the wages due to the guards for the past five quarters[100] cannot be settled with the office or the amount ascertained of what is due for their letters.

Memorandum

The words of the Postmaster General Commission are these, 'he shall settle, establish or allow such constant salaries or allowances to the said officers or any of them for their respective services in the Commissioners of our High Treasurer for the time being shall first approve extract from the commissioners report.'

Guards

The guards are now also paid by the Comptroller General or his deputy, and warrants are issued to them for the amounts according to an account exhibited by them without any check or control, except that for one for the other and without sufficient evidence of all the payments being actually made to the parties a copy of this warrant for the pay of the guards is inserted in the appendix over page – a comptroller office ought not to have the disburse of any money whatever the reason assigned for this practice is to render the contractor as dependent as possible upon those under whose immediate direction they act, at first setting this out might have been necessary, it is now no longer so and may be subject to abuse and therefore ought to be discontinued.

We shall hereafter propose a proper officer to pay the incidental mileage and wages of the guards, they should be paid by the deputy postmasters and credit given in the quarter accounts for the same when the payments are duly vouched.

NB this is proposed for the wages but cannot be done for the contingencies.[101]

The outcome was settled and the guards were thenceforward paid by the Deputy Postmasters, although there were some problems in settling the accounts due to both over and under-payments. The whole business dragged on, come 29 August 1791 the Postmaster General was again in contact with the Treasury on the subject of guards and their payment:

> This letter was intended to be sent to the Treasury to explain the Postmaster Generals reason for absorbing the Guards Fund and for issuing the money in the manner proposed but as the authority of the Treasury was deemed unnecessary for this regulation the letter was not sent, however the PostMaster General think it right to have it entered for the purpose of recording their reasons upon the subject.[102]

The letter states that they were applying for a warrant for 10s 6d per week, the monies being intended for the guards' weekly wages. They went on to explain how they proposed to pay in future for the items that used to come out of the Guards Fund but which were now in arrears, as they had previously refused to issue warrants for these amounts. Money was collected by deducting the 2s 6d a week from 140 guards, making a total of about £900, so that although they were officially wages, the monies were actually being used for other purposes. No receipts were being produced and money was used with no checks on the value of goods. They mentioned clothing in particular, as £559 had been paid out in January 1789 and £255 had been spent on hats.[103] Saying that no proof had been offered as to whom the goods had been delivered and that in any case this type of finance was unacceptable, the deputies decided that they would pay the guards their 10s 6d and any bills for treatment of injured or sick guards would be forwarded to the Postmaster General for approval. Payment and the same would apply to pensions[104] for retired guards.

On the face of it the letter was a clear attempt to introduce some financial order into the very haphazard system used by Palmer and Bonner. It is clear from the letters opening phrases that the Treasury were happy, and the system was then established on the suggested lines. Equally it is obvious that Palmer could well have seen this as an attempt to curtail his control. The problems left by the changeover from Guards Fund to the newer system, and the accounting of the deputies for the guards' wages, were to continue. This problem was long-lasting, and at one point in February 1794 the Postmaster Generals refer to it as 'this disgraceful and longstanding account.'[105] It seems that not all the Deputy Postmasters paid the guards, but the country was divided into nine divisions including a number of the guards in the area. Thus the Second division covered the South West, Bridgewater, Bodmin, Plymouth and Taunton and the Third Division covered Wales and the south-west, Hereford, Newbury, Pembroke and Windsor.[106] From then on the Post Office paid all charges for uniforms and weapons directly to the suppliers.

In 1838 there were plans to change the basic salary, and in November George Stow (the Surveyor) and the Superintendent sent a circular to all guards saying that the new rate would not always apply. He also attached a list of guards showing the length of service of each. The longest serving guard had thirty-seven years' service. The grand total of guards at the time was 213, but there is no breakdown as to how each was employed. One list given in 1838 gives a total of 293, but with the 93 crossed out and 79 written in, at this point they were also being paid on a length of service basis:

Under three years	£70,
Three – ten years	£100,
Ten – fifteen years	£115,
Above fifteen years	£130.[107]

By this date the number of coaches in service was diminishing. It is of interest to note that the vast majority of the guards had over ten years' service, with five having served over thirty years. Stow also points out there were ten guards without regular appointment who were not included on this list.[108]

There were opportunities for the best of the guards to gain promotion to the rank of inspector, but such chances were rare. On 17 August 1812 a notice was issued saying that the best guards could be offered jobs as extra superintendents of coaches. They would receive the same pay as guards, with a fairly small travelling allowance.[109]

In 1837 Louis (the secretary) received a petition from five inspectors from London, Manchester, Exeter, Edinburgh and Carlisle expressing their grievances over pay. The petition pointed out that inspectors still only received the same wages as guards, with an additional allowance of eighteen shillings a day when travelling, which had then been cut to fifteen shillings. When it was at the higher rate they were able to save a little, but now this was difficult. The inspectors pleaded that the nature of the work made them liable to gout and rheumatism. They asked for £100 per annum for the two seniors and £70 for the juniors, it was calculated that this would only cost £213-2-6 extra per annum.[110]

All the evidence suggests that the guards were rather more than merely the cheerful, beaming figures so often depicted on Christmas cards. Most were hard working and their job carried a great risk of physical injury, but they certainly served their purpose. The success of Palmer's scheme, as far as security on the mainland was concerned, cannot be doubted. In 1838 a Constabulary Force Commission was set up by Parliament to consider the future policing of Britain. The Commissioners wrote to the Post Office in December 1837 asking them for a list of mail robberies on the road, since 1790 or as far back as they could go.[111] The idea was to compare the safety of the roads over the period, and the Commission thanked the various offices in March 1838 for the information they had provided.

The results of the returns[112] are quite surprising: very few robberies are listed anywhere, with the notable exception of Ireland. The General Post Office could only offer English details from 1824 to January 1838: in this period they said there had been only nine cases. This was obviously a great improvement on the eleven to thirty-seven a year that had been recorded in the early period. Edinburgh listed thirteen entries and all offenders had been caught. Their sentences ranged from six weeks in prison to transportation for seven, fourteen years or life, and even three death sentences. Ireland's list dates from 1801 and runs to fifteen large handwritten pages, making a total of around 500. Almost every one is described as involving violence. This is despite the fact that the Irish coaches were often accompanied by two armed guards.

The Post Office was conscious of its obligations to the guards, and in 1794 there was a query as to what pension might be paid to disabled guards. Five shillings (25p) a week was suggested.[113] The Postmaster General wrote in January 1794 that:

> Mr Freeling has to state is that the P M Genel took it on themselves pay the guards the real wages, instead of impressing a sum to Mr Palmer for that purpose from whence Mr Palmer proposed to pay such provisions as he might think fit to allow the disabled guards, to this the P M Gen objected but said they would recommend such objects as appeared on certificates laid before the Board to be fairly entitled to it. Their Lordships recommended one viz Roberts but the Treasury refused it, none have been recommended since, Does Mr Pitt approve of the P M Genl paying 5 sh a week to disabled guards without making separate applications to Treasury on each case or will he have each case laid before him for such sum as the person may be thought deserving to receive. Mr F will explain to Mr Long that the P M Genl object is to save the Treasury as far as is possible the trouble of any applications from the Post Office which can be avoided of which applications they complain so much.[114]

In one case a guard showed signs of mental instability and in consequence Hasker was reluctant to trust him with firearms and so the Postmaster General retired him and granted a pension of 7s 6d (37½p) in recognition of his past services. Pitt was asked if the Postmaster General might pay such sums without further reference to him.[115] The Postmaster General seem to have had a genuine concern for their staff. When Read, one of the guards, was in trouble and due to appear before the magistrate, they thought he should have a counsel so 'that he may not suffer in the opinion of the judge or jury either from his ignorance or from his poverty.' They made sure that he was represented as:

> Their Lordships thought it was their duty to enable their own officer who is unable to defend himself to make his defence by counsel that he may have the

Although of a much later date, this net and hook system for picking up and delivering the bags of mail on the railway is essentially the same as that used on the early nineteenth-century railways. (PO 51676)

full protection and benefit which the laws of this country and the mercy of his jury may entitle him to expect.[115]

The guard was, on odd occasions, in danger for reasons other than those associated with his job. In December 1792 the guard on the York coach had laid information against a 'disaffected person', and the news seems to have reached his associates. Hasker was told to inform Parkin, the lawyer, that threats had been made against the guard by 'fishermen, smugglers & c who had a rope ready for the purpose of dragging the guard thro' the harbour if they could find him.' It was suggested that Parkin write to the Mayor of Dover and call upon him to discover, 'by reward or otherwise and upon this being discovered the Mayor should take the proper means for punishing those persons as the law directs.'[116] Similarly, when the Oxford guard was 'ill-treated by a Mr Barker a passenger' in October 1798, the Postmaster General was most emphatic that the solicitor was to take out a prosecution on Barker.[117]

The Post Office paid the surgeons' bills and also tried to care for those employees who suffered injury or death whilst on duty. These accounts were placed before the Postmaster General who had to approve them, they clearly demonstrate the risks involved in guarding coaches:

> 1788: 16 July, paid J. Edward surgeon for treating Lewis Williams guard of Newmarket coach whose leg was much bruised in fall from coach 19/6.[118]
> 1792: 12 June, attendance to Alex Young Norwich mail guard who had his scull fractured by a fall £6-7-6.
> 1792: 13 June, to R.E. Mason for the eating washing & c of the above Alex young before he was able to be removed £2-2-10.
> 1791: 10 August, to T. Robertson for medicines and bleeding J. Denys Portsmouth guard who was hurted (sic) by a fall from the mail coach £2-3-0.

As the transport of mail was taken over by the railways, so the number of coach routes was reduced and more and more guards were made redundant. However, in general the Post Office was generous to them. It was their policy to pay pensions to those whose jobs were abolished. The guards were granted a pension when they retired and a list of Irish mail guards dated 26 February 1848, placed on the superannuation list since 1831, shows they were getting pensions of £18-4-0 (£18.20), £15-12-0 (£ 15.60) or £13-0-0. A note says that while these guards were pensioned the wage was 13s a week.[119] In the 1840s there are records of superannuation being paid to the guards. In April 1844 the total of the guards' wages was £4695-11-6, and the superannuation paid was £140-19-11.[120] Answering a petition for an increase in the pension in January 1807, the Postmaster General stated that the principle was that an officer who served well would, on retiring, get two thirds of his salary as a pension, if he had served for over thirty-five years then he would receive three quarters.[121]

The number of serving guards varied over time, at the beginning of the mail coach system there were around 140 to 150 permanent guards. The number of guards seems to have stayed fairly stable until the early part of the nineteenth century when figures get confused. In 1791, in addition to the regular guards there were six supernumerary guards on permanent stand-by, in times of crisis during bad weather this number was increased to nine.[122] There are references to 'the guards', or 'the mail guards', but no distinction is made between coach guards and riding guards. From the late 1820s and early 1830s the generic term is also used to include rail guards. By the 1840s and 1850s the majority are indeed railway guards. One list of 1831 gives the figure of established guards as 245, amended in red to 234, and a note says the figure was 236![123] Interestingly, there is a listing of five police officers and two Street Keepers. The list of 1838 records 293 'Mail Guards', later amended to 279. The duties of one inspector were then confined to the railways.[124]

The honour of being the last known survivor of the mail coach guards went to one Moses Nobbs,[125] who wrote his memoirs in 1891. Unfortunately, he gives really very few details of the life and times of the guard. He certainly makes no mention of the question of tips, but at least he offers a flavour of the times of what has become a Christmas card icon.

4

THE GUARD'S GEAR

In his plan to reform the Post Office Palmer made two major claims, he promised a faster, more regular delivery of mail and he offered a more secure delivery; he fulfilled both. The speed came by careful planning and the security was ensured by having an armed escort on each coach. Both improvements were long overdue, for the mail was then in a rather parlous condition. Palmer commented on the state of the post in his *Plan for the Reform and Improvement of The General Post Office*, written in 1783:[1]

> 2.) It is likewise very unsafe as the frequent robberies of it testify, to avoid a loss from this people generally cut Bank Bills and Bills at Sight, in two and send the parts by different posts
> 3.) The Postmaster lately advertised directions to the public of the best method he could devise of dividing a bill in such a manner as to prevent it's being of any uses to the Robber.

This advice, accompanied by a diagram showing a diagonal cut, was published in the newspapers and approved by the Secretary, Anthony Todd. Todd performed this duty once in February 1782 and again in March 1790. It is of interest that some six years after the introduction of the mail coaches Todd still felt it necessary to advertise this procedure. Each piece of the bill was then sent by separate post, so increasing costs which had the unfortunate effect of making it unpopular with businessmen.

In the first outline of his plan Palmer was adamant that the guards used on the coaches would be regular soldiers and he described how they would be placed:

> 10.) The guard should by no means be left either to the postmaster or master of machine to provide, as those they could procure, would be little relied on in any respect. A soldier is accustomed to the discharge of firearms, to keeping them clean, and to watch and fatigue in late hours; a sufficient number of them, well recommended by their officers, should be distributed over the kingdom and

one quartered at the inn of every stage or every other stage where the diligence stops to change.

It might be queried, knowing the British Army's reputation for drinking, whether stationing a soldier in an inn was a good idea. Palmer continues:

> ...he might be seated on the top of the coach with the mail behind him, here he could best command the road and observe suspicious persons, he might have two short guns or blunderbusses and the Coachman might have Pistols to use if necessary, they should have some extraordinary pay and be liable to military punishment for neglect of duty.[2]

Had his plan been adopted then the number of troops involved could have been quite high, during the Napoleonic Wars this would have represented an unwelcome extra drain on the Army. However, as has been pointed out, for reasons of his own Palmer changed his mind and used 'civilian' guards.

The mail coaches first ran in 1784, and as security had been such a feature of Palmer's plan it must be assumed that each coach carried an armed guard. If the engraving of the very first run is to be believed that certainly carried an armed guard, and it is reasonable to assume that all other coaches carried one. How were they armed? The first payment for firearms traced so far in the Post Office accounts does not appear until March 1786, 'Mr John Bennett for firearms for guards £4-14.'[3] A gun maker of this name is recorded as working at this date in Threadneedle Street, close to Lombard Street where the Post Office was situated.[4] It is therefore most likely that the purchase was made from this maker. In 1788 the price of a blunderbuss and a pair of pistols from Mortimer, the armourer, was £4-19-0 (£4.90). Since the cost of this purchase from Bennett was almost identical, it strongly suggests that it was for similar firearms. As only one set of weapons was bought it is possible that the purchase was made to ascertain costs and perhaps examine the proposed weapons. Those coaches running between 1784 and 1788 were ordinary stagecoaches, supplied by the various contractors and pressed into Post Office service. In the circumstances it seems very likely that the guards were also supplied by the contractors, although this was something that Palmer had specifically rejected in his original plan. Stagecoaches frequently carried a guard, although it seems they were not normally armed. These early mail guards were presumably armed, and there is good reason to believe that the contracts bound those supplying the coaches and guards to supply the weapons (see below). However, when Besant's patent coach[5] was approved in 1786 Palmer and Bonnor insisted that from then on contractors should use only this model. There is enough evidence to suggest that it was about this time that the guards first became employees of the Post Office, the organisation which now became responsible for supplying the uniforms, arms and other equipment.

Handwritten note by Hasker passing on the Lord Mayor's restriction on the blowing of horns during times of divine service. (PO 10/5, no.42)

Further support for this idea is given by a minute from the Postmaster General to Mr Freeling on 25 February 1791, when they apparently first became aware that the office was paying for the guards' firearms:

By the printed contracts the contractors are to find firearms The Postmaster General have no official notice of these printed contracts being discontinued nor are they in possession of any reasons from the Comptroller General why this expense should now be brought upon the public. The Comptroller General had better state it and let it make a paragraph for the Treasury in the Port Patrick Mileage draft.[6]

There is another reference to the Port Patrick Mileage, dated 19 April 1792, which suggests it was some sort of memorandum dealing with queries and explanations to the Treasury. So far, however, the document has not been traced.[7]

This reference seems to indicate that the Postmaster General had only just become aware that the Post Office had been paying for the guards' firearms since 1788, a period of three years. This in itself is a little surprising, since the accounts were normally looked at closely and clearly show payments for firearms. Any further relevant, associated correspondence to this minute has not so far been found and there are no further references to the matter. In a letter to the Treasury on 8 May 1790, the Postmaster Generals, in the course of the long missive defending themselves against accusations made by Palmer, state that:

… it has been the practice ever since the mail coaches were adopted for the Comptroller General (Palmer)to make and execute the contracts without our ever having seen or signed them or been parties to them or to the covenants they contained.[8]

This change of policy over the supply of arms would appear to be just such an occasion. The fact that there is no record of any further correspondence on this subject suggests that the situation was accepted as a *fait accompli*.

There is one indication that the coach maker Vidler may have been somehow involved in the early supply of arms for the coaches. Hasker refers to him as claiming payment for holsters but the reference itself is not specific. Hasker wrote to the Postmaster General:

> My Lords,
> I did not intend to have troubled your Lordships with the enclosed bill of Mr Vidler for firearms cases that have been made for about three years to the mail coaches but that Mr Vidler is so very importunate.
> He says that Mr Palmer promised him payment at a guinea each and that I directed them made at your Lordships desire I believe this to be very true but I was in hopes when you agreed to take the payment of oiling and greasing and drawing the coaches to the office to the great ease of him and the Coach Contractors that it would have covered every trifling expense of this sort and have kept me from further importuning but as it does not I refer it to your Lordships with his letter.[9]

The letter is dated 25 September 1795, in which case Vidler was apparently supplying these cases either towards the end of 1791 or the start of the following year. In the Incident Bills for January 1792 there is an entry that seems to be the first recorded purchase of holsters by the office, this may well mark the time when Vidler stopped supplying them.

> Mr Thomas Foster for mails & c £31-0-0
> Ditto for pistol cases & C to 5 Jan 1792. £9-18.[10]

The first major payment for firearms for the coaches is recorded for the quarter ending 5 April 1788[11] and is listed below:

> An Account of money paid for Fire Arms & Accoutrements from 5th January 1787 to 5th July 1789.
> Mr Wm Henry Mortimer for 59 setts (sic) of arms consisting of a blunderbuss and pair of pistols with powder horn, bullet mould & screw driver at £5-3-6 p sett: £305-6-6.

Seven blunderbusses at £1-7-6: £9-12-6.

One pair of pistols at £3-1-6.

Repair for one year at £4-14-6: £322-15.

1789 To the Deputy of Exeter paid by him for repairing: 7-6.

To the Deputy of Grantham for fire arms: £11-9-8.

1789 Jan 5: To Mr Mortimer for 64 setts of arms consisting of a blunderbuss pair of pistols with powder horn bullet mould & screw driver at £5-3-6 each: £331-4

To Mr Mortimer for repair of fire arms from Feby 1788 to 31st Jany 1789: £16-11-6

Mr Tho. Foster for Belts and cases for fire arms in the Qtr ended 5th April 1789: £9-8-6

July 5 Do in the Qrt ended 5th July 1789: £16-17-6

Apr 5 Paid by the Postmaster of Coleshill for a cover for a Blunderbuss 9th Aug 1788: 2/6

Total for 2 & ½ Years: £708-16-2

Which for one year is £283-10-5

This grouping of payments would also seem to substantiate the idea that the guards became part of the office establishment around 1787. This first payment was made for the quarter ending 5 April 1788 and was for weapons supplied from January 1787. The proximity of the orders for firearms and belts suggests a connection.

The initial price for a complete set of firearms and accessories was £5-3-6 (£5.17), in January 1808 the firm of Mortimer & Son petitioned the Post Office for an increase in the price of mail coach firearms. This suggests that for the previous twenty years' prices had stayed the same. Mr Freeling wrote to the Postmaster General questioning their claim:

> For the Postmaster General:
> I do not see that we shall be justified in giving to Mess Mortimer a greater sum for the arms in question than that at which the Ordnance Board has valued them. If these gentlemen will undertake to furnish them at 6 guineas being half a guineas more than hitherto paid, it is well. If not, I should suggest the propriety of getting arms supplied from Birmingham or Sheffield
>
> *Approved*, signed Sandwich and Chichester

As Freeling's suggestion was approved and since the Mortimers continued to supply the weapons, they presumably accepted the offer.[12]

No source has shed any positive light on why the Mortimers were chosen as the official armourers to the Post Office. It has been suggested that there may have been some external religious contact, for apparently there was a strong Methodist association between the Mortimers and some officials at the Post Office.[13]

> **GENERAL POST-OFFICE,**
> *July* 1816.
>
> ## TO THE MAIL GUARDS.
>
> ———
>
> AS many accidents have happened by the improper loading of the Fire Arms, although Guards have positive orders not to fire them wantonly, it is deemed proper to state to them—That the Top of the Powder Horn is a sufficient charge for the Blunderbuss, with ten or twelve shot, the size of a pea,—That for the Pistols two-thirds of such a charge is proper,—That they must be particular to ram the charge well that air may not be confined between or beyond the charge,—And that they keep their Arms clean, and never loaded above a week.
>
> If these rules are strictly observed, the like accidents will be avoided.
>
> **THOMAS HASKER.**

Hasker seems to have been especially concerned with the guards' firearms and issued many reminders and warnings about their care and safety. Although he refers to many accidents, very few are listed in the records. (PO 10/6/107)

The firm held the contract to supply the Post Office with firearms between 1788 and 1816. On 3 October 1816 Freeling reported to the Postmaster General that Mr Mortimer:

> …who has supplied arms for years, has declined business and had called into his office, to return thanks to your lordships for the favors (sic) he has received.[14]

This surrender of the contract appears to have been associated with family matters and a change in business arrangements.[15]

Obviously a new supplier was needed, and the accounts for the next quarter, which came on 5 April 1817, record the first payment to the Mortimers' successor, J. Harding.[16] The choice of the Harding firm may well have had its origins in an earlier trade association between the two gun makers. A trade label for John Harding indicates that at one time he was working either with or for Mortimer.[17] There can be no other reason why this particular supplier was chosen, he was not even local to the Post Office as he worked from Blackman Street, The Borough, across the River Thames in South London. The firm was to remain the principal supplier of arms to the Post Office until 1842, and retained the Post Office contract for the care and repair of firearms right through to 1846.

This is an example of a guard's timepiece which was carried on the Leeds coach. It was enclosed in a locked wooden case to prevent the guards interfering with the setting. (P 9481)

All the evidence suggest that until at least the early nineteenth century there were never more than 150 full-time mail coach guards employed by the Post Office. A number of supernumeraries are recorded on occasions, but the references suggest that they were used for odd jobs and were not in fact regularly employed on the coaches. Since the number of items in the initial purchases of firearms is so closely proportional to the number of guards, this surely may be taken to indicate that a set of firearms and accessories was issued to each guard. There is support for this hypothesis in later correspondence, much of which clearly indicates that later post riders made a personal issue of their pistols (see p132). Each guard was supposed to report for duty with his firearms, and it would seem to have been far more practical for each guard to have his own set rather than to have a scramble to issue them before each run.

One of the rules set out in the list of *Instructions to Guards* states:

It is a guard's duty always to have a bag of tools complete; and every week when they go to receive their wages the Postmaster has orders to examine their firearms, to see if they are perfectly clean. Barrel, lock and every part, that they have a blunderbuss and case, a pair of pistols and holsters, a powder horn, bullet mould, screwdriver, touch-hole pricker and lock for his mailbox.[18]

The number of guards fluctuates throughout the nineteenth century, but the records do not make clear whether the stated figure refers to all types of guard: i.e. coach, rider or railway. No more large individual purchases of arms are recorded, but as both the regular gun makers were under contract to repair and supply firearms for the mail guards, new weapons would have been purchased as and when required. Hasker mentions in his petition (see p42) that one of his first jobs was to record the firearms and their 'numbers registered',[19] sadly this ledger seems not to have survived.

Some coaching pistols and blunderbusses survive in both public and private collections, the vast majority conform to a standard pattern. They are essentially plain, sturdy weapons with stocks of walnut and brass barrels and furniture. As these weapons would be carried in all weathers, brass was presumably preferred to iron because it is far less prone to rust or other exposure-related deterioration.

The typical coaching blunderbuss had a substantial brass barrel, 35cm (14in) long, often rather thick-walled, that belled at the muzzle to a diameter of about 2.5cm (1in). Around the muzzle was engraved 'For His Majesty's Mail Coaches', modified after 1837 to 'For Her Majesty's Mail Coaches'. The style of lettering and spacing varies slightly, and there are occasional mis-spellings and changes in layout, but as each legend was engraved by hand that is not surprising. Along the top of the length of the barrels the maker's name and address is engraved, this can be a useful pointer when dating examples. There is also an engraved number, the style of which varies greatly and was sometimes executed extremely crudely. The significance of these numbers has been a matter of some debate. It is almost certainly not a coach or route number, and on balance it seems to be sequential numbering. The reasons for this assumption are discussed at length in Chapter 10.

The plain stock is of walnut and all the furniture, side plate, trigger guard, ramrod pipes and butt plate are of brass. The lock is of conventional form, with both a full and half-cock position that locks the cock in a safe position, thus preventing accidental discharge. Some surviving examples are fitted with the usual swan-neck cock, whilst others have the later ring-neck style. On the Royal Armouries weapons the majority are fitted with swan-neck cocks, but it is dangerous to assume that this was always the case, for some locks could obviously have suffered damage during their lifetime and had the cock replaced. The lock plate is engraved with the maker's name and sometimes had some simple incised line decoration. The surviving weapons have wooden ramrods which fit into a slot cut in the stock under the barrel. The original ramrod was almost certainly of wood and, since the guards were ordered to draw the charges at the end of each journey,[20] it can be assumed that the original ramrods were fitted at the tip with a worm or jag. This was like a small corkscrew; as the ramrod was pushed down the barrel and turned the worm bit into the bullet, thus allowing it to be pulled out. Drawing the charge meant pulling out the lead bullet and emptying out the gunpowder from the barrel.

Mr. HART's Report of Riding Work in the Month of April.

TIME BILLS.	Departs from H. M.	Arrives at H. M.	Miles	Armed or not.	Observations.
Beccles and Wangford	3.45 PM 9 — AM	10 — AM 5 — PM	9	not	*Nell*
Bedford and Woburn	8 — PM 5 — AM	7 30 AM 10 — PM	15	armed	*Mell*
Brandon and Fakenham	7 — AM 2 15 PM	7 30 PM 11 30 AM	33	not	*Nell*
Bury and Thetford	4 — PM 5 30 AM	10 — AM 9 30 PM	26	armed	*Mell*
Cambridge	6 30 AM	9 — PM			*Mell*

Part of a surveyor's monthly report on his Riding Work when he toured his area checking on the quality of service. These reports were submitted to the Postmaster General. This one dates from April 1826. (PO 40/324)

A distinguishing feature of these coaching weapons was the sliding-bolt safety-catch set in the lockplate just behind the cock. With the cock vertical in the half-cock position, this small sliding bar, known at the time as a stop, could be pushed forward to engage with a slot cut in the rear of the cock. In this position the stop locked the cock firmly in the safe position and the weapon could not be fired. Many surviving Royal Mail weapons have damaged stops, and it has been suggested that these may have been deliberately modified by the guards. On balance this appears unlikely, as there was little to be gained from removing the projecting arm – so often the only missing part.

The significance of the stop was the subject of impassioned debate after an unfortunate accident in Ballina, Ireland on 27 October 1835.[21] The mail coach in question was loaded and ready to go, the guard was placing his blunderbuss at the rear of the coach when for some reason it fell to the ground and accidentally discharged. An unfortunate bystander, a Mr Terence McDonagh, 'a very decent person', was shot through the body by one ball and expired very quickly. An inquest was held and the guard, Samuel Middleton, was exonerated and a verdict of accidental death returned. On 5 November Dublin Castle sent a full report to Freeling and expressed the hope that some help could be given to the widow.

During the course of the inquest the jurors examined the blunderbuss and decided that it was in an 'imperfect state of repair', given that it had fired from the half-cock position. On 3 November George Louis, the Secretary, wrote that he did not think there was any imperfection, he suggested that the sheer weight of the blunderbuss hitting the ground could have caused the shot. The gun maker, Thomas Calderwood,[22] was asked to examine the weapon. In his letter of 7 November he stated that:

According to your directions I have carefully examined the blunderbuss sent up from Ballina. It was an old blunderbuss and the cock stands so near the hammer when at whole cock that it has the appearance of being only at half cock which circumstance may have caused the accident but the lock will not go off at half cock as stated by the jury.

As a means of preventing further accidents I would strongly recommend a general inspection of all the Mail Coach arms and would advise stops put to the locks of those found servisable (sic) the same as they are in England. The unservisable (sic) arms to be replaced by new ones on the same plan.

I am sir with great respect yr obt servt,

Thomas Calderwood

His report implies that although the lock may have looked as if it was set at the safe, half-cock position, it was in fact ready to fire.

Louis was delighted when the armourer said that the weapon could not go off at half-cock. If there had been any doubt then the guard might not have been totally exonerated and the Royal Mail held responsible for the accident. The same letter contains the information that, 'before the Superintendence in Ireland formed part of the duties of this department the locks of the firearms were without the stops that those furnished subsequently have been supplied with.' This clearly indicates that the lock had no safety catch. He goes on to suggest that all surveyors be told to carry out the inspection, firearms found fit for service should be fitted with stops and all others sold off with the money to go to the office. The Postmaster General disagreed and did not think it would be worth the expense, as such an accident was very unlikely to happen again. He thought that having enough weapons was the primary necessity over technological innovation. However, new blunderbusses were to have stops and the Postmaster General went on that, 'I do not think in the state of Ireland it is advisable to sell the unserviceable ones.' He was probably right, since fitting a stop would involve quite a lot of work and it might well have been cheaper to fit a new lock. His comment about the sale of surplus weapons was an oblique reference to the unrest in Ireland.

The unfortunate guard involved in the accident was held in high regard and did not fear any conflict with the local people, nevertheless he was transferred to another route at his own request. The question of compensation was raised by local supporters, and although McDonagh was not a Post Office employee it was felt that the family should be helped. The Postmaster General was apparently favourable to the idea of providing a pension for the widow, and there was a precedent in that other accidents involving mail coaches in Ireland had killed three people, in each case pensions were paid.[23]

A blunderbuss was chosen as the main coach armament because, all things considered, it offered the best chance of the shooter hitting his target. The normal load was a number of small lead balls. When the shot was fired the balls leaving the muzzle tended to spread out, so covering a much larger area than a single ball. To achieve this effect the bore, the internal diameter of the barrel, increased towards the muzzle, so allowing the balls to begin fanning out. The amount of spread was not greatly increased by widening the barrel beyond a certain size, although some makers were not convinced and some blunderbusses have enormous muzzles.

Accompanying the guard's blunderbuss was a pair of pistols of similar design, with a barrel 9in (23.5cm) long and a bore of 15mm. The stock, furniture and locks are very similar in style to those of the blunderbuss, and there is little to distinguish them from holster pistols of the period, except the slightly sharper, more hooked curve to the butt. These too have the engraved legend around the muzzle, and the barrels carry the gun maker's details and a number.

The mail coach firearms produced by the Hardings differed very little, if at all, from those made by the Mortimers. Obviously the name on the barrel and lock is different, but apart from that the pistols and blunderbusses have the same style of construction. However, there is one distinction on many of Harding's weapons, they are engraved on the barrel or lock with a mark of a crown above an arrow head. The tip of the arrow points upwards to the crown, the opposite direction to that found in Government marks. The symbol is not found on all the mail coach firearms by Harding, but it is in place often enough to suggest that Harding could conceivably have been using it as a semi-official Post Office mark.

Several smaller, overcoat-sized flintlock pistols made by Harding are recorded, and many of them carry the crown and arrow mark which may well indicate ownership by the Post Office. It was suggested by the late firearms expert, H. Blackmore, that these smaller pistols were probably carried on their journeys by the mail office inspectors or surveyors. Another, perhaps more likely possibility, is that these pistols were carried by the Foot Post, since the larger coach pistols would have been bulky and very inconvenient to carry about their person. None of these smaller pistols have the engraved legend around the muzzle.

These smaller pistols are far less common than the larger coaching type, information which ties in with the fact that only a comparatively small number of Foot Posts are listed as being armed. The few surviving records for April 1826 for *Riding Work* detail the runs and whether they were armed or not:

Mr Scott: covering south east England, thirty-two rides. nineteen armed. Eighteen Foot. Eight armed.

Mr Fletcher: covering Lancashire and north west, forty runs. Seven armed, Foot not shown separately but four entries amended from unarmed to armed.

Mr Churchill: West country and Wales, thirty-three runs. three armed, Foot not separated.

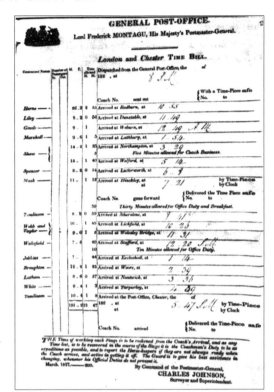

Time bill for the London-Chester run in March 1827 with very precise timings and very short stops. (PO 10/203)

Mr Rideout: Oxford and south west, thirty-three runs, four armed, Foot not separated.

Mr Louis: Bristol and west Country, forty-four runs, twelve armed.

Mr Hart: East Anglia and his lists separates the Foot Posts.[24]

West and Wales notes only three armed out of thirty.[25]

In his original proposal of 1796[26] Freeling specifically excluded the Foot Posts from his planned arming of the Horse Posts. The first time that the armourer's entries included a specific mention of Foot *weapons* is in Mortimer's account of 1814[27], but from then on they are regularly listed, certainly until 1838.[28]

Although the Post Office guards were armed by the Mortimer's and the Harding's between 1788 and 1846, it is of interest to note that the design of the weapons hardly changed at all. This suggests that Mortimer may well have set up something approaching a production line to meet the demands of his customers, and that this was simply taken over by the Hardings.

As pointed out above, in his original plan Palmer had said that the guard would have either two short guns[29] or blunderbusses and that the coachman was to have pistols. A contemporary engraving purported to depict the first coach of August 1784; it shows a guard[30] in a feathered hat, wearing a rather quizzical look, sitting to the left of the driver with a leather belt slung across his shoulders. From the belt he dangles a flintlock blunderbuss, apparently set in the half-cocked position. Cradled in his arms he holds an object that could well be a second blunderbuss, for the end appears to flare slightly, suggesting that it is a barrel. There are no signs of the proposed coachman's pistols, and indeed when the system was in action it was the guard who was issued with the pistols. This would seem more sensible, for the driver would surely be more concerned with the horses than the robbers.

The majority of surviving pistols and blunderbusses show signs of having endured a hard life. Many have broken stops and the stocks are often dented, bruised, cracked or lacking pieces. This indicates that they had had some rough usage. It is perhaps not surprising that their condition was often poor, for the weapons must surely have been frequently loaded and unloaded, carried from office to coach and, no doubt, occasionally dropped. The regular entries for repair and supply of guards' firearms in the records suggests there can be little doubt that the mail coach weapons suffered rough handling, for there is little indication that they were fired on a regular basis:

5 July 1792
Mr H.W. Mortimer: for repairing firearms & for new firearms for the mail guards from Jan 1791-July 5th 1792 £ 117-6-0.[31]
2 February 1817
Harding: for repairing the firearms used by the Mail guards: £23-18-6.
Apr 26
Harding: for repairing the firearms used by the Mail guards: £ 23-5-0
£ 37-10-0.[32]

According to their instructions, every guard was supposed to show his pistols and blunderbuss to the Deputy Postmaster when he reported for duty. Over the coaching period a number of the weapons must have been lost or mislaid, these would have been replaced. In the case of coach overturns or other accidents they may well have been thrown out and lost. There are two or three cases detailed in the archives which mention the loss of firearms, one is in a handwritten letter dated 3 December 1792, signed by John Harraden, it is addressed to the Postmaster General:

My Lords
I have this instant received your minutes of the 23 rd Nov and now inform your Lordships in answer thereto that on my quitting the conveyance of his Majesty's Mails in carts I much wished to deliver up the firearms and applied to Mr Hasker's office for such purpose and desired receipt in discharge thereof. When I found their answer more arms outstanding against me than I had to account for from the following reason:

The drivers of the carts not being permitted to enter the Inland office with their arms loaded they were obliged to leave them in their carts in the office yard from whence some were taken.

This was reported to Mr Palmer who told me in Mr Hasker's presence that from such an unforeseen event he did not consider me as responsible for what was already lost but that he should for whatever might be lost in future.

And on such grounds I thought it best to Them and when I was last at Harley Street your Lordships may recollect I expressed a wish to mention two or three circumstances to your Lordships among which this was one and which I now beg your Lordships will determine upon.[33]

On 6 March 1794 Hasker wrote to the Postmaster General:

I have the honour to enclose your lordships a letter from Mr Harraden and I have to inform you that the arms he had from the superintendents office as per receipt given were three setts and two pistols. The arms he returned were one blunderbuss & one pistol – Mr Aush says Mr Busby did not receive any blunderbuss which, if admitted, there is now due from Mr Harraden to account for two setts (sic) and three pistols, in reduction of which I submit to your lordships what he says of their being lost from the Comp Gens, which if your lordships admit there will only remain for him to account for two blunderbusses and three pistols.

On 4 December 1792 the Postmaster General firmly said that Hasker must find out how many firearms were issued and how many were returned and that Harraden must either deliver the firearms or:

…if a guard loses his firearm does he not replace them? and is there anything in Mr H report that is different from a guard but Mr H must deliver up all he has immediately to Mr H.[34]

This statement could be taken to mean that the replacement of lost weapons was regularly necessary, and this could perhaps explain the apparent inconsistency in the numbering of weapons. If one of Mortimers' pistols was lost after their contract was surrendered then the replacement would be made by Harding, since it is known that a numerical list was kept[35] it could well be that the new pistol was given the old number.

The matter of Mr Harraden's responsibility rumbled on, and in the Postmaster General's report of 28 February 1794 is a letter stating firmly that, '…Mr Harraden must account for the missing arms viz. two blunderbusses and three pistols.' A little later it was further added that, 'Mr Harraden to make good as all the guards do the arms he is to account for except such as were found to be left in Mr Palmer's house and lost there.'[36] Mr Harraden did not give up easily, and in a let-

ter dated 10 February 1797 addressed to the Postmaster General he said that his
Counsel thought this account case was not suitable for trial by jury and could be
referred to arbitration. On the back of the letter Walsingham rejects the idea, and
Harraden is now bound to pay £25-9-6, but he cannot find the money and suggests that it be held over until the case is settled. If he won then this money could
be taken from his damages, if he lost then it could be added to his costs.[37] The
suggestion was rejected, and the Postmaster General commented that Harraden
was, 'to make good as all the guards do.'[38]

Hasker obviously thought that the guards' firearms should be properly cared
for and was very worried about the casual way in which some of the guards
treated them. He wrote on many occasions about the correct care and use of
firearms and one such example is given below:

> To all the guards. March 25th 1793
> Sir,
> I have the honour of the Postmaster General's Commands, to direct you to be
> very attentive to your Arms that they are clean, well loaded, and hung handy.
> N.B. These orders have been given before, but I have now the particular
> Commands of the Postmaster General to repeat them and to desire you will
> read over your instructions.[39]

The phrase 'hung handy' is so vague that it cannot be interpreted. Did Hasker
mean hung in holsters on the guard or were they somehow to be affixed to
the coach? So far no evidence to support either interpretation has been found.
However, his instructions about the care and loading of the firearms were less
ambiguous:

> July 1816   To The Mail Guards
> As many accidents have happened by the improper loading of the firearms,
> although guards have positive orders not to fire them wantonly, it is deemed
> proper to state to them – that the top of the powder Horn is a sufficient charge
> for the blunderbuss with ten or twelve shot, the size of a pea, that for the pistol
> two thirds of such charge is proper – That they must be particular to ram the
> charge well that air may not be confined between or beyond the charge – And
> that they keep their arms clean and never loaded above a week.
>   If these rules are strictly observed the like accidents will be avoided.
>   Thomas Hasker.[40]

Strangely enough, although Hasker speaks of 'many accidents', the archives contain very few references to the accidental discharge of firearms throughout the
entire period. There are one or two references to guards discharging firearms, as
in a letter of 26 January 1801 from the Postmaster General to Freeling:

It is hoped that a letter has been sent to a Mr Hamilton representing the conduct of the guard of the Dover Mail Coach in firing a blunderbuss, the ball of which entered through one of the windows of his house.[41]

There is one intriguing entry, for which no details have so far been located. Late in 1792 the Postmaster General wrote to Freeling, saying:

…let the Secretary in conformity to Mr Kirkmans letter enclosed to Mr Hasker write to Mr Walker surgeon of Duke Street St James's and say that if Mr Jones who was shot in the leg by the mail coach guard wants any extra assistance or food which the hospital does not usually find & which may be necessary for Mr Jones case Mr Walker will have the goodness to order it for him and the office will pay for it.[42]

Hasker felt so strongly about the guards and their firearms that, in October 1793, he proposed to the Postmaster General that a new law be introduced. He wanted to make it an offence for a guard to travel without his firearms being properly cleaned, loaded and primed. If the guard was found guilty Hasker wanted a tough sentence: he was to be sent to a House of Correction for a period not less than a month and not more than three, with hard labour as an added punishment.[43] Presumably the Postmaster General did not support the idea, for there is no further mention of it and it was never implemented.

The original payments for the firearms include a number of items, all of which would have been in common use during the period: powder horns, bullet moulds, turnscrews and prickers are all mentioned. However, few examples, if any, have ever been positively identified as being of Post Office issue. So far only one powder horn with an apparent association with the coaches has been located. It is of conventional cow horn form and is engraved with a picture of a coach and the inscription: 'John Davis Royal Mail 1815' within a wreath. It may be a presentation piece or a standard issue horn that was modified (see p251). Instructions to the guards mention 'the top' of the horn, and this suggests some type of removable cap which is lacking on this specimen. It is, however, likely that the normal issue powder horn would have been very similar.

The mould would probably have been of iron made in two halves and hinged at the top, each half would have had a semi-circular recess. When the two halves were closed together molten lead was poured through a small hole to fill the globular space. When cool the mould was opened, and out fell a ball with a small tail from the entry channel. This was cut off and the bullet was ready for use. Nowhere is it made clear as to how the guards acquired their ammunition, or whether they were expected to cast their own bullets. Since they were supplied with a mould this may well have been the case, and if so it was a job that most men of the period would have been used to. When the armourer was employed this may then have become part of his duties. The pricker mentioned would have been a short pointed metal rod, probably fitted with a small wooden handle and used for clearing the touch hole. It is likely that the turnscrew was the same as those found in fitted cases of firearms of the period, a small screwdriver with a wooden handle and a short broad 'blade'. Were these items marked in any way and did they carry the Post Office or maker's name? Pistols, blunderbusses and the weapons carried on the packet boats were usually all clearly marked as Post Office property, but perhaps these small everyday objects were not thought worth the effort. There are no specific references to the accessories apart from the original purchases in the records, although replacements may have been covered in the repair bills.[44] It is clear from the documents that the guards were often lax and uncaring about their firearms. The accounts cited above clearly show a constant need to repairs and replacements of firearms. Mr Hasker tried hard to improve matters with appeals and orders, but sadly with little success:

25 Sept 1793

My lords, for some time past my attention has been a good deal employed in correcting several abuses into which I find the guards had fallen respecting their arms.

Upon my taking opportunities of unexpectedly examining them, I found some very indifferently and carelessly loaded and others extremely dirty, some of the guards had neglected to bring all their arms to duty and others having lost some of their arms had absolutely travelled several journies (sic) with only a part.

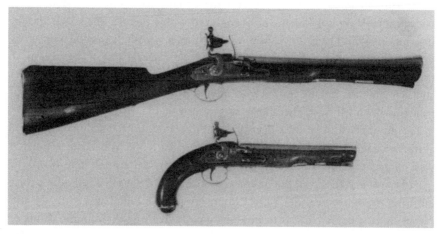

Blunderbuss and pistol of a guard, as supplied by Mortimer or Harding from 1788 until 1842, during which period the design remained unchanged. (XII291, XII855 Courtesy of the Trustees Royal Armouries)

In parts of the country where the danger of being attacked may not be so great and where the duty of superintendent calls him but seldom, it is not impossible but that the guards may become at times negligent. Yet wherever we meet them their arms etc are examined; but it requires that the greatest attention should be paid to the arms of those who come into London in order that they may be constantly in readiness to use them with effect in case of an attack, and which there is great reason to be prepared for the many daring robberies that have recently been committed in the neighbourhood of the Metropolis, and the probability of the road being very much infested in consequence of the number of felons lately discharged from the hulks.

I was very much alarmed in finding that several of the guards, instead of attending to the loading and management of their arms, have incautiously left that very necessary part of their duty to be executed by a man which they casually pick up in an inn yard or at a public house they frequent, to whom they allow six pence a week each. The danger to be apprehended of entrusting such characters with the cleaning and loading the Guards arms must appear obvious to your Lordships.

In order to prevent such misconduct in further I beg leave to submit to your Lordships consideration the propriety of obliging the guards coming into London to pay the six pence a week to a man that I may provide and on whom I can rely, and be answerable for his cleaning and properly loading all their arms before they go upon duty instead of paying it (as they now do) to a person in all probability of very indifferent character and connexions (sic) unknown to the office and over whom there can be no control.[45]

The Postmaster General accepted the suggestion but with some reservations, saying in September 1793 that:

Let the guards pay 6d & c a week to the man for taking care of the firearms and loading them if they prefer that to taking care of them themselves. But if a man does not take care of his own arms already it is hard to tax him £1-6-0 per annum to make up a sum for a man who is to take care of all it is punishing the innocent for the guilty – if a man undertakes the care of them if to him this option and does not execute it he will have no case. Mr Hasker may appoint a man if he pleases to examine them all and see that they are kept in good order.[46]

Hasker appointed a William Broadrib to the position of office armourer. However, matters did not go smoothly at first and Hasker wrote to the Postmaster General stating that:[47]

Overcoat pistol by Harding, which may well have been carried by the Foot Posts, or possibly the surveyors. Harding's mark is visible on the lock plate. (XII1865 Courtesy of the Trustees Royal Armouries)

GPO Apr 28 1795

My Lords

I have the honour to inform your Lordships that Wm Broadrib, the person fixed upon to clean the fire arms, has been employed in the actual duty since Monday 6th Inst. He was engaged and at the GPO ready to do this duty 4 wks before that time. But not having a room to work in till the 6th Inst at which time I hired one at 3s a week – his pay of 6p set 19/6 a week could not be deducted from the pay of the guards till then, when he really cleaned their arms. Therefore there are 4 wks to pay him during which time he attended the office and cleaned the extra arms, which I submit to your Lordships if he should not be paid by me and such expense charged in my incident bill I have not yet ordered the 6d wk to be deducted from the Guards wages but will if your Lordships approve from the 6th Inst.

I also submit to your lordships if I am to charge the 3swk in my incident bill for the room he works in till such time as he can get an apartment in the office Hasker.[48]

This request was approved on 2 May 1795 and the allowance started. But the waters had not been entirely calmed, another problem for Mr Broadrib cropped up later:

March 8 1796

My Lords

The weather being so very cold Wm Broadrib the 1st Instant informed me he could not clean the guards fire arms if he had not a fire – for immediate use I directed him to take a scuttle of coals from my office and have now the honour to solicit you Lordships to allow him a fire when necessary in such very cold weather.[49]

Safety seems not to have been too great a concern, having an open fire in a small room with gunpowder lying might be viewed by many as being somewhat hazardous!

The appointment of an armourer seemed to have worked, for there is no mention of him for nearly twenty years, but then there was a shock. Acting either on suspicion or from a tip-off, the Customs men visited the armoury on 3 November 1814 and searched the firearms cellar,[50] however there is no way of knowing whether this is the room referred to by Hasker and Baines.[51] The Revenue men found some 500lbs (226 kilos) of cocoa hidden there. Cocoa had been introduced into London in the late seventeenth century and soon became very popular. The Napoleonic Wars must have affected supplies and presumably it was now worth smuggling into the country. Sellick, the Portsmouth coach guard, confessed and was found guilty of smuggling. Freeling informed the Postmaster General, who felt that Broadrib must have known what was going on and ordered that both men be dismissed.[52] The armourer was evidently blessed by good personal representation, for just over a year later – on 28 November 1815 – he was reinstated on account of his very large family and the fact that he had previously been of good character.[53]

No more of Mr Broadrib's life has been traced in the records, but in 1814 there is the first appearance of another name to be associated with the guards' firearms when the Ashkettle family appears on the payroll. The initial entry is:

Mr Geo Ashkettle: two quarters rent of a room on Lady Day 1814 for the use of the armourer to the mail coaches, £10.[54]

Whether this is the same room as that mentioned above is not clear, but the fact that it is mentioned at all could be taken to indicate a change of circumstances. Perhaps after the discovery of the contraband cocoa it was felt that a new storage room was necessary. Similar payments continue to various members of the family until October 1823 when no payment is recorded. There is a long period without any reference to an armourer, but then a letter of December 1829 remarks that a 'Pike' inspects the guards at night.[55] There is then a reference in 1845 to a gentleman with this name, but it is by no means certain that the two are the same:

5 Jan 1845 Mr J. Pike messenger for cleaning and attending to the mail guards firearms and store arms from 28 Sept 1844 to 5 Jan 1845 £7-1-6.[56]

Permission was given by the Treasury on 17 October 1838 for the Mail Coach Office to take on Pike as a messenger on their establishment.[57] This is confirmed in the volume of *Miscellaneous Disbursements*:

Typical inscription around the muzzle of the guard's blunderbuss and pistols. After the accession of Queen Victoria in 1837 it was changed to Her Majesty's. (XII1080 Courtesy of the Trustees Royal Armouries)

18th September 1844: Jas. Pike the messenger attached to the Mail Coach Office to clean the arms used by the guards & c to receive at the rate of 5s a week and a further allowance at the rate of 3d for each of the guards working coaches out of London both amounts to be paid from revenue.[58]

This would suggest that there is a good chance it was the same man. Similar payments are recorded until 1854 when the records cease. The room used was presumably in the new premises at St Martin's-le-Grand, which opened in 1829.

There is one very big mystery associated with the guards' firearms. There are frequent mentions in the accounts to 'holsters blunderbusses' and 'pistol cases'[59] among many others:

Incidental bills 1794-96
5 April 1794
Chas Enouy for leather bags £244-4.
Mr Thos Foster for mails etc £80-3.
Ditto for pistol and blunderbuss cases £9-6.[60]
30 January 1828
Mr Walter for timepiece pouches & holsters for mail guards.[61]

What were these 'blunderbuss cases' and 'pistol holsters'? In the late eighteenth century personal firearm holsters carried on the body were rare, yet the Post Office accounts record their frequent purchase. Most of the holsters were supplied by a number of regular leather makers such as Hurst, Walter, Fisher and

Enouy (there are various spellings), who are all recorded as supplying bags, cases and leather straps. This suggests that the holsters and cases were of leather. There are too many references in the archives to doubt the existence of the holsters but a close and detailed examination of contemporary illustrations has, so far, found no obvious sign of guards or riders wearing holsters, either round the waist or slung across the chest. If they were not carried by the guard where were they stored on the coach? There are references to the guards keeping them in the post box. A circular of 22 January 1813 to mail guards reminds them that nothing should go in the box apart from the mail and certain specified items. These items included firearms.[62] Storing them in the mail box seems unlikely as they would not be readily accessible in an emergency. In the report of the accident at Ballimina there is a reference to the guard putting his blunderbuss in the sword case on the coach (see p100).

The waters are further muddied by an incident on 29 August 1836; a report of an accident to the guard on the Grantham and Yarmouth coach. As guard William Aldis was climbing back onto the coach he grasped a strap which came loose and caused him to fall back and under the coach. A wheel passed over his leg, breaking it just below the knee. The investigating inspector reported that as Aldis was ascending the second step and catching the 'holster strap', his weight pulled out the securing nails and he fell.[63] It is not known what is meant by the term 'holster strap', it could be a term for a means of attaching luggage or it could mean a pistol holster, although so far no illustration has indicated such a fitting. It is also possible that the holster was the container for the guard's horn, but this can only be a supposition. In the below extract, 'The Coach', there is a very full specification of a coach in existence around this date, but there is no mention of holster straps.

An illustration of what might be Royal Mail holsters appears in *The Story of the East Riding of Yorkshire*, published in 1912 and written by Horace B. Browne. A pair of flintlock pistols, together with a belt and holsters, are shown on page 245 and captioned as being carried on the 'Hull Stagecoach'. Although the photograph is not too detailed, the shape of the pistols suggests that they could just be mail coach ones. However, the caption makes positive identification uncertain, for the question is whether the author was referring to the mail coach or to a private stagecoach. Despite various enquiries these items have not so far been traced.

A possible explanation of the phrase 'blunderbuss case' is given by Stanley Harris in his book *The Coaching Age*, published in 1885. He stated that he saw the guards' firearms and mentions 'leather cases enclosing locks'. If this was what he saw then it may be that the cases so often referred to were no more than leather sleeves slipped over the lock to protect them from damp and damage. This was a feature used by the British Army on some of their rifles and carbines in the nineteenth century, but once again there is no positive confirmation for this hypothesis.

Matters are not helped by some early writers and Haworth[64], writing in 1882, states that the guard had a blunderbuss, pistols and 'a short, dirky looking sword.' As indicated elsewhere, no original source has been found to support this quote. The same writer adds that the coach had 'a round seat behind, covered with a skin for the guard, pockets for pistols being placed on either side.' This description does not match any illustration or coach plan. As far as can be seen in the many illustrations, the seat was semicircular but none show any sign of holsters.

Until 1842 Mortimer and Harding were the only regular suppliers of firearms to the Post Office. There are occasional references to the purchase by a Postmaster who talks of a 'blunderbuss' or 'firearms', and it is quite likely that some 'unofficial' arms were used by the staff (see p96).[65] A number of pistols and blunderbusses by makers other than Mortimer and Harding are recorded, they have the usual engraving found on Royal Mail weapons. Unfortunately, with some there must be a query as to whether the inscription is a later addition, since it is known that ordinary flintlocks have, in the past, been embellished with a bogus engraving or two to enhance their value.

In 1841 there were surprise additions to the guard's armoury and reference is made to the issue of weapons and holsters from the Government supplier the Board of Ordnance:

1841
5th July: To the Account of the Paymaster General at the bank for Firearms supplied by the Board of Ordnance for the use of mail coaches etc to June 1841 to the credit of vote 7 year 1841-2: £43-11-6.[66]
10th October 1841: (Under conveyancing item 288). The Paymaster General for firearms supplied by the Office of Ordnance for the use of the mail coaches etc £43-11-6.[67]
5th Jan 1842: 289 The Paymaster General for firearms supplied for the use of mail coaches on the 28th January 1842 £38-0-2
Ditto on 29th October 1841 £18-5-4.[68]
April 1842: 273 The Paymaster General for pistol holsters supplied by the Board of Ordnance for the use of the mail coaches on 10th February and 9th March 1842 £17-8-0 (Post 6/31).[69]

Why there was this change to the Board of Ordnance as a source of the guards' weapons is not clear, matters are made even more confusing by the fact that Harding was still being paid for the maintenance of the pistols:

289 Messer Harding & Son repairing mail coach firearms one qtr. 5 Jan 1842 £19-3-6.[70]

Harding & Son were still actively involved in repairs right through to July 1842, as is shown by a list summarising various payments.[71]

Harding & Son
Firearms

Date of Warrant	£	s	d
Jan 5 1838 – Feb 6 1838	24	16	–
April 5 1838 – April 30 1838	43	2	6
July 5 1838 – July 25 1838	24	13	–
Oct 10 1838 – Oct 29 1838	17	18	–
Jan 5 1839 – Feb 18 1839	32	16	–
Apr 5 1839 – Apr 24 1839	55	7	6
July 5 1839 – July 17 1839	23	5	6
Jan 5 1840 – Jan 27 1840	55	11	–
Apr 9 1840 – May 14 1840	58	14	–
July 5 1840 – July 28 1840	8	4	6
Oct 10 1840 – Oct 24 1840	23	3	–
Jan 8 1841 – Jan 30 1841	13	0	6
Jan 5 1842 – Jan 27 1842	19	3	6
July 5 1842 – July 28	8	9	–

In 1841 and 1842 the amounts are very low, which happens to have been the time when the Board of Ordnance first took over the supply of arms. Whether any conclusion can be drawn as to the relationship between the two events is difficult to say.

It is interesting to speculate as to what type of firearm might have been supplied by the Ordnance as, by this period, the old flintlock system was very much out of date. By the 1820s a simpler ignition system using a small metal cap had been perfected and the Army firearms were converted to the new system. Did the guards get the latest in design or did the Board of Ordnance use some old flintlock pistols? Unfortunately, there is nothing mentioned in the records about the type of firearms.

The orders to the guards about the use of their firearms were quite specific, as shown by rule number 5 in the 1829 Guards Instructions:

He is to take care that his Fire Arms are kept in clean and good Condition: that they are always properly loaded and primed when on duty, and on no account whatever to be wantonly discharging his Blunderbuss or Pistol as the carriage is going along the Road or through a Town; for every such Offence he forfeits Two Guineas, agreeable to an Act of Parliament, he is also to draw the charge of them as soon as he has ended his Journey.

It would seem that the guards' firearms were not the only ones held by the Post Office. In 1848 the Chartists planned a massive demonstration over their lack of political rights. It was feared that the demonstrations would degenerate into violent riots and plans were made for the defence of public buildings. The Post Office took the risks seriously and there is an entry for 13 June 1848 detailing payments for:

> Extra services 7 to guard against the intended Chartist riot of 10th April
> For casting bullets for pistols at 34 days 9 h at 4/8 a day: £8-2-10
> Guarding the office and gunpowder 36 – 1 at 2/6 a day: £4-10-3
> Refreshments for the men: £6
> For branding the staves 20 –9 at 4/8: £4-17-6
> Assisting the staves 20 –9 at 4/8: £1-1.[72]

The staves were another measure to protect the office and staff:

> 12th May 1848 constables' staves supplied by T.Harding on 10th April/48 1250 at 1/3 each £78-2-6
> 12th May 1848 constables' staves supplied by J.Griffiths 1000 at 1/3 each £62-10.[73]

The number involved, 2,250, would suggest that these truncheons were intended for all staff rather than just those at Headquarters. The low price almost certainly means that these were plain, simply turned, wooden truncheons such as were issued to the Special Constabulary on similar occasions. The mention of branding indicates that the truncheons were probably heat impressed with some sort of legend, such as 'Post Office' to indicate ownership. There is another reference to staves on 1 September 1848.

> Staves: the constables attached to the department supplied with pocket staves expense about 11s each.

The high price, eleven shillings as against one shilling and three pence, indicates that these were either painted truncheons or more probably tipstaves: carried as a badge of office by many civil officers.[74]

There were frequent orders to guards about the care of their firearms, but there was still another item about which he was warned to attend to with care – the timepiece. Since the whole system of delivery and collection of mail depended on the punctuality of the coaches, special timepieces were used by the guards. They carried them in leather pouches suspended on narrow, shoulder cross-belts. That the guards' equipment was subject to rough handling is shown by an entry:

> Mr W. Wiles for chains, snaps and buckles supplied for the repair of mails and mail guards' pouches one quarter to the 10th October 1840 £5-6-6.[75]

The guards were strictly forbidden to tamper with the timepiece, for apart from any other considerations they were quite expensive items. They required constant maintenance and winding was undertaken by a specially designated member of staff. Hasker, in his petition, says that he had to ensure, 'that the timepieces are kept in good order for the roads and the spare ones in repair and ready for service and the new ones as per contract annally (sic) made.'[76]

To prevent any tinkering with the clocks by the guards, perhaps to cover up delays, each of these timepieces was numbered and enclosed in a locked wooden case with a glass front. The case was evidently altered, for in August 1792 the Postmaster General approved Mr Hasker's change in design to prevent the guards from opening them with false keys, any guard who did so was to be dismissed.[77] On 11 December 1814 a guard, Benjamin Robinson, was discharged for interfering with his timepiece.[78] At first he was fined one guinea, but as the rules stated that a guard who broke the seal on a timepiece should be dismissed the Postmaster General did not consider this to be a penalty proportional to the gravity of the offence.[79] A letter of 20 November 1793 said that in the robbery and overturn of the Plymouth coach John Mathews, the mail guard, lost his timepiece. Although it was customary if that happened for guards to pay for a new one, in this case he was excused.[80]

Since standardised time did not come to the whole of Britain until quite late in the nineteenth century, the timepiece mechanism could be adjusted to lose or gain time depending on the direction in which the coach was travelling. In a letter dated September 1795 to the Postmaster General, Hasker states that:

> …we have them regulated to gain about 15 minutes in 24 hours that when they are travelling eastward they may be with real time therefore they gain about 10 mins in their way to W (Weymouth) which added to the clocks so far most being a few minutes slower than in London is the cause of the variation in the time bill at Weymouth.[81]

Hasker commented in the same letter that whilst every effort was made to keep them in good order, the timepieces were 'ill used on the road by guards and others – guards frequently throw the timepieces in the pouch from one to the other where they change.' He said that if caught doing this they were punished, but admitted that this happened very infrequently. The maintenance of the timepieces was important and expensive, and the records list regular payments for their winding and repair:

> An Account of money paid out for timepieces and repairs from the 5th Jany 1787 to the 5th July 1789
> Oct 10: To the Postmr of Dover for repairing timepieces 2/6
> 1788
> Jany 5: To the Postmr of York for do 12-0

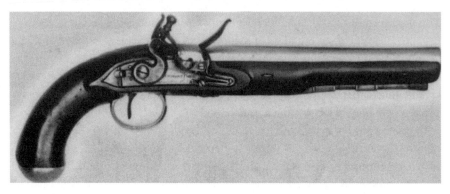

Guard's flintlock pistol by Mortimer, supplied between 1788 and 1814. (XII3984 Courtesy of the Trustees Royal Armouries)

> Octr 10: To Mr Delafons for timepieces & repair to the 10th Octr 1788: £356-19-10
>
> 1789: Jany 5 To Mr Delafons for timepieces and repair £17-8-8
>
> 1789: Jany 5 Mr F. Delafons for timepieces & repairs from 30th Novr 1785 to 31st Decr 1786 £316-12-6
>
> Apr 5 – Do – £48-0-6
>
> July 5 – Do – £67-14-0
>
> April 5 Paid the Postmaster of Exeter for repairing timepieces in Nov 1787 £ 7-0
>
> Haverford for Do 15th March 1789 – 2-0
>
> Total for 2 years and ½ – £757-19. For one Year £343-3-7.[82]

The size and spacing or payments etc. offers support to the idea that these were also early orders, made when the guard system was first being established by the Post Office. The next mention in the records is in January 1790, when £303-3-7[83] was spent on them. The value of the purchase suggests that quite a number of timepieces were acquired. In comparison, by 1848 the bill for repairing and buying seven new timepieces was only £95-13-6, a figure that, even allowing for inflation, indicated that a small number of items had been purchased.

Obviously, as the timepieces travelled backwards and forwards they suffered from a deal of wear and tear. Sometimes it was the fault of the guard, as with Kelly on the Lancaster coach. In November 1796 his timepiece was, 'much broke', as he had apparently strapped it to 'strap irons behind the coach.'[84] Like the firearms they were constantly being repaired, on 14 August 1839 Lord Lichfield wrote:

> It having been stated to me that there is reason to suspect the accuracy of many of the time pieces in use, the times by which I believe frequently disputed when parties are written to . I submit it would be expedient that a survey should be held on them & those which are no longer trustworthy should be condemned as in

case of any prosecutions we should certainly depend upon our time pieces & the consequences of them not keeping time correctly would be serious. August 9.[85]

To the Postmaster General 9th August 1839
The time pieces must be thoroughly examined and new ones supplied in the place of those that are found to be inaccurate.
Lichfield (ibid).

The inspection was undertaken by a longtime supplier, George Littlewort of Rahere Street in London, who sent a covering letter:

In submitting this statement I beg humbly to state from my daily examination of the time pieces, I believe I have given a true return of their performance, but I should state from the number of hands and rough usage which many time pieces appear to receive leaving my hands that it is surprising how many perform as they do. The time pieces are made very strong to bear the usage they meet with which is very much against good performance, if not they would be broke every journey. There is a great difference exists in the performance of them being through so many hands.

I have marked those with a cross which I consider should be substantially repaired, the others that perform well I have ticked and have placed them the order of the book in use.

I regret most sincerely to have brought before your notice my time & occupation is solely given to the department & I assure you that my best attention shall be given to ensure if possible the time pieces perform with accuracy.

Waiting your commands, I beg most respectfully to remain your most humble and obedient servant,

George Littlewort

The inspection began:

Bath N 10, 80, 85(X), 127 – these time pieces work to Devonport and pass through six guards' hands, N 10, 80 and 127 good order. 85 requires considerable repair.
Birmingham night railway Ns 20 & 196, these time pieces work to Preston and back and both good.
Brighton night N 9 & 154(X) both these time pieces go well but '154 is 'an old vertical one.'
Bristol N 55, 78(x), 125, 143(x) these time pieces go to Pembrook and pass thro' six guards hands are old ones but perform pretty accurately 7 &,143 require repair.

Devonport N 51,94,111(X),124 these time pieces go to Falmouth and Penzance pass thro' four guard's hands and one coachman's hands all perform well but 111 an old one and requires repair.

Dover Nr 74(X) ,157 these time pieces go to Romney from Dover by the cart 74 is much out of repair.

The other is good.

Edinburgh N 79, 86, 104, 142 these time pieces go thro' ten hands and all perform well.

Exeter N 12, 100, 106, 107(X),these pass through six hands to Falmouth and back, three of these time pieces perform pretty well, 107 is an old one.

Gloucester N 28(X) 58(X) 81, these time pieces go to Carmarthen & back perform well.

Hastings N 3 156 both perform well.

Hull N 39 76(X) 82(X) these time pieces are much worn, N 39 not so much as the other two.

Leeds N 108(X) 133 144(X) these perform well N 108 & 144 are old ones & much worn.

Louth N 46 69 166 perform well.

Lynn N 123(X) & 175,123 is an old one & much worn the othere perform well.

Manchester N 84(X) 112(X) 121(X) 128(X) these time pieces go to Carlisle & back 84 & 112 much worn, the other two perform pretty well.

Ipswich N 102(X) 197 – 197 goes well 102 very old.

Norwich N 148(X) 160 these time pieces go well 48(sic) is an old one.

Portsmouth N 4 129(X) N 4 good the other an old one.

Poole N 19 22 – both good.

Stroud N 51(X) 135(X) – 135 good the other are old one.

Worcester N 77 87 187 – all go well.

Yarmouth N 5 145(X) – N 5 good 145 an old one.

Birmingham Day N 201 204 – both good.

Brighton Day N 212 213 – both good.

The first recorded supplier of timepieces was F. Delafons. He supplied timepieces from 1785[86] and evidence shows that he had a contract in 1790 and 1791, since the Postmaster General queried why it had not yet been taken up.[87] John Delafons appears in 1792[88] and remains in the list until 1809 when the initial of the supplier (still of the Delafons family) is given as T.[89] From 1810 it is Mrs Elizabeth Delafons[90] who is recorded, changing to Henry in 1813/14.[91] The Post Office Directories list watchmakers with this surname at 66 Threadneedle Street in 1798 with John resident at 'the corner of Bartholomew Lane Bank' between 1809 and 1814. On 24 September 1811 Mrs Elizabeth Delafons asked for an increase in pay for repairing timepieces. Hasker admitted that pay had not increased since coaches were established, nevertheless, their price of fifteen guineas – although a lot – was considered to be fair. It was suggested that Hasker make further enquiries.[92]

The other main supplier was Littlewort (in some directories he is given as Littleworth). The name Littlewort first appears in the records in 1802, on this occasion he was paid for helping load the mail carts, but whether this is the same man is not known. From around 1817 a man of this name is listed as winding and repairing timepieces,[93] which he continued to do until 1850 when Mrs Mary Ann Littlewort was listed, presumably she was his widow.[94] Unusually, the name Littlewort does not appear in any of the lists of clock or watchmakers in the Directories, although it is known that he was in Rahere Street in 1839 (see above).

Generally the timepieces were supplied and maintained by Delafons or Littlewort, but some were handled at the main post towns such as Exeter, Manchester or Liverpool. The main office was very cost conscious, and on 7 July 1796 it was set down that they had found a repair man in London who charged less for a year's work than Mr Rule (?) of York had for two months of his labour. In future, York were to send their timepieces down to London for repair.[95] In 1797 the office purchased four new patent lever timepieces for £33-12-0 from Messrs Sutherland, Whiteside & Banning.[96]

The list submitted by Littlewort shows 213 as the highest number, this was in 1839 when the coach system was being run down, which suggests a maximum of perhaps 215 to 220 timepieces. His report refers to 'the book', which indicates that a record was kept as new pieces were acquired. The logical conclusion must be that numbers 3, 4 and 10 enjoyed a long working life, for they are still in service in 1839 some fifty-five years after the system started. However, they may have been a renumbered piece, as suggested by the pistols. The latest reference to traced timepieces dates from 1850, when a Mr T. Collingridge was paid £29-19-4 for the quarter: his job was the winding and repairing of timepieces.[97]

Apart from his timepiece and firearms the guard had one other item of equipment – his coaching horn. Traditionally these are shown as long tapering horns housed in a holster of leather or wicker and fitted to the side of the coach. Surviving examples would seem to suggest that they were around four feet (1m 20cm) long. Strangely, although much emphasis is placed on their use, the records contain practically no references to the object itself. There is a payment mentioned on 3 July 1722[98] for three dozen horns at a price of £3-16-6 (£3.82) and there are payments in 1845 for horns for use in Canada at Halifax (Nova Scotia), St Johns and New Brunswick.[99] It is likely that the 1722 purchase was for the bugle-like horn depicted in some caricatures of the post boys.

Whilst the great majority of prints show the guard with the long, tapering horn, there are one or two that show a bugle type. Writing in 1903, Harper states that the bugle horn was imported from Germany in about 1818 and that the valve type was a later development. However, this particular type was forbidden by the Post Office. There is some doubt about the use of the bugle style, and in the 1870s *The Field* magazine carried a number of letters dealing with the question of which type of horn the mail guards used. An ex-mail guard of advanced years categorically stated that only the long type was allowed by the Post Office. This provoked a number of 'I remember' letters recalling tunes played by the guards on their bugles. The initial effect of these letters was later diluted when writers recalled that they were thinking of the procession. Malet[100] states that he was told by an ex-guard of the Brighton mail coach that the horns were provided by the guards themselves, he added that they were their own property and that both types were used. Apparently it was difficult to blow the horn if front teeth were lacking. On a commemorative trip Nobbs, the oldest guard, attempted to blow his horn as of old, sadly he failed due to the loss of his teeth.

The horns were almost certainly made by some of the many musical instrument manufacturers in London. Writing in 1882,[101] Harris tells of a shop near St Martin's-le-Grand that offered a wide range of horns. There were the cheap tin ones, straight copper ones, others with a single twist and some with a double twist. The same writer claims the Post Office supplied the guards with the cheap tin ones but that the guards themselves privately purchased the copper ones. He also claims that the only means of securing the horn was by a leather loop nailed to the side of the coach, indeed one painting does show such a fitting.[102] Other illustrations clearly show wicker baskets on the sides of various coaches.

There seem to have been three possible supply methods, although so far none has been confirmed. The guard may have supplied his own horn, as suggested above, although there is no reference in any of his instructions as to their acquisition. The instructions mention other items like tools and lamps that he must have, and given their inclusion it might be expected that the horn would have been mentioned if the guards were officially required to possess one. It may be that the contractors or mail coach makers supplied them, but in the specification for the coaches there are no references to such parts (see Chapter 8). The guard may have been given an allowance to purchase the horn, but so far there are no references in the accounts to a 'horn' allowance or mention under 'Tradesmen'. There is one indication that the contractors may have supplied the horn: Hasker, writing on 23 October 1794, refers to a coach driven by Cook – Mr Weeks' coachman – overturning at Salisbury. Hasker had not been happy about this driver, having heard a bad account of him before the mail started. He had asked the contractor – Mr Weeks – to replace him, but this had not happened, so Hasker hoped that he would improve. He goes on to say that Weeks, 'had been in business so long and he knew he had bought some horns I did not like to look for another person at Salisbury.'[103] This statement is the sole reference to contractors supplying the horns, so unfortunately it cannot be taken to show that this was normal practice.

The guards were instructed to blow their horns as they left town and approach the turnpikes so that the gate could be open ready for them.[104] Harris (*op. cit.*) states that the guards were supposed to blow their horns at a distance of 250 yards from the gate, but this seems just a little pedantic. In 1796 Hasker reprimanded some guards for neglect in blowing their horns and so nearly causing accidents.[105] However, following a complaint from the Lord Mayor of London they were warned in 1803 not to blow them during the hours of divine service.[106] In September 1796 one of the central points of a murder case was the sounding of the horn. William Clark was accused of killing ten-year-old Michael Connel on 16 August. Clark was the driver of the Newmarket mail coach as it dashed along Bishopgate Street in London. Some children were in the street and one seems to have been knocked down by one of the horses. The guard, Bolt White, was questioned as to whether he had blown his horn, to which he replied that he had. The driver was given a good character reference by his employer, and after two hours the jury returned a verdict of not guilty.[107]

The blast from the horn also warned other road users to get out of the way, for the mail had priority, a fact which drivers were often very keen to emphasise. There were stories of the mail breaking-through troops on the road and drivers were often very reluctant to yield to other coaches. On 20 October 1794 the Preston Deputy Postmaster reported that, 'a mail coach and a gentleman's carriage were running together on the road and that both were overturned.' Cooper the deputy feared that there might be a case brought against him and sought assurance that the office would reimburse any costs. Hasker was a little indignant but it turned out that he had misunderstood the letter – he thought Cooper was asking the Postmaster General to bring an action. He was corrected by the Postmaster General, who pointed out his error and said in general that the office should be supported if any such action was taken.[108] The horn was also used to signal the end of meal breaks on the longer journeys, thus summoning passengers back to the coach.

The use of horns was not limited to the Post Office coaches, and a Mr Wolmer wrote in suggesting that the Post Office be granted the sole right to use them. On 2 March 1801 Hasker reported that he:

> …had every wish to promote the object of this letter, I fear that great objections might be urged against a monopoly of horns to the General Post Office & its departments. I perfectly agree with Mr Wolmer that horns are a cause of frequent alarm and confusion in most post towns, but an exclusive patent for the commodity would not be attainable.[109]

Tombs[110] illustrated what is purported to be the horn carried by the guard Richard Griffiths, who served on the London Norwich coach until 1846 and died in 1870. It is marked 'J.A. Turner 19 Poultry'.[111] He also quotes a newspaper report of November 1822 praising the musical skills of the mail guards, they now played a tune instead of the old ' discordant blasts'.

Blowing the horn was an acquired skill which did have its problems: whilst the guard was standing up, blowing his horn, during a journey in 1813, somebody broke open the mail box and took the bags. This happened whilst the coach was still in London trotting along the road between the famous pub The Saracen's Head and Whitechapel Church.[112] In another case, reported in March 1796, the guard was shaken off the coach whilst blowing his horn.[113]

Whilst there is some doubt over the issue of the horns there is none over the matter of uniforms for the guards. The very first time they are mentioned reference is made to the 'great coats'. The cost of these coats was high, originally they were red or scarlet top coats while in the contemporary illustrations some are plain but others have some gold facing. However, there is no clear description of the coat, while various illustrations are quite unhelpful. The coats are depicted in a variety of colours and it is clear from other references that the guards often wore another coat on top of their standard issue one. When a batch of uniforms were delivered in 1790 the Postmaster General expressed doubts as to their personal ability to judge the quality of the coats or decide whether they were good value. On 17 November 1790 they asked a Mr Pearse to examine the coats:

> Let the office seal and Mr Pearse's seal be put upon the pattern suit immediately and seal one set of the guard's clothing as the standard pattern and style.[114]

Pearse approved the quality and sealed a set, for which the Postmasters later wrote and thanked him. They were, as always, very conscious of the cost. Mr Bonnor was asked to supply an account of the money paid for uniforms to Mr Beanie, dating from the first establishment of the mail coaches to 4 June 1787.[115] This was the date when he submitted the three accounts (as above). It can be seen that the first purchase came some three years after the coaches first ran.

An additional item of uniform appears to have been introduced early: in April 1792[116] the Postmaster General queried an order for guards' clothing as it included waistcoats. From this date on waistcoats feature regularly in the accounts:

> July 1809
> Dickinson for uniform coats & waistcoats for the mail guards & cloaks for the messengers £1594-17-0.[117]

The two items, coat and waistcoat, continued as standard issue for the guards. This is evidenced by the quarter ending July 1833[118] where Dickey and Shaw are recorded as receiving £1,128-1-0 for uniform coats and waistcoats. These prices represented a heavy cost over the years, they reached a maximum of £1357-4-0, paid to Messrs Dickinson & Finch in the quarter ending 5 July 1815.[119]

Illustration of what may have been a guard's holster, as pictured in a book on the history of East Yorkshire. Unfortunately the details lack clarity and it is impossible to be sure of their origin.

Photo by] [C. W. Mason,
PISTOLS AND HOLSTERS FORMERLY USED ON THE HULL AND PATRINGTON STAGE COACH.
(Now in the possession of Dr. J. Wright Mason, Hull).

There was a change of supplier in 1816, Freeling wrote to the Postmaster that year saying that the former contractor was relinquishing the business. On 26 October 1816 Samuel Dickinson, of 32 Great James Street, had written in to say that he had furnished the guards' uniforms for nearly thirty-nine years but was now too ill to cope with the order and was giving up the tender.[120] However, there is a problem here, for if his memory was right he first supplied them around 1777, but the coaches did not run until 1784. He may have been referring in general terms to uniforms rather than those specifically for mail coach guards.

Tenders had been received from both Pearse and Dickey, Hasker sought guidance over his choice. Pearse based his quote on the idea of using the 'Army system' of production, where the uniforms were put together by people who were not tailors. If 'proper' work was done, presumably meaning the use of skilled workers, the charge would be twenty shillings, the price would be double if the Army system was used. The cheaper version would look just as good but the general wear might not be of the same quality. Dickey, tendering in October 1816, offered coat and waistcoat at £4-9-6 (£4.47p). He said that his company would supply uniforms of the pattern submitted to good quality while still being superior to those produced by the Army system. Pearce quoted £4-5-0 (£4.25p) and Freeling suggested that the higher quality was the better buy. However, the Postmasters said that as both firms were respected clothiers standard practice must be followed, which meant that the lowest tender had to be accepted.[121] The price fell over the years, and in May 1831 Dickey and Shaw quoted £3-17-0 for 289 mail guard uniforms for the annual procession.

The high number of guards is a little confusing, but is perhaps explained by the number of guards serving on the railways (as well as on foot and horse) by this period. However, there is no indication as to whether all those mentioned took part in the procession.[122]

The uniforms remained the property of the Post Office, and in the event of dismissal or retirement the guards were expected to return them. On 16 July 1796 S. Nichols of Manchester received a letter saying that, though it was customary for guards quitting the service to leave their uniforms for their successors:

> Mr Hasker in consequence of your good behaviour while in the employ of the office makes you a present of them and your leaving it with propriety gives you a fair claim to future employment if you desire it.[123]

There were also problems about old coats, for there were reports of them being worn by non-postal staff. Hasker did make casual enquiries as to what the Army did about discharged soldiers' uniforms but came to the conclusion that there was nothing that could be done about it.

The red coat and waistcoat were set off by a top hat, also depicted in prints in various colours, but predominantly black with slight variations in shape. Certainly it was embellished with a gold coloured hatband and a cockade. The hats were not cheap, the earliest payments recorded are:

Robert Partridge for mail guards hats to 20 May 1789 £112-16
Robert Partridge for mail guards hats to 20 May 1790 £104-17
Robert Partridge for mail guards hats to 5 July 1791 £112-3.[124]

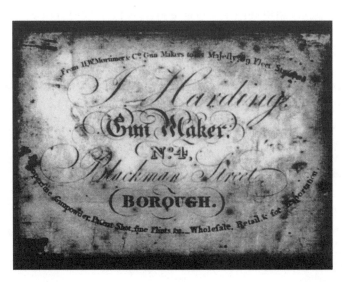

Trade label which seems to establish a working relationship between Mortimer and Harding, which might explain why Harding took over as armourer to the Post Office when Mortimer gave up. (R. Dale)

THE COMET COACH,
To IPSWICH, COLCHESTER, HARWICH
And CHELMSFORD,

LEAVES the RED LION INN, CAM-
BRIDGE, every Tuesday, Thursday, and
Saturday Mornings, at Eight o'clock, as usual ;
through Linton, Haverhill, Clare, Melford, Sud-
bury, Boxford, and Hadleigh, and arrives at the
Old White Hart, Haxell's Coach-office, and the
Coach and Horses, IPSWICH, and the Waggon
and Horses, COLCHESTER, at Half-past Three.

Leaves IPSWICH and COLCHESTER every
Monday, Wednesday, and Friday Mornings, at
Ten o'clock, and arrives at the Red Lion Inn,
CAMBRIDGE, at Six o'clock.

W. MITCHELL and Co. Proprietors,
Who will not be accountable for any Packages or
Parcels above the value of 5£. unless entered as
such and paid for accordingly.

Advert for a stagecoach of the late eighteenth century. (Permission of Bath Postal Museum)

The prices vary from £166-12-6 in October 1798 to £150-2-6 for the quarter ending 5 January 1797. This fell to £82-1-5 by June 1849.[125] The individual price of hats by Dickey was 15s 6d (77p) in 1816 while hats by Pearse were priced at 12s 6d (62p) at the same time. In October 1816 a new firm, Wagner, Gale & Co. of Pall Mall, tendered at 12s (60p). On special occasions the hat was embellished, as indicated by a payment on 12 February 1820 for 'crape hatbands' for inland and foreign letter carriers as well as mail guards. Presumably they were black to mark the death of George III in January that year.[126] On 8 November 1794 a letter from R. Partridge of 12 Tavistock Street states that he has invented a waterproof hat,[127] in 1795 he repeated the claim but without giving any details.[128] Come 1 September 1826 it was reported that repeated complaints had been made by guards and letter carriers about the quality of the hats provided for the procession. It was decided to advertise a tender for waterproof hats, several samples were examined and those of Mr Smith of Deptford, priced at 15s each, were accepted. Those he supplied were found to be satisfactory, as well as his bands and cockades, and Mr Smith now wanted to know if he could rely on an order for the following year. His request was approved.[129]

The Postmaster Generals kept a close eye on uniform accounts, and on 12 July 1791 they raised a query with the Deputy Comptroller, saying they recalled that:

...168 hats were supplied along with 140 suits of cloathes (sic).

A French view of the early English post boy. He is shown here with a straight horn but other depictions show a curved bugle type.

What had happened to the twenty-eight extra hats? They were still waiting for an answer on 24 July.[130] There was a similar enquiry on 14 October 1792,[131] when Hasker asked for 148 guards' uniforms with a 16 April minute having mentioned 137 hats. The Postmasters wanted to know if the supernumerary and extra guards had been included, for now the number was 160 hats.

The guards' uniforms saw hard wear: they were exposed to all weathers as well as facing the normal wear and tear of climbing on and off coaches, heaving leather bags about and general everyday life. The coats and hats were replaced annually, and, judging by the various cash accounts, orders were usually placed in the summer, or in time for the annual mail coach procession. There is no reference to the guards being issued with trousers and top boots, as had been stated by Harper.[132] The guard, with his top hat and red coat, has come to typify what was a romantic, colourful, but hard working system – the Royal Mail coaches.

By the 1830s it was clear that the day of the mail coach was drawing to an end. More and more railways were being built, with more and more mail being transported by a system that was generally faster and more reliable than the coaches.

Mail coach guards were either made redundant or transferred to rail duties, horns, pistols and blunderbusses were no longer needed. No official note of their disposal has been traced, but in Ireland some of their coach weapons were surrendered to the Ordnance. A note says that:

> ...all the arms at present unused to be given up to the Ordnance Office in Dublin and the allowance of £50 per an for cleaning and taking charge of them to cease 20th April.

The entry is dated 1 April 1848 in the Volume of *Miscellaneous Disbursements*.[133] It is possible, but by no means certain, that a similar disposal may have been carried out in England and Scotland.

There is some supportive evidence: an acquisition by the Board of Ordnance can be found in the inventories of the Royal Armouries. In the collection there are twenty-nine pistols and twelve blunderbusses, it is known that a number were sold-off in the 1920s. This could well indicate that in the 1840s and 50s, as the Mail Coach Office was closed and Mr Pike's salary disappeared from the accounts, the weapons were handed over to the Board of Ordnance. It is certainly unusual for such a large number of the same type of firearm to be held by the Armouries. The condition of most of these pieces indicates a hard working life with varying degrees of damage and wear, a feature common to nearly all recorded example of the Post Office weapons. It cannot be imagined that this damage was caused whilst the pieces were in the Armouries, but is certainly consistent with weapons that for many years were passed from hand to hand, dropped and generally misused by guards and Post Office staff.

The fate of the timepieces is similarly uncertain, for of the couple of hundred or so that are known to have been in service – 207 is the highest number (recorded in 1839) – very few seem to have survived and they are now quite rare. Again, no official disposal procedure has been recorded. Genuine coach horns are also rare, many of those offered on the market are either late copies or fakes. Since it is possible that these horns were the guard's personal property, when he left the service the horn went with him, and it was probably disposed of by the family of the guard at some later date.

5

GUARDING THE HORSE MAILS

Between the sixteenth and early nineteenth centuries the roads of Britain were very unsafe, lone travellers were always at risk from highwaymen and footpads. In an early attempt to improve safety, the Statute of Westminster in 1265 ruled that a space should be cleared of all vegetation on each side of the main roads, thus reducing the chance of thieves being able to ambush the traveller. Wars and rebellions generated a variety of armed bands of villains, and although the legends of Robin Hood and others paint a picture of a gallant outlaw, the facts were very different. As commerce and industry developed, so the risks for the traveller grew, and highway robbery flourished. Since there was, in effect, no real policing, the Governments of the day tried to encourage the public to take action. One way was to offer rewards to any persons who successfully tackled a highwayman. In 1692 an Act for encouraging the Apprehension of Highway Men (4 & 5 W & M c8) was promulgated. It applied to the whole country, and from March 1693 anybody who captured a highwayman received a reward of £40, as well as the villain's horse, furniture, arms, money and their goods.

Despite the fact that they were criminals, the highwaymen gained a certain false glamour and were regarded by many as anti-heroes. Myths grew up about their gallantry, their humour and their generosity. Dick Turpin, Claude Duval and Dick Sheppard were little more than petty thieves, but folk stories about their exploits took root and blossomed. They became celebrities and people paid quite large sums to visit villains like Sheppard in the condemned cell at Newgate Prison. The evidence given at their trials shows they were no more than vicious villains.

Lone travellers were obviously at the greatest risk and the post boys fell into this category. The majority were young, commonly less than sixteen, and consequently were unlikely to offer a serious threat to the villains. They were defenceless and stood little chance in a confrontation with desperate men. Coaches, especially private ones, were obvious targets, for they carried passengers who might well have valuables and money. However, they also represented a potential threat to any robber, for the travellers could well be armed and ready to defend themselves. The post boys were unarmed and represented easy targets, but the proceeds from mail robbery were uncertain; the mail might contain cash and some negotiable bonds, but equally there might just be letters of no real value. What was certain was that with every robbery many people and businesses would lose letters, possibly resulting in financial loss or personal inconvenience. Apart from the annoyance that they provoked, these robberies reduced public confidence in the mail. Whilst the robberies were perhaps not quite as common as some accounts might lead us to believe, there were enough to upset people and make them reluctant to use the ordinary mail. Public complaints and petitions were common, and in 1797 the merchants of Manchester wrote to the Postmaster General declaring that post between Warrington and Chester was suffering greatly from depredations. Important mail and money was entrusted to a post boy at night, and they asked a mail coach to go from Manchester and Chester through Knutsford and Northwich.[1]

From the adoption of Palmer's plan to use coaches to carry the mail, together with the introduction of armed guards, the mail coaches were immune. The weak link in the security chain was still the post boys. The archives contain no more than one or two reports of what may just have been attempts to stop and rob a mail coach. Nobbs, in his autobiography, tells of one apparent attempt on his coach that was unsuccessful, but the event itself was confused. Nobbs claims that he fired his blunderbuss, remarking that it had vicious recoil because it was probably loaded to the muzzle. Here is an apparent discrepancy for, according to the Guards' Rules, each weapon had to be unloaded at least once a week and was checked by the Deputy when the guard reported for duty. There is no way of knowing if Nobbs was mistaken or if, by his time, standards had slipped and checks were not made.

The records detail another case in July 1796 of what might have been an attempt, although once again the reported evidence is confused and disputed. Hasker received a letter demanding that a guard, Waldron, of the Manchester and Liverpool coach, be dismissed for misuse of his firearms. In typical fashion he wrote back saying it was unfair to dismiss him without first hearing Waldron's side of the story, he further added that he wanted accounts from witnesses and coachmen. Waldron claimed that three men had stopped the coach and refused to let go of the reins, despite the coachman lashing out with his whip. The guard dismounted, presented a pistol and threatened to shoot them if they did not let go of the reins. This account was disputed and directly contradicted by other witnesses; Hasker was convinced that Waldron was lying and said that he was not happy trusting such a man with firearms. On 21 July 1796 Waldron was dismissed and ordered to 'give up his cloaths' (sic), or else his bondsman would be sued for their value.[2] There were various thefts from the Royal Mail coaches but they were opportunist and usually took place either while the coach was stationary, when the guard was distracted or was not following the rules. Although they were classed legally as highway robbery, none could be so described in the conventional sense of the coach being halted by the robber.

Freeling, writing in 1796, said that since 1784 there had been no robberies from coaches,[3] but that sadly the same could not be said of the riders who delivered the post by cart or on horseback. He was very conscious of the problem and anxious that something be done, but whilst most people agreed with him getting the officials to take action was not easy. He put together a report in 1792 and circulated it to the main surveyors seeking their comments. On 16 November 1792 he then placed his simple plan together with the surveyors' remarks before the Postmaster General.[4] One point on which all agreed was that to provide some protection the messengers would have to be armed, but there was also common agreement that there was no way the present post boys could possibly be issued with firearms. Freeling thought that arming the guards would not be necessary in the daytime and suggested that 6 p.m. to 6 a.m. would be an appropriate timeframe. In winter the start time might have to be earlier, perhaps 4.30 p.m. He proposed that the equipment issued should be a pair of pistols in holsters and a strong cap to protect the head. He did not think they should be supplied with a uniform and he proposed that their pay be 1½d a mile.

He examined the districts covered by the various surveyors, assessed the situation and made an estimate of the areas' protection needs.[5] Hodgson's area would need coverage on one section for 136 miles – involving nine stages – and another of 127 miles with seven stages, this latter district had already suffered three attacks. Wilkinson's area had one section of 308 miles with twenty-five stages and one of forty-one miles with two stages, the shorter section having been the scene of three attacks. Lott's sector included a length of 217 miles with thirteen stages and one of twenty-one miles with one stage, with the shorter section having had three attacks. Saverland's area had 148 miles with nine stages while Western's two areas were listed as 215 miles with seventeen stages and twenty-two miles with one stage, again the shorter length had seen three attacks.

Hodgson's note to the Postmaster General suggested that the night riders be armed with pistols and a sword, he did not think them really necessary during the day but thought they might be carried as a deterrent. He queried the cost and suggested that some areas might find it difficult to find the cash if they were made responsible for the payments. Wilkinson, writing on 10 September 1792, stressed they could not possibly arm the existing post boys. If they did there would certainly be accidents 'from their not taking proper care of them both upon the road and at home.' This last comment is interesting, since it seems to suggest that the weapons were to be a personal issue and would be retained by their owner both on and off duty. The surveyor Lott, from Honiton, was in favour and agreed that it was not possible with the present boys. Woodcock, writing from *Gloster* (sic), agreed that boys were too young and that:

...if firearms are to be carried none but men of a proper age and light weight who can produce a very good character should be employed in the business – such men would expect higher wages than under the present allowance could be afforded them.

He thought that 'a pair of pistols carried in holsters before them is the readiest and the best.' This comment suggests that the riders would be equipped with a pair of saddle-mounted holsters similar to those used by the British cavalry of the period. These were of leather with brass furniture, and were fitted at the pommel of the saddle so that one hung on each side of the horse with the butts of the pistols just projecting from the top. Saverland, of Claybrook, was also totally opposed to the post boys being armed and stated that any such guards would have to be well chosen, given a uniform jacket and a great coat as well as light horseman's cap:

...something in the same way in which His Majesty's Hanoverian Post Riders are claothed (sic). The arms would only be carried at night but day riders would get the uniform.

He favoured pistols and a hanger. Surveyor Western also favoured the pistols and hanger, he also proposed that the riders get better horses, higher pay and should be a minimum of eighteen years old.

On 17 November 1792 Freeling presented his plan, with some reservations,[6] to the Postmasters. They expressed their appreciation of the report, saying at the same time that there was no call for him to apologise for any inadequacies as this was an entirely new subject. They agreed with the broad outline and in their enthusiasm felt that the more information they could gather the better the case they could make. They therefore suggested that every surveyor circulate a note within their districts asking people to write in offering any ideas they might have on the subject. They would also seek ideas as to how best to do the job and, most importantly, assess the possible costs. The Postmaster General also felt that the advertising of the scheme would be useful since it would demonstrate to the public just how determined the office was to improve security. Freeling produced an estimate of the prosecution and law expenses marked down in their accounts as the cost of robberies over the previous three years. The Postmaster considered it a fair estimate but thought that it perhaps needed a little more examination. Clearly everybody agreed that at night the riders should be armed with a brace of pistols, a cutlass and a hard hat. However, they did not think that a special uniform was appropriate. Their only real query concerned the probable costs.[7]

Freeling thought that the Postmaster Generals were perhaps being a little premature and that more planning was needed before any action was taken. Consequently he was not keen on this advertising and pressed the Postmaster Generals to delay. They agreed in February 1793 not to take any such action,

Freeling and the surveyors subsequently made it clear they were opposed to the idea and had not intended to advertise it as a separate duty. They regretted any misunderstanding they may have caused and accepted that, with calculations of rates of pay and costs still to be agreed, it was too soon to press ahead.[8] They also expressed their appreciation of Freeling's care in seeking estimates of costs from the surveyors, postmasters and others; the Treasury would certainly want to know the probable cost before they even considered the scheme. The Postmaster General was convinced that whatever the cost the scheme would offer good value if, as a result, the number of robberies was reduced.

Time passed but still no action was taken, despite continuing robberies and a constant flow of complaints from the Deputy Postmasters and the public. In July 1793 the Postmaster General hoped Mr Freeling was making progress with his plan.[9] No progress on implementing the plan was forthcoming from higher authorities, and on 14 March 1796[10] Freeling made one more determined effort to get some action. He reminded the Postmaster General that he had raised the subject in 1792, 1793 and 1794, and he now produced another long, twenty-page treatise on the problem. He stressed the potential benefits of a scheme that would both increase security of the 'vast property conveyed by the Horse Mails', and prevent mail robberies 'at once a disgrace to the office and the nation, saving of prosecution costs' leading to an improved service all round. The benefits would more than cover the Treasury's inevitably increased costs.

In his report Freeling claimed that he had sought advice and opinions from 'surveyors, Postmasters and every intelligent person from whom I could gain information' on the problem. The unanimous opinion was that 'the person who conveys the mail should be equal to the protection of it.' If, as he suggested, the riders were to be armed, he thought that it would be very wrong and dangerous to entrust firearms to the present riders, 'many of whom were barely fourteen years old.' Some riders were even younger, and in one case in March 1796 a letter from Leicester reported that one boy of twelve was charged with stealing a letter worth £100. However, the jury threw out the indictment, saying that at twelve the boy was too young to have felonious intent. The jury suggested that a fresh charge be made out using a lesser crime, a misdemeanour, but the lawyers said this was not possible since taking the mail was a serious crime, a felony.[11]

Freeling wanted to employ only people of good character, aged between eighteen and forty-five. He thought that with such people, if they were armed, the defence of the mail would be complete. Both day and night riders would be armed, Freeling proposed that each rider should:

> ...be furnished with a cutlass, brace of pistols, strong cap for the defence of his head and once a year with a jacket of blue cloth with a red collar for the day and a thick coat once in two years for the night.

These riders were to be employed by the Deputies, after previously being approved by the surveyors or their superior officers. Their employers were to provide horses, 'of a better description than those now used.' He anticipated that the coats and pistols would be purchased in towns 'where they could be furnished better and cheaper than in the country. The cutlasses to be made at Birmingham unless any can be procured in London at a reasonable rate.' He did not envisage arming any Foot Posts (*ibid*).

One slight mystery about these proposals was the hard hat. Nowhere is there any description, and so far it has not been possible to find an illustration of one. The name hard hat seems to preclude metal helmets but it might refer to a leather one. There is one other possibility, for about this period gamekeepers were some-times given a plaited hat, this would have been light and less uncomfortable than other types. On the other hand, elsewhere in the archives the word helmet is used. It seems most likely that this hard hat was a leather helmet, something similar to that worn by Light Cavalry of the period, but this is pure conjecture.

Freeling was unable to offer any really firm estimates as to the probable cost of his scheme and the surveyors' projections also fluctuated widely. Some thought that three farthings[12] a mile for nightriders was fair, with one penny for those travelling partly by day and night and halfpenny for day riders. Others thought that a flat wage of 10s and 6d (52.5p) a week was better while yet more dissenting voices said a flat rate of 1s and 6d (7.5p) a journey was best. He pointed out that conditions varied greatly from area to area, as did the price of local labour, and this made it difficult to set a flat rate. In the circumstance he felt that it was not possible to set an overall rate, but that it should be left to the surveyors to discuss and set the figure.

However, to give the Postmaster General a rough idea as to probable costs he suggested a working figure of one penny a mile. Estimating that some 3,800 miles would be covered every day this gave a total of £5779-3-4 a year. In addition, there would be the cost of 'arms, holsters, ammunition, caps and cloathing (sic).' He excluded Scotland as he did not think it a good idea to extend the scheme there but offered no reason for his reluctance to go north of the border. Freeling accepted that this figure was perhaps a little high, but he was convinced that mat-ters would balance themselves, as some areas would no doubt prove less expensive than others. He pointed out that less robberies meant that the costs of prosecu-tions would be reduced, this would represent an overall surplus, the expectation of which he further inflated by adding, 'especially as the mail coaches have not once been attacked since their establishment.'

Prior to 1794 Freeling calculated the cost of prosecuting arrested robbers over a ten-year period to be around £1,500 per annum. It was now around £1,250 but a couple of very expensive cases were in prospect and so he set the future figure at £1,570. If this amount was saved it would reduce the overall cost of the scheme to £4279-3-4 per annum. He also anticipated that when the public realised there was greater security more people would return to using the Post Office instead of other means of sending letters and valuables. He thought it not unreasonable to assume that this would produce an increased income to the revenue of £1,000.

He admitted that, in addition to the mileage price, the pistols, cutlasses, caps and clothing would cost money. However, he estimated that 6d (2.5p) a week would cover the costs of ammunition and running repairs, this would run to approximately £300 per annum. He pointed out that the weapons would be a one-off expense. Caps and clothing would be a recurring expense, which he put at £450 per annum and he also allowed £300 per annum for incidental expenses. After all his calculations, and factoring in savings on prosecutions and increased revenue, he expected the final cost to be £4,029-3-4. He was sure that the gains in public confidence and security would be worth it, as citizens' lack of confidence in the existing system was clearly shown by the number of petitions and memorials forwarded to the Postmaster General. He suggested that the Treasury be asked to allow them to spend a maximum of £6,529-3-4 per annum.

Freeling had originally thought that only the nightriders should be armed, but on reconsidering the risks he now felt that both day and night mail should be protected. In the event of the plan being approved the arming would be introduced gradually, starting on those routes most at risk; namely the Barton Mills to Lynn, Bristol and Portsmouth, Chester to Warrington and the posts to and from the great manufacturing towns. Night rides would take priority over day rides. The riders might be asked to supply a bond for security, but under all circumstances they should be considered Government employees.

Robberies continued and the Postmaster General was at pains to point out that there was a form of insurance for:

> ...the sum of, or under five guineas, take a check from the Clerk of the Road, if in London, or from a Postmr if in the country and they will for 3d in the pound insure its going safe. This has been found particularly useful to the families of soldiers and sailors in time of war who often wish to send almost their all to their relations in a single letter for any sum above five guineas sent in gold or in silver enter it with the Clerk of the Money Book if in London or upon the Letter Bill of the Postmr if in the country. All drafts and bank notes may be cut in half and the second half may be sent by the next post it has never happened that the mail has been robbed on two nights together but even if that is apprehended wait till the receipt of the first half is acknowledged before the second is sent and then the security is complete. As however these precautions will not be universally attended to the Postmaster General have long had in consideration a plan for guarding the mails all over England on Horseback effectually as that are already by the coaches but hitherto from the difficulty and expense of so extensive a plan though it is in forwardness it has not been possible to make it so complete and perfect.[13]

Despite Freeling's reasoned statement and the Postmaster General's support the Treasury still took no action. On 15 August 1796 Hasker replied to a request that the Chester to Liverpool ride be armed by saying that his plan was 'under consideration', and that until a decision was taken there was nothing to be done.[14] The Postmasters agreed to write, yet again, to the Treasury, and on the back of one of the letters they express their frustration with a handwritten note:

> We can do no more than we have. If the Treasury will neither consent to the guarding of the X mails nor give us an answer – it is their fault not ours.
>
> (Both put their initials to the letter.[15])

Robbery was not the only problem with the riders: time keeping was a constant source of difficulty. If the riders were late with the bags they collected from the various offices then the coach had to wait, or was obliged to leave before its full collection was ready. The surveyors did their rounds, checking on all the offices and taking such action as they deemed necessary, and then submitted reports to Lombard Street detailing the situation. In June 1795 Mr Lotts, covering the West Country, submitted just such a report.[16] He reported on nineteen riders, five of whom were not doing as well as they should. The Bath and Portsmouth rider was singled out for particular criticism:

> ...this duty has been most shamefully done and great inconvenience in the correspondence has been occasioned thereby.

Lotts visited the Postmaster at Warminster 'who had performed his stage frequently very ill.' He wrote to the other deputies, all of who promised to improve. One very bad stretch was between Winchester and Salisbury, and apparently the post boy often turned up without his way bill, which Lotts thought was just an excuse to avoid filling it in and showing where the delays occurred. He pointed out that this part of the ride was done at night, and if the Poole coach was delayed then the riders had to try to make up time by riding at 6mph; a feat which he admits was difficult in the dark. If they were late then the bags had to be forwarded by express, which was an expensive undertaking.

In the meantime matters were not improving, with post boys as young as twelve still being used. There was still no decision by 1 March 1798, and, according to one letter of March 1800, on one twelve-mile stretch of road near Wigan there had been four robberies in three months.[17] Hasker, writing to the Postmaster General, pointed out that this would hardly encourage people to use the post, perhaps it was time to push his plan with the Treasury. The Postmaster Generals signalled their intention to raise the matter at their next meeting.[18]

Things were so bad that on 8 March 1800 the writer at Liverpool, discussing the robbery of mail, says there were many 'bad Irish in town'. In conversation with

General Nichols there was much talk of providing an escort of Light Dragoons. He would consult the Duke of York first, but feared that this would send a bad message to the public about mail safety (*ibid*).

The policy of executing offenders had little obvious success as a deterrent, and some people were beginning to question the value of capital punishment. A letter of 18 July 1801 from Freeling, announcing the death sentence for Atkins and Lomax for a Winchester robbery, provoked a response from the Postmaster General:

Mr Freeling,

I sincerely wish that these awful examples had a better effect. The mail for Brighton Lewes was robbed this morning by two men the other side of East Grinstead I still indulge my favourite hopes that all the mails may yet be guarded – I am willing to give up my own plan to any other with the same object.

I receive such an account with pain and with real regret but it may be doubted whether in this instance of a mail robbery by three soldiers the crime would have been prevented if the post boy had been armed. Possibly that circumstance might have occasioned the additional crime of murder. Auckland and Charles Spence.[19]

On 21 August 1801 a letter to the Treasury from Auckland and Spencer, the Postmasters General, reminded them that the plan of 1796, with an estimated cost of £6,500 per annum, had been submitted for their approval. The case was even stronger now as prosecution costs were running at £2,000 to £3,000 per annum. There had been some modification to the original proposals as it was now suggested that not all routes would need to be guarded. The specified age range was now set at twenty-five to thirty-five, and each applicant would have to be backed by a recommendation from a clergyman or Justice of the Peace. The letter made the point that the mail coaches were not being robbed and repeated that each rider would get 'a strong cap a brace of pistols and a hanger.' The letter sought financial approval.[20]

At last, some nine years after Freeling's first report, on 16 December 1801 I.H. Addington of the Treasury Chambers wrote to the Postmasters General, telling them to put their plan into operation with them to report on its progress in one year's time. On 29 December 1801 the Post Office were officially informed that the Treasury had approved a sum of £1,500 per annum for guarding 'the principal mails which are conveyed in the night and especially upon those roads where they have repeatedly been robbed.' The scheme was to be introduced gradually, all guards were to have their references checked and they were to be paid fourteen shillings (70p) a week. It is interesting to note that these guards were to get a higher rate of pay than the coach guards (*op. cit.*). This may have been tacit acknowledgement that tips regularly swelled the mail coach guards' income whereas the riders could not expect tips. Having received permission Freeling wasted no time circulating the surveyors. A note from the Postmaster General approves the circular but points out that this is, in effect, only an introduction to the scheme, and that there will be 'many explanatory details before the machine can be put in movement.'[21]

The approved scheme was obviously much more limited than Freeling's original plan but it was a step in the right direction. In September 1802 it was pointed out that pistols and swords would not be an annual expense and that the helmets might well last two or three years. The scheme was certainly implemented, for a circular of 3 September 1803 refers to one guard – who had refused to wear his helmet or carry his arms – and another who had been found to have only one pistol with him, which turned out to be useless since it had no flint or ramrod.[22] The care of the weapons was one problem that was constantly referred to, and in a circular of 27 October 1804 Freeling exhorts all surveyors to ensure that the arms are kept in good order.[23]

The issuing of weapons for the horse riders raises a number of questions. The records indicate very clearly that Mortimer – and later Harding – supplied pistols to the riders. The various account books refer to separate payments to these makers: on the one hand for repairs and on the other for new firearms – for both the mail coaches and the riders. What sort of pistols were they? So far no example has been positively identified as being that which was issued to the riders.

In 1801, when the scheme was first introduced, Mortimer, as the established arms provider, must surely have been asked to supply the pistols, and indeed he was the only one regularly paid for the purchase and repair of firearms. Since the records of payment do not include any sudden high-priced order, it may be assumed that when the new system was implemented he began by supplying small numbers of pistols at a time. Common sense and practical considerations would suggest that as he had a pattern pistol in production for the coaches then the output of the same pattern weapon would simply have been increased as required to meet demand.

If Mortimer, and later Harding, did follow this straightforward plan, then is it possible to distinguish rider from coach pistol? The answer may be that only those weapons specifically marked 'For His Majesty's Mail Coaches' were carried on the coaches and that all others were carried by the riders. As pointed out in Chapter 10, this hypothesis has its flaws. A small number of the brass-barrelled coaching pistols are engraved with the names of the apparent starting and finishing locations. The distances between the named places are fairly short, e.g. Norwich to Cromer, suggesting that these were local routes and therefore that pistols these may have been carried by the Horse Posts. There is no evidence that the guards changed their weapons at the various stages, what evidence there is suggests they kept their own personal weapons. If this was the case then there would seem little point in engraving the name of these places on them: however there is no firm evidence to support any such supposition. There is one other confusing feature; for so far no recorded ride has been found to match the details of these engraved runs.

No positive evidence of any differences in the types of weapons used has been traced so far. This use of pistols by both horse and coach guards might possibly explain why the numbers engraved on the barrels of the Post Office weapons run to more than 380, a figure nearly three times the original number of guards. Backing for the idea of sequential numbering is perhaps slightly strengthened by the records of the result of an attack on a rider by two men near Marlborough in October 1826. The offenders were not traced, despite a thirty guineas reward, but the entry then states: 'I have ordered a brace of pistol to be supplied to the rider.'[24] The problem is further complicated as there is some evidence that in the past a few pistols and blunderbusses had been embellished with bogus inscriptions to increase their potential value.

The costs incurred in arming the coach and rider groups are quite similar:

Harding: for repairs etc. to Horse Posts
| 1821 Apr | £15-16 |
| 1821 July | £25-4 |

Harding for Mail Guards
| 1821 Apr | £30-10 |
| 1821 July | £29-19[25] |

There is no way of assessing just what is covered by the recorded prices, but as a yardstick: in 1788 a pair of pistols cost £3-12-6 (£3.62p). Using this figure it seems that at £30 the number of items involved was unlikely to be very high. For the mail coaches there was also the blunderbuss to be considered.

The cutlass is another mystery as yet unsolved. Only one reference to swords has so far been traced in the Post Office archives, that was on 16 September 1821: 'William Parker £8-6-6 cutlasses and belts for mail guards.'[26] The term 'mail guards' is unfortunately non-specific, and foot, horse and coach people all worked as guards of the mail. From the records it is impossible to know to which group the charge referred, but the riders would seem to be the most likely recipients. William Parker was a well-known gun maker with a shop at 233 Holborn, London. He produced weapons ranging from pairs of top-quality duelling pistols to handcuffs and cheap pocket pistols. He acquired the contract to supply the Metropolitan Police when it was formed in 1829 and he also supplied swords to police, prisons and local watches. These swords – known as cutlasses or hangers – were fitted with a fairly short blade, slightly curved, single-edged and with one broad fuller or central groove. The blade was usually etched with the name of the prison or police force. The hilt had a knuckle bow, either D or stirrup-shaped with a grooved wooden grip covered with sharkskin. The sword was normally supplied in a brown or black leather sheath, with brass or iron fittings and a leather frog to fit onto the belt. Some of these swords had a spring loaded clip on the hilt so that it could be held securely in the scabbard. If the riders were issued with a sword it is more than likely it would have been one of this pattern. Parker is recorded as working in Holborn from 1792-1834, he was followed by his son-in-law who traded under the name of Parker Field. However, this reference is for a date some twenty years after the introduction of the horse riders plan and is for a small purchase. As far as is known no example of a sword with any inscription or marks suggesting Post Office ownership has been found, and no contemporary illustrations seem to show a sword worn by any of the Post Office guards. It could be that the reference quoted above (p113), was in fact describing this sword as carried by the riders.

The same may be said about holsters, for there seems to be no pictorial evidence of them, although the numerous references to them in various records leave no doubt as to their existence. References to holsters apply first in the late 1780s and continue through to 1842. The concept of a holster was not new, they were commonly used in the sixteenth century but were not actually carried on the body. The majority were fitted to a saddle, as indicated by an Elizabethan proclamation of 1575. Permission was given for gentlemen, 'which be without spot or doubt of evil behaviour', to carry a pistol when travelling, but they had to be openly displayed 'at the saddle bow'. Since the pistols of the period were large and carried by the gentry – most of who were anxious to impress onlookers – their holsters were usually highly decorative.

The flintlock pistols carried on the coaches, and probably by the Horse Post, were also large. The holster would have been fairly sizeable but undoubtedly plain and almost certainly of leather. However, lacking any direct evidence as to size, design or style, one has only the references to go on, such as this letter from Uckfield:

23 Oct 1803

Dear Sirs, in answer to your circular letter on the prospect of the horse mail guards I have to observe that when I armed the riders on the different lines I gave a much directions to the deputies and contractors that the guards not only constantly wore their arms but that they were kept in good order, I have every reason to be satisfied from my own observations with the condition in the which the arms are in upon this and the Hastings Road and shortly after the receipt of your letter I wrote very smartly to the deputies at Epsom Haselmere upon the prospect of the guards under their direction. I find a pistol had been lost by the guard between Uckfield and ?Chichester but a very proper one was immediately supplied by the deputy and much enquiry made after the one which was lost also it appears that one of the pistols had been lost by Mr Coles son on the Kingston to Horsham a fresh one was immediately supplied and direction given that he had to pay for the loss of his carelessness. I also found that just before my arrival on this roads one of guards had lost one of his pistols, but as they work alternately hath two less they were armed and for the present to make the equipment complete. As the guard on this and the Chichester road both ascribed the loss of their pistol to 'the very imperfect and unacceptable connection of the holsters I judged it right to order new ones to go across the breast which are now used by all the guards under my direction but as the men before alluded to have rather at making good the loss contend the fault was in the equipment and not with them and as I am putting the whole of the guards upon a decided footing I could wish to have your decision whether this claim can be admitted as both men are of excellent character and I am satisfied in this instance it would be quite right an inducement.

Signed L. Maidstone and addressed to Freeling.[27]

This letter is interesting, it speaks of lost pistols being replaced but unfortunately gives no details. If a new weapon was supplied was it given a new number or the one previously in use? If a new number was issued it might help explain the lack of correlation between numbers and makers as shown on p248.

What this holster looked like is unknown, indeed it is unclear as to whether it was a single or double holster. This type of cross-breast holster is extremely unusual, although an early eighteenth century engraving of Edward Teach, Blackbeard the pirate, shows him with a broad belt across his chest, to which a number of pistols are attached. A similar holster carried by some members of Napoleon's army is illustrated in Funcken.[28]

Payments for holsters continue to appear in the various accounts, even in a contract drawn-up as late as 31 August 1858.[29] This was with George and William Almond of 14 St James St, Piccadilly, John Nutting of 93 Regent Street, Westminster – button maker, and William Nichols of 22 St James Street – Army outfitter. The contract was to supply white leather bags, brown leather bags, knapsack canvas bags, portmanteaus for special areas, canvas bags, leather straps, pouches with gussets, saddle bags, timepiece pouches with labels and firearms holsters with labels. The labels referred to were probably small brass plaques riveted on to the holster. By this date the coaches had long since been retired from Britain's roads, as such this order was almost certainly for an overseas postal service. There are records of other items, such as horns, being sent to Canada around this date.

For most of the nineteenth century matters continued to run their usual course, with the official gun maker supplying and maintaining the firearms for both coaches and riders. However, in 1842 an apparent change of policy emerges from the records, for the Board of Ordnance become involved (see Chapter 4). The same entry also makes reference to Harding & Son supplying 'firearms for the mail guards'. It is not clear whether these weapons were for the coaches or the riders. Some guidance may be deduced from the other reference to the Ordnance to mention holsters. During this period the Board of Ordnance are not known to have stored personal holsters. This suggests that the holsters being loaned may well have been the saddle type, as used by the cavalry, in which case they would have been for the riders. There is no positive verification but the supposition is reasonable. There is more backing for this idea: when the horse riders were being discussed there was mention of a brace of pistols carried in 'holster before them', exactly like the existing cavalry. The date may back this hypothesis, for by now the number of coaches still running was fairly small, whereas the riders were still very much in use.

A contract drawn up in September 1847 – between the Postmaster General Clarincarde and Tomas John Bolton of 32 Harrow Road, Marylebone, London – casts no further light on this problem. The contract was for five years and was to supply horses, carts and wheeled carriages, riders, drivers, harnesses and other equipment, uniforms, hats and coats for horse riders, saddle bags and pouches for letters. There is no mention of holsters. The contract also says that the guard was appointed and paid by the Postmaster General and had sole charge of the letters. The carts and riders were to fetch and carry the mail between the various Post Offices and the main headquarters at St Martin's-le-Grand. The date, 1847, is at a time when the mail coach was nearing its end, but the post boy was to continue for some time as he dealt with the minor routes.[30]

6

THE JOURNEY

Until 1829 the control centre of the entire mail coach operation was based at the premises of the General Post Office in Lombard Street in the City of London (see p44). A large house was built here around 1675 by the family of Sir Robert Vines, and on 18 March 1678 the *London Gazette* announced that the General Post Office had moved from Bishopgate to Lombard Street. It was here that regular meetings of the Governing Board were held to decide all manner of matters while the complicated process of controlling the coaches was also located here. Despite these important functions it could not be described as a carefully planned, streamlined office.

The premises were an irregular hotch-potch of buildings, acquired on a piece-meal basis over the years. Some rooms had been converted into offices and there were also three large sorting rooms. They were bound by Sherborne Lane, Abchurch Street and Lombard Street. Some of the buildings were owned by the Post Office, others were leased and some were 'at will'. The buildings were con-nected by various courtyards and staircases and the amount of office space seems to have varied. Houses were regularly given up as, for example, no.20 Sherborne Lane was in October 1792.[1] Space was limited and consequently every metre had to be utilised. Some rooms were set aside as the living quarters of various officials, including at one time the Postmaster General and the Secretary of the Post Office, Anthony Todd, as well as various members of the domestic staff. Poor Hasker was less fortunate and was not allocated a living space, in June 1790 he was still looking for rooms to rent near the office.[2]

On 21 July 1801 Freeling petitioned the Postmaster General on behalf of a Mrs Colledge. Her husband had been a storekeeper in the bye office but had been dismissed. He and his family had an apartment and kitchen, situated on the fourth floor under the roof, with an allowance of £60 per annum for two servants to clean the various offices and rooms. As the husband had been dismissed they no longer had any claim on the accommodation. However, Freeling suggested that they be allowed to stay as long as the husband behaved himself, the Postmaster General agreed to this suggestion.[3]

One of the few original coaches that still survives, although it has been somewhat modified. This example was at one time owned by London Gunmakers. It was later presented to, and is now housed in, the Science Museum, South Kensington.

THE "YEOVIL" MAIL.

One of the illustrations from *Road Scrapings Coaches and Coaching* by Captain M.E. Haworth, 1884. Despite its simplicity it does show the main features of the coach.

At times the Post Office was paying rent on these premises to six different land-lords, and every so often the various officers would press the Postmaster General and Treasury for permission to acquire more room. In August 1786 they wrote bemoaning their lack of space and pointed out that the lease on several of their buildings was due to expire in January 1787. On Tuesday 7 August 1784 a fire in the vicinity burnt down a number of houses, leaving two derelict spaces – one between the back part of the existing office and Abchurch Lane – and another on the other side by Sherborne Lane.[4] This seemed a good time to consider purchasing the land made available by the destruction, but since it would involve spending money the Treasury was not keen on the idea. By May 1787 they had reluctantly agreed to purchase the land of a Mrs Bowes for use as offices by the Inland Office and Letter Carriers. The owner of part of the property, a Mr Vyner, did not wish to sell on the same terms, but later on an agreement was reached and that land was also acquired.

This Akerman engraving of the Leeds coach shows the guard with a bugle-type horn instead of the conventional long type.

"THE DEFIANCE HAS GONE 10 MINUTES!"

Although this illustration shows a specially designed cart intended for a well-known disabled rider of the period, it is fairly typical of dog carts of the period, all of which were exempt from paying the tolls. (From *Road Scrapings Coaches and Coaching*.)

In the 'before and after' listing, the working conditions in the Inland Office were outlined, the office was described as being much too small – which meant that the clerks were in each other's way. The 'Window Man', or 'Clerk of the Paid Letter Office', had to work in the same room and was seated by a window that opened on to the paved court. This created the opportunity for fraud if he was so inclined, and he was constantly being interrupted by questioners.[5] The 1788 listing indicated that things were a little better: the office had been extended by taking over part of the backyard. A Paid Letter Office had been erected in the forecourt, where the clerk could work without interruptions.

Some idea of the casual way in which the offices must have developed is given in a letter to the Treasury from the Postmaster General in June 1790. It stated that Mr Wynn, the owner of a dwelling house and premises in Abchurch Lane situated next to the office that had been rented as part of the premises since 1733, was prepared to sell. However, enquiries had elicited the unwelcome discovery that the office premises encroached on another person's land by some 9ft (3m). If the Post Office did not purchase this land then it would be obliged to demolish some of the office, and they were not sure just how much work and expense this would involve. They had agreed to purchase the property on what they considered advantageous terms and hoped that the Treasury would approve.[6]

These cramped offices were lit by candles, and some idea of the numbers involved may be gained from the size of the bills for their purchase. These were: £418-12-2 for the quarter ending 5 April 1786[7] and £263-17-5 for the quarter ending March 1788.[8] One report speaks of between seventy and a hundred half-pound tallow candles burning at night in the Inland office, and goes on to highlight the unfortunate effect that this had on the wellbeing of staff working there.[9] The heat and soot generated by all those burning candles must have been considerable, while the associated fire hazard with all those naked flames is obvious. Thankfully this was appreciated at the time as the Post Office maintained fire engines either on or near their premises. In March 1793 an official query was made as to whether anyone was checking on the condition of the fire engines.[10] Later on there was mention of one engine cared for by Messrs Hopwood and Telley, who were paid £2-2-0 for their years service in June 1820.[11] The salary of many of the top officers included an allowance for candles, and in 1782 the Secretary – Mr Todd – received ninety-six dozen (1,152) candles as well as thirty-six chaldrons of coal.[12] A watchman was employed to attend to some twenty oil lamps, he was paid £50 a year for supplying the oil and looking after the lamps.[13] It is most likely that these oil lamps were fitted on the outside of the buildings.

A substantial number of people worked in the offices, and there was a considerable traffic of people collecting and delivering mail. If conditions inside the Lombard Street offices were crowded and cramped then the approaches to the offices were little better. The customers' entrances were via narrow passageways; one from Lombard Street was about 8 to 9ft (3m) wide, another from Abchurch Lane was even narrower whilst one from Sherborne Lane had a width of a mere 5ft (1.5m).[14] These led into an open courtyard which, most of the time, was filled with a milling crowd of customers and officials. An architect's report of 1814 stated that:

...access for the public to the various departments is mean, obscure and unintelligible.[15]

Keeping the offices reasonably hygienic was achieved by the use of vinegar and other substances thought to be effective disinfectants:

Quarter ending October 1825:Vinegar for Chief Office £3-2-6.[16]
Quarter ending January 1827:Vinegar camphor and charcoal £5-13-6.[17]
Quarter ending October 1853:Vinegar and chloride of lime £17-0-1.[18]

These substances were periodically scattered or sprayed around the floors. In 1814 a petition was presented to Parliament by a Mr Butterworth on behalf of 4,000 of the merchants of London. He claimed that the Lombard offices were so closely confined as to be injurious to the health of those concerned. Another claim he made was that two guineas a week were being expended for vinegar to fumigate the rooms and prevent infectious fevers.[19] Judging by the figures quoted above this seems an obvious exaggeration.

A night soil man was employed and his malodorous job earned him £9-15 (£9.75) in 1767,[20] rising to £11-10 (£11.50) a quarter in 1785.[21] Included in the list of staff in 1807 is a Watchman who, after all the staff had left, took over at eleven o'clock and closed the gates at midnight; admitting any officers or residents, accepting care of any mail and generally ensuring the security of the offices.[22]

As might be expected the offices' stationery bills were high and quite complex, one dating from the 1780s has a list detailing sixty-five items, including more than fifteen different types of notepapers. The lists include intriguing items like 'Brazil sandboxes', 'folders in ivory', 'folders with handles', 'pins Dutch', 'pins large' and 'flat ebony'.[23] In 1792 the Postmaster queried a demand from Bonnor for 5,000 pens in one order.[24] The office staff were presumably encouraged to economise where possible, and in October 1837 the office received £6; the proceeds of the sale of waste paper in the Mail Coach Office on the sixteenth of that month.[25]

As business expanded the situation at Lombard Street became more and more difficult, and eventually it was realised that little could be done to improve matters. The Post Office architect reported in 1814 that redevelopment of the current premises was just not worth considering and that there was no alternative but to relocate.[26] The Post Office was by now seen as an important part of the life and industry of the country, so that it was felt that the new building should reflect its status. The first steps of the move were taken in 1815, when an Act of Parliament authorised four commissioners to find a site for the new headquarters. There was a meeting at the Crown and Anchor Tavern in the Strand on Monday 11 May 1814; the meeting convened at one o'clock to state the case for moving the Post Office and consider the virtues of the proposed new site. The notice says that there was some opposition from foreign merchants but that it was not really serious, the move was only about seven hundred yards from the existing site.[27]

The Commissioners settled on an area at the junction of Newgate Street and St Martin's-le-Grand, not far from St Paul's Cathedral. The selection was perhaps partly influenced by the fact that it was an area of poor repute and presumably the land would be reasonably cheap. Sir Robert Smirke, one of the leading architects of the time, was commissioned to produce the plans and a fine Grecian style was chosen. The first stone was laid in May 1824 and the building was completed and opened for business on 29 September 1829, Baines (*op. cit.*) states that Freeling led the staff into the new offices, 'carrying the staff and the secretarial chair.' The move was made without too many problems and the staff settled down to work in what would hopefully turn out to be more comfortable quarters. Even in their new premises ventilation was a problem, but this time they had new technology to call on. Messrs Easton and Amos erected a small steam engine – at a price of £135 – for ventilating the Inland and Letter Carrier offices, as authorised by the Lords of the Treasury on 20 July 1840.[28]

After the officers and staff had transferred to St Martin's-le-Grand the old premises were offered for sale by Mr Hoggart[29] at the Auction Mart on Friday 6 May 1831. The premises were divided into fourteen lots, of which the first was the Mail-Coach Office:

> ...adjoining the church with a frontage to Lombard Street of 16 feet 6 ins, by a depth of 44 feet and abutting on entrance to court of late Post Office, and immediately adjoining the Branch Office retained by Government.

The premises were on four floors; the top three comprised six bedrooms and water closets. The first floor had two sitting rooms which were, 'conveniently fitted up.' The ground floor 'had an entrance hall, parlor (sic) or shop in front and a sitting room at the back.' In the basement there was a kitchen, larder, coal cellar and an 'arched vault'.[30] The other lots comprised the Two Penny Post Office, Ship Letter Office, Letter Carriers Office and Board Room, various other premises were described as residences while three plots were designated as freehold building ground.

The basic system of operations in the new building continued much as it had done in Lombard Street. The officers in charge of the Inland Office were known as Presidents, and in September 1795 they drafted a list of duties for the information of all the clerks. They noted all the procedures to be followed[31] and each clerk was to keep a book listing all current orders, it was to be checked daily and kept in a locked bookcase. The document gives full details of charges and defines what were to be considered 'double letters'.

The letters collected from across London and those brought in by the coaches were taken to Lombard Street and later to the new headquarters by the officials. There they were sorted and packed into the various bags, each of which was labelled with the name of its destination. There was a long tradition of packing the letters into leather bags, going back through the seventeenth century and beyond to medieval times:

> Oct 1681: Mr Richard Evans his bill for leathern bags (sic) from 3rd of September 1681 to 13th Oct foll £ 04-02-00.[32]

July 31 1722 paid Mr Roby for 6 mailes £8-05-0.[33]
...paid John Geymor for leather bags to Jul 3 £12-10-0.[34]

The majority of the bags were made of leather, although in July 1819 there is mention of some being made of canvas for the Ship Letter Office[35] and in July 1817 there are references to linen.[36]

Most bags were fitted with brass plaques engraved with the name of their destinations, and each Deputy Postmaster would receive a batch of these bags to be distributed to the various addresses served by their offices. They would have similar groups of such bags ready to be passed onto the coach for delivery to other offices along the route. The number of bags in use at any one time was very high, and this total obviously increased as the service developed. Reports of robberies from the post boys often mention the large numbers of bags being taken by the thief and these would have to be replaced. In one theft in June 1772 sixty bags were stolen.[37]

During the mail coach period there were several recorded suppliers of bags, the names of Hurst, Turner, Fisher and Enouy (there are various spellings) regularly appear in the accounts, and the costs were quite substantial:

April 1778: Muly leather bags £10-16.[38]
Foster: £53-10-6.
January 1794: Enouy £192-12.[39]
April 1794: Enouy £ 244-4.
January 1817: Hurst £126-4.[40]

Although these are a random selection of prices, similar figures are recorded over the years.

In addition to the cost of these newly made bags there were regular payments for repairing them. One supplier, Hurst, offered to rivet brass plates on them, he was also involved with a special security bag that was mentioned, but not described, in 1816.[41] The usual Post Office bags were available in, amongst others, brown, white, black and red. On 15 December 1792 Freeling was told to order red bags from the stationer, 'not as large as our black ones', with F. Freeling on them. There were also to be ten green bags with A. Scott on them, they would have different locks and keys. Ten new brown bags were to be ordered for the Postmaster General, which would be nearly as deep as the West Indies bags, they would have brasses with 'The Secretary Gen. Post Office London' on one side, and the 'Postmr Genl Staines' on the other. The stationer was to be sure to number all the pouches 1,2,3 right up to 13. It was also stated that no bags were to be made for specific individuals, with the exception of Cabinet Ministers.[42]

The accounts mention various types of containers like bags, – presumably the small ones – mails and portmanteaus, which were obviously larger. Hasker,

Until the nineteenth century gibbets and gallows were to be seen dotted around the countryside. Carey's maps showed the sites of them, as with this one near Wells in Somerset. It was hoped that they would provide a visible deterrent, and on some the corpse of the villain was left until it rotted away.

answering a query, asked if the Haslemere and Petworth office wanted a portmanteau mail or a white leather sack or bag.[43] In December 1828 an order dealing with passengers' luggage said that none was to be put on the roof of the coach until the boot was full. The number of items was limited to three, and the largest portmanteau (or carpet bag) was to measure no more than 2ft 4in (75cm) by 1ft 6in tall (45cm). A portmanteau was defined as any article 'covered with leather or hair', and these containers were to be very securely fastened to the coach.[44]

The procedure for handling the bags at the beginning and end of a run were clearly detailed in a case heard at the Old Bailey Court in London on 16 April 1795.[45] A Mr Thomas Thomas was accused of stealing bank notes from the mail. In giving evidence various clerks explained their procedures as the bags were passed along the line of delivery. On 3 October 1794 at Bristol the letters were bundled up and placed in a bag which was then tied with 'pack thread' and sealed. This bag was then placed in a large leather sack, presumably the mail or portmanteau, which was also tied. This large sack was given to the guard, Lewis Williams, who was to escort the coach from Bristol to Marlborough. If he followed his orders then the sack would have been immediately put into the coach mailbox, which would then have been locked.

When the coach arrived in London, at the Gloucester Coffee House in Piccadilly, the bags, accompanied by the guard, were taken by cart to Lombard Street. When the mail reached Lombard Street the clerk noticed that the portmanteau was untied and there was no trace of a seal, so he took it straight to the President of the office. The guard, Lewis Williams, when cross-examined in court, reported that he had gone from Bristol right through to London on 2 October. This was unusual as he normally changed at Marlborough, but that day he had business in London. He guarded the mail from Bristol to Marlborough on the following day and remembered seeing the bag of London mail tied and sealed, noticing this he proceeded to place it in the corner of the box under the guard's seat. He travelled from Bristol to Marlborough whereupon another guard took over.

The accused, Thomas Thomas, travelled on this coach from Bristol sitting with the coachman. Shortly before the coach reached the small town of Calne he changed to the roof of the coach. He told the guard that he was very tired and then the guard, contrary to strict orders, said that he might ride in his seat for a while. It is not clear why this was thought a better seat. The guard then sat with the coachman until they got to Backington, six miles from Marlborough, at which point the guard told Thomas he must move back to his seat. There he stayed until the coach reached Marlborough and he handed over to the new guard, Thomas Hawkins. The guard admitted that the box was not locked, another breach of the rules, but he said the box was locked while he went into the office at Bath. He did not think that anybody could have got to the box at Calne because he was away for less than a couple of minutes. He had jumped off the coach while it was moving, delivered the bags, collected the new ones and was soon back up on his box. The coach stopped at Chippenham to change horses, and again the guard admits the box was unlocked.

The new guard, Thomas Hawkins, also admitted that he had allowed Thomas to ride on his seat when they stopped at the top of a hill to give the horses a breather. He stayed in that seat for about twenty miles until the guard retook his place, but at Thatchum they again swapped places until they reached Hare Hatch. There the guard again swapped with the driver, who then sat on the guard's seat whilst Hawkins drove. At Colnebrook they all moved back to their correct seats and Thomas eventually got off at Hyde Park Corner.

The coach stopped at the Gloucester Coffee House in Piccadilly and the guard took the mail to Lombard Street in the cart provided, he claimed that at this point the mail was in the same condition as it had been when it was delivered to him at Marlborough. The prosecution went on to prove conclusively that at some point Thomas had opened the box and extracted the bank notes; consequently he was found guilty and sentenced to seven years' transportation.

On getting the details of the robbery Hasker wrote to the Postmaster General on 12 October 1794 saying that Thomas Thomas was being held for questioning. It appeared to Hasker that the guard was in the habit of riding with the coachman and that this had permitted the villain to get access to his mailbox. Hasker suggested that the guard be suspended or dismissed, as well as the coachman who had allowed him to drive. However, he pointed out that coachmen were not appointed by the Post Office, which meant it had no direct control over them, while it was also clear to him that contractors should not support the coachmen in such cases.[46] If this case is at all typical it is apparent that, despite all the oaths and warnings, regulations were poorly observed by some of the guards. It also indicates that the coach would stop to allow passengers to dismount at locations other than Post Offices, since Thomas left the coach at Hyde Park Corner.

This practice of allowing passengers into the guard's seat was not uncommon, on 17 March 1840 a female was reported by a member of the public as sitting there and an inspector was told to investigate. The complaint was verified and the guard admitted his guilt. He was apparently well known as his name featured in the Black Book.[47]

Highway robbery, in which the mail coach was halted by an armed robber, had never been a problem with the mail coaches, that crime was usually reserved for the post boys. Robbery from the coach was usually, in one way or another, an opportunist snatch of the bags from the box whilst the guard was distracted, from the carts it was usually far more blatant and direct. In one fairly typical case of robbery from a mail cart, on 8 December 1780[48], the charge states that twenty-three bags were taken from the Norwich mail. The robbery took place in London whilst the driver, a boy named Jacob Byner, was in the Coach and Horses public house on the Mile End Road. He stated that all the bags were in a portmanteau and that he had not missed it when he got back in the cart. From his evidence it seems that the portmanteau was not secured in any way. Some of the stolen banknotes from the mail eventually turned up in Dublin, presented by a Mr James Jones. He – real name Thomas Roberts – and two accomplices were arrested. One of the accomplices, Edward Sutton, turned and gave evidence against his accomplices. Roberts and his accomplice Archer were brought back to London for trial. Archer was found guilty and condemned to death.[49]

Before any run started from London, conforming with a long-standing Post Office agreement, the coaches were taken to Vidler's workshop at Millbank where they were cleaned and inspected for wear or damage. Moving parts were coated with grease for lubrication and the coaches were then driven to Lombard Street or other starting points of the run. When the coach arrived at its departure point the guard's duties included checking the condition of the coach, the harness and the horses, and then reporting any problems.

The harness was extremely important; a broken strap could do anything from halting the coach to overturning it. The poor condition of many of the harnesses was a considerable problem in the early days and many sets had to be replaced. In October 1792 Hasker was ordered to keep half a dozen reins in stock so that if the guard found a problem it could be quickly remedied. The contractor would be charged for the reins.[50] Efforts were made to ensure good runs, and in 1790 Hasker was reminded by the Postmaster General that:

...from the accidents that have happened lately to the Royal Mail coach Mr Hasker to remember that in future a report is to be made by the Superintendent or Deputy if all the horse, harness are in their place previous to the coach starting and that the coach shall run three of four times at least previous to the regular day of its starting that the coachmen and horse may be used to the road and each other.[51]

It was also the guard's responsibility to check the passengers and ensure that no more than the permitted number were on the coach. For the normal coaches four inside passengers were allowed and one outside, this was later increased to two. On some runs there were larger coaches which held more passengers. Booking places on the mail or stagecoaches was not an easy or pleasant task, and Charles Dickens in *Sketches by Boz* describes the depressing process. His account is for a stagecoach, and it seems likely that the mail process would have been slightly less discouraging. The fares were higher and this may well have made for a slightly more sober or cultured traveller.

According to De Quincy,[52] in the early days of the mail coaches there was certainly a social divide between inside and outside passengers. Those travelling inside had paid more for their ticket, often twice the 'outside' fare, and consequently were probably wealthier. De Quincy believed that they therefore considered themselves superior. In 1789 the fare for a run to Bristol on a Royal Mail coach was £1-18-0 (£1.80p) for an inside seat and 18s (80p) for an outside seat. An inside seat for Carlyle cost £2-11-0 (£2.55p). He claims that when the coach stopped at an inn 'outsiders' were not even allowed to sit at the same table as the 'insiders'. Obviously 'inside' made for a more comfortable ride, for the seats were padded whilst 'outside' it was essential to ensure one had a firm grip on some part of the coach. One passenger sat on the box with the coachman, this was usually considered the prime place, and the other sat upon a small, bench-like seat on the roof.

If there was a spare inside seat it was not unknown for the guard or coachman to turn a blind eye and allow a passenger to swap from the outside in return for a donation. In November 1825 Freeling warned the guards that if there was a change of seating then the excess fare was to be collected and handed in.[53] In February 1801 one coachman collected money but failed to pass it on to his employer. He was tried, found guilty and sentenced to be transported for seven years.[54] On 5 February 1801 Hasker issued a circular to serve as a warning to guards by giving details of another case: John Sperink, a coachman employed as the driver of the Banbury Coach by the contractor, Thomas Fagg, had kept money taken after leaving the Bell and Crown Inn, Holborn. Under an Act of 12 July 1799 he was found guilty and sentenced to be transported for fourteen years.[55]

During the eighteenth and nineteenth centuries there were plenty of stage as well as mail coaches traversing the country, and whilst there were similarities in the service there were also marked differences. The two were in competition for paying passengers and it was not unknown for the private coaches to poach the Post Office customers. One trick was for the stagecoach to arrive at the inn shortly before the mail coach was due, 'then by a person behind blowing a horn many passengers take it for the mail coach.' The waiting passengers would climb aboard to be whisked away just before the real mail coach arrived. Mr Hasker reported just such a case at Hounslow in May 1794 and said that it would not happen if the guards wore their distinctive red coats or did not cover them with heavy, darker weatherproof coats.[56] According to Harper (*op. cit.*), the guards sometimes wore box coats which were stitched in five or six rows and were fitted with large buttons. It is apparent from the records that the guards did not always wear their regulation uniform, and there were reminders in April 1845, 1846 and 1848 that this was not acceptable (Vol. 4, Raguin).

The coachmen or drivers were employed by the contractors and not the Post Office, so presumably they could wear any clothing deemed appropriate by the contractor. However, some contemporary illustrations show them wearing a similar overcoat to the guard. De Quincy[57] (*op. cit.*) states that some drivers did have red coats and implies that they were granted this right almost as an acknowledgement of the length of their service. There is some evidence to support this idea, for in 1792 the Postmaster General expressed the opinion that:

> …although by the universal custom of the office the guards only have uniforms at the expense of the office (if one coachman has it will not others expect it) but if he drives the mail well and lower than the usual price in consequence of it the PMG have no objection to it if Mt F and H see none.[58]

Unfortunately there is no indication as to which driver they were referring to, but the entry does suggest that some drivers may well have been allowed the official red coat. Some of the earlier writers, such as Joyce and Harper, say that the coachmen of the nineteenth century often had a reputation for looking rather dandy-ish in their very smart clothing. Since the drivers were not employees of the office there are comparatively few details about them in the archives. It is not clear whether the drivers always did the same run or whether they rotated. On the whole the relationship between guard and driver appears to have been fairly amicable but there were occasional problems. In February 1793, at Warrington, when the guard went to change bags the coachman drove off without either him or the mail. The guard obtained a horse and overtook the coach at Congleton. Hasker suggests that the driver be sacked and 'never be allowed to drive again.'[59] No reason for this lapse is given.

Coping with four horses was no easy task, coachmen were highly regarded for their skill and there was a certain glamour associated with them. The seat next to the driver on a mail coach was considered very desirable and it was not unknown for a little bribery to be used to get that seat. Sometimes quite distinguished men would take over the reins and drive the stage, something that was recorded as happening very rarely on mail coaches. There were plenty of amateur drivers who delighted in showing off their skills and there were a number of clubs devoted to the craft. A good coachman would walk around his team, checking all the harness was correctly in place and connected, and then he would take hold of the reins, known as ribbons. These had to be held correctly – normally in the left hand – and then he mounted to his box.

Every driver had his whip and its use required some skill, for each horse called for a particular blow, the strength of that blow and the point at which it was struck were all-important. According to the contemporary writers, the less the whip was used the better the response when it was needed. It was also used as a kind of signalling device; indicating to another driver one's attitude, favourable or otherwise. Malet declared that no driver should go more than seventy miles a day, and even this was thought to bring about premature ageing and infirmity. As the driver was not a Post Office employee the archives have little or nothing to say abut their wages, general life and expenses, but if a driver wanted to ensure a quick changeover it was as well to tip the ostlers.

When the letters had been sorted at the office and packed into the appropriate bags they had to be taken to the waiting coaches. The guards were supposed to wait in the guards' room until their bags were ready and they were then called to collect them. The report of 1814[60] says that the room was only '132 superficial feet', and into this small area were eighteen guards complete with great coats, tools and firearms, together with the assistants. This made a total of some twenty-eight to thirty people. In 1895 F.E. Baines states in his book *On the Track of the Mail Coach*, that the guards' room in the old office was less than 12ft (3.7m) square.

There just was not enough room, and some of the staff went to public houses to wait:

> …it must occur to every person that no place can be so very improper recollecting that they (the guards are on the point of performing long journies(sic) and the great importance of the trust confided to them.[61]

This seems a somewhat short-sighted solution to the crowding problem, knowing that many of the guards had a well-earned reputation for being hard drinkers.

According to Hasker, in 1814 there was space in Lombard Street for only seven coaches to wait for their mail. Two more stood at Cornhill, a nearby street, while all the other coaches were located at the various inns. He pointed out that the mail for other coaches had to be taken by cart from Lombard Street, so increasing their vulnerability. To counter this each guard had to have an assistant or two to help carry and – after poor Fagan's experience (detailed below) – guard the

PARTICULARS, &c.

LOT 1.

A VALUABLE FREEHOLD DWELLING HOUSE,

FORMERLY OCCUPIED AS THE

MAIL-COACH OFFICE,

ADJOINING THE CHURCH,

With a Frontage to LOMBARD STREET of 16 Feet 6 Inches, by a Depth of 44 Feet,

And abutting on Entrance to Court of late Post Office, and immediately adjoining the
Branch Office retained by Government,

AS DESCRIBED ON PLAN;

CONTAINING

On the UPPER FLOOR Two Bed Rooms and a Water Closet.

THIRD FLOOR—Two Bed Rooms, with large Closet on Landing.

SECOND FLOOR—Two Bed Rooms, with Closets on Landing.

FIRST FLOOR—Two Sitting Rooms, conveniently fitted up.

PRINCIPAL FLOOR—Entrance Hall, communicating with the Passage from LOMBARD STREET, Parlor or Shop
in Front, and a Sitting Room at the Back.

BASEMENT—Kitchen, Larder, Coal Cellar, and arched Vault.

Page from the sale catalogue advertising the 1831 auction of the old Post Office
premises in Lombard Street. This was no longer required when the new office in St
Martin's-le-Grand was built. (PO 91/12)

bags during the loading time.[62] These extra men increased costs to the office and
meant that there were more people milling about in the area, thus increasing
crowding and confusion.

The waiting coaches also created traffic problems, especially in the Lombard
Street area. The coming and going, the milling crowds and the general confusion
afforded the villains a good opportunity for a little thieving. To reduce the danger,
Hasker had a strong lamp placed at the end of the passage in Lombard Street, and
on 25 January 1794 he asked for another to light the passage from Abchurch Lane,
Sherborne Lane and the Inland Office.[63]

The new lighting, sadly, did not prevent every incident, and on 20 February
1794 the dangers were clearly demonstrated. Fagan, the Norwich guard, was about
to carry three bags from the office across Lombard Street to his coach – standing on the other side of the road. Smart, another employee, waiting in Lombard
Passage for the York mail, told Osman, an extra guard, to help Fagan load the bags.

Fagan crossed the road with the bags but, at that moment, a hackney coach passed along the road just behind him and prevented Osman from following immediately. Fagan was by then on the opposite side of the road, standing at the back of the Norwich coach and had dropped the bags onto the pavement in order to climb onto the coach – ready for Osman to hand up the bags. In that brief moment before Osman crossed the road and reached the coach the bags were spirited away, 'probably by three men dressed in drab' who had been seen standing about. Mr Roberts, a book-keeper who witnessed the incident, said it happened in not more than half a minute. A boy saw the whole business, Bow Street took a statement from him and began the process of looking for the three men – including one Whitemore – who was well-known at Bow Street.[64]

Naturally there was consternation over the robbery, and on 24 February Hasker presented a three page report on the incident along with his plan to reduce the chance of it happening again. The Mayor was to be asked to have a patrol or constable at the Mansion House end of Lombard Street along with a chain across the road to stop passing traffic. In this report he points out that there is a great deal of activity whilst the coaches are loading, but says that all are ready to go within, '6 or 8 mins except the York which takes 10 or 12 minutes to load.' Seven coaches were loaded in Lombard Street during the process, and henceforward as each guard loaded he was to have another guard with him to serve as an assistant and lookout. Hasker wanted another guard for the Liverpool, Chester and Newmarket coaches. These extra guards were to wear red jackets and have an identity label.[65]

When informed of the theft the Postmaster General did not look kindly on Fagan, he said that he should never have let go of the bags, unless they had been in the care of some other person.[66] They also approved Hasker's suggestion that he apply to the Lord Mayor to let a patrol or constable:

> ...stand at the end of Lombard Street near the Mansion House, with a chain across the road to prevent carts and drays entering from a quarter of an hour before 8 till the mails are all off and for another officer to be placed in the Post Office side of Birchin Lane in Lombard St (*ibid*).

The Mayor agreed to a trial of the scheme. The Postmaster General also asked if Hasker could not use three porters to help with the loading, rather than hiring supernumerary guards at extra expense.

When the new premises came into use security became less of a problem during the loading of coaches, for they were all held within an enclosed area. The extra supernumerary guards hired to help load the coaches in the past were no longer necessary. Pike, a messenger, was there to inspect the guards and another man checked that no bags were overlooked. The New Police[67] were helping and apart from a couple of other men there was no need for more.[68]

Ralph Allen, the pioneer in improving and developing the cross posts during the eighteenth century. (Permission of Bath Postal Museum)

The guard was held responsible for any loss or delay of the mail and faced the possibility of dismissal in the event of a failure – but the authorities did not always enforce this rule. On 12 May 1794 the tender-hearted Hasker interceded on behalf of the Bristol guard. Whilst loading his bags into the coach at Thatcham the guard was called away to 'attend some other duty', in consequence he forgot to load the bags for several posts on his route. Another guard saw the bags, took them with him to Newbury and handed the bags into that office. The Deputy Postmaster quite rightly sent his assistant to town with the bags. A chaise was hired and the cost of this, together with the tolls paid, amounted to four guineas. Hasker suggested that the guard be ordered to pay these costs as his punishment and he, described by Hasker as a 'very sober guard but for this a very careful one and is willing to pay the expenses and hopes that no greater punishment will follow.'[69] The Postmaster General replied on 20 May that, in view of Hasker's good report on the guard, the penalty was a little harsh. Hasker then suggested that the guard pay half and the office at Newbury pay the rest.

In the normal course of events, when the bags of mail reached the coach they were to be immediately placed in the box, which was then locked. As shown in the above mentioned trial, this important step was not always taken and at one point Hasker remarks that some guards only locked their boxes when they thought a supervisor might be around checking.

It was not unknown for the guard to take a chance and try a little smuggling or some private trade. On at least one occasion this led to a complex situation. In April 1805 Hasker had a tricky problem, for a guard was found by the Excise people to have a hundredweight (nearly 45kg) of coffee in his mail box. In the event the Excise men seized both the coffee and the coach, the unfortunate owners pleaded that this was unfair as the guard was a Post Office employee and not under their control. The contractor demanded compensation.[70]

In October 1838 Richard Butler, the Dover coach guard, was committed for having in his possession two carpet bags containing some silk lace goods. He was fined £181-7-0, a quarter of the value of the goods. Unfortunately he could not pay the fine and so was imprisoned. He wrote to the office saying he knew nothing and that the bags could have been put in the box before he took over the coach. The explanation was not accepted and he was told on 25 October that he had been dismissed.[71]

It could be to the advantage of the coachman as much as the guard to indulge in a little private enterprise. In March 1838 illicit spirits were being traded on the London to Stroud route. The suspicions of a Revenue man had been aroused, he intended to stop the coach and search it. Upon hearing this the guard, William Turner, sought advice from the office. The Excise Office investigated, found some strong evidence and established that a coachman had already been sent to prison. Apparently the Excise Office had the power to search coaches. However, as it was only the coachman who had been involved the office was not really concerned, nevertheless the contractor should still be told.[72]

When the mail had been loaded at Lombard Street the coaches were then driven to the various inns to collect their passengers. When all were aboard, when the bags had been locked away and the coach and horses checked, it was the guard who gave the order to start. He carried the timepiece and a time bill which set out the precise schedule for the run. These time bills were very exact; they specified just how long was allowed for each stage and how long a break was permitted for each stop. In the event of a late arrival then the signatories – for the bills had to be countersigned at various points – were expected to give full reasons for the delays. Among the details on the time bill there were spaces to insert the number of the coach and the timepiece carried. Although some of the later time bills survive most do not have all the details fully entered, so that individual coaches and timepieces cannot be identified. On 11 July 1792 the Postmaster General, perhaps feeling a little put out, wrote:

> ...tell Mr Hasker he should leave out the printed words in his new time bills 'by order of the Surveyor and Comptroller General' and insert the words 'Postmaster General'.[73]

The journeys were carefully planned and it is apparent that each stage was generally the responsibility of one guard. Harris (*op. cit.*) states that sections of up to one hundred miles were covered by one guard, but the records suggest that most routes were covered by a number of guards, each of whom normally served the same section. Thirty or forty miles seem to have been the normal distance. A list, unfortunately without a date, lists the posts in England, twenty-nine in all, with their length and the number of guards allocated. The longest is Liverpool to London – 205 miles – which had eight guards detailed. Another column lists the number needed if each guard did thirty miles, which suggests that on this occasion Hasker was asked if he could reduce the number of guards. The analysis suggests that the service could possibly do without six or seven.[74] Another list differs only very slightly in the detail and is dated 1792.[75]

Hasker and Freeling were often asked by the Postmaster General if the number of guards could be reduced to save costs[76], but only on the condition that the service did not suffer. In August 1793 Hasker was authorised to remove one guard from each of the Portsmouth to Chichester, Manchester to London and York to London coaches as long as it did not negatively affect the quality of the service.[77] There was also some discussion as to whether the length of each guard's section could be altered. The working stage for each guard seems to have been rather varied, and in May 1792 the Postmaster General queried with Freeling whether some Scottish stages were simply too short, could Hasker reduce the number of guards?[78] The reply indicates that the length of the stages ranged from eighteen to twenty-eight miles.

Berwick to Edinboro': 54 miles 3 guards
Carlisle to Moffat: 46 miles 2 guards
Moffat to Glasgow: 57 miles 2 guards
Glasgow to Ayr: 35 miles 2 guards
Carlisle to Dumfries: 40 miles 2 guards

There is evidence that the system could, if the guards so wished, be modified to suit the circumstances. As each stage finished the guard for that sector was replaced by the next one, although the evidence suggests (see above) they could vary this arrangement. The records show that the guard then escorted a returning coach back to the previous changeover point. The guards were not allowed to change their schedule without permission, and in July 1796 Hasker reprimanded two for doing so without his permission.[79]

During the journey the guard was expected to keep his eyes open for any danger and blow his horn to warn traffic to clear the way; for it was an offence to impede the mail. Any person who delayed or obstructed the Royal Mail could be prosecuted, although it seems that the Post Office was often satisfied with just a public apology and a promise to be more careful. There are several such occasions

Handwritten statement by John Twopenny. The driver admitted to taking unofficial stops and that this had led directly to an accident. He thanks the officers for accepting his apologies and not prosecuting him. (10/5 63)

recorded: including the public apology given by Edward Monk, who damaged the York and Liverpool mail coach and caused an accident. He expressed his contrition and gratitude that the Postmasters were allowing him to apologise and so avoid further punishment. The document was signed with the cross of Edward Monk and dated 2 August 1804.[80] There are other similar documents in the archives.

On 11 October 1794 Hasker warned three guards about their failure to sound their horns. He told them that they should blow their horns when passing through towns or villages, they had been negligent and had nearly caused accidents:

Take care that I hear no more of these complaints or I shall be obliged to punish you be careful especially thro Wellington.[81]

It was also noted that on occasions the guards became a little exuberant. In a letter of 9 August 1837 a correspondent complained that on the Hounslow Road there were occasions when the coaches engaged in an unofficial race, with the guards sounding their horns in encouragement.[82]

As the coach neared the tollgates the guard was duty bound to sound his horn. This was to give the tollkeeper time to swing open the gates, as mail coaches were allowed through free, except on Sundays or if they were not carrying mail. This privilege was established by law 25 Geo III cap LVII, with effect from 15 July 1785:

> …and all Turnpike keepers and toll collectors are hereby directed and required and to permit such carriages and horses to pass through all and every Turnpike Tollgate or bar without demanding any toll or duty whatsoever.

Later a legal query was raised over the question of liability to pay toll on chaises or extra horses when they were hired in bad weather or other adverse circumstances. Freeling sought legal advice on 16 February 1828, and was told that when post horses were taken and paid for by the office then duty was not payable, but when part of the charge was paid by contractors, 'the case is so complex better not to open it.'[83]

Although the toll keeper was supposed to assist the coaches there seems to have been little love lost between some of them and the guards were often the victims of abuse if not worse. A minute of May 1811 complains about the tollgate keepers who abused the coachmen and guards as they passed through.[84] On 12 November 1841, in Kendall, Edward Throw, the guard on the Carlisle coach, was taken before the magistrates for assaulting the keeper of the Netherfield gate. Apparently, when the coach reached the gate the keeper, who was drunk, refused to open it until he had measured the height of the luggage on top of the coach. The guard demanded that he open it, and when this request was refused he pushed the keeper aside and opened it himself. The guard was found guilty and fined one farthing[85] but had to pay costs of one guinea. The Post Office was assured that under an obsolete – but unrepealed – Act the keeper could demand the measuring.[86] A law of March 1811 had set down the maximum permitted height from

The proprietors of the travelling menagerie (owners of the escaped lioness) sought to benefit from the publicity and featured it on their posters. (P 8167)

ground to the top of the roof luggage as being 8ft 9in (2m 62cm). There was some legal confusion as whether the Act 2/3 Guil 4 *c.* 120 applied to mail coaches or not and whether height was relevant. The Office solicitors thought the toll keeper could be prosecuted and was liable to a £5 fine under Vic c36 sec, 9. It should be remembered that each mail coach passing free through the turnpike represented a financial loss to the turnpike company, which did not make for a happy relationship.

If the weather was fine, the road in good repair, the horses in fine fettle and the driver sober, then the coach probably had no great trouble maintaining its correct speed and would arrive punctually at the inn. If all was well then the ostlers would have the new team of horses harnessed and ready for the changeover. This operation involved unhooking the team of horses from the coach and replacing them with a fresh team. It was often a matter of pride to ensure a rapid changeover, and it was claimed that it could be done in minutes. The process was not simple, for the arriving team had to be unhitched and led away and the new team moved into position. The reins had to be carefully sorted and passed to the driver; traces were attached to the coach and if the horses proved frisky the whole swap could become tricky. This could delay the coach, which would certainly not please the coachman or the guard who would have been handing over the bags of letters and picking up passengers ready for the next stage. The next team of horses were supposed to be ready and waiting for the coach when it arrived, but some inns were not quite as prompt as they should have been. On 21 September 1796 Mr Hasker wrote a strong note to one Deputy Postmaster:

> Your housekeepers at Hertford Bridge & Basingstoke very inattentive never ready when the coach arrives and frequently the guard and coachman harness the horse themselves. I dare you was a stranger to this but have no doubt you will remedy the evil now you are informed of it.[87]

The changeover was a particularly risky time. Hasker told guards that they should stand by the head of the horses while the changeover was being made, and there were one or two cases where the horses ran away when they were left unattended for a moment.[88] In one notorious case in July 1792, at a stop between Wakefield and Sheffield, the driver was not on his box while the guard was attending to the mail. The horses bolted and as the coach rushed along one passenger panicked, tried to jump out and broke a leg. Hasker thought that the guard and driver should be dismissed unless they could present a good defence.[89]

On Thursday 22 November 1810 Walter Price, the driver of the Chester and Manchester mail coach, left the horses to help a passenger with their luggage. The guard had gone to the office leaving the team unattended, and the horses reacted by bolting through Chester on the road to Holywell. The guard was taken before a magistrate and fined £5 on 26 November 1810.[90] The time bills indicate that the coach – as well as the horses – was changed at some of the stops.[91]

Cash receipt from late 1836 with only one mail coach listed. (Permission of Bath Postal Museum)

On the longer journeys there were set breaks for refreshments. In 1827 the London to Bristol coach was allowed a fifteen minute break at Marlborough. On the London to Leeds run only ten minutes were allowed at Nottingham, while on the London to Edinburgh route there was a forty minute break at Grantham and another of the same length at York.[92] On the Carlisle to London run the coach, which left at 7 p.m., was allowed a break of precisely forty-six minutes at Leeds. The breaks were very finely calculated and in 1827, on the Gloucester to London run, there was a break at Oxford, where the coach arrived at 11.32, set for precisely twenty-eight minutes.[93] On the London to Chester run the total time for the journey was twenty-one hours forty-seven minutes, of which five minutes at Northampton, thirty minutes at Hinckley and ten minutes at Stafford were the only breaks allowed (*ibid*). The coach left London at 8 p.m. and reached Chester Post Office at 5.47 p.m. the next day, so that for nearly a whole day a 'through' passenger would have been seated on a not very comfortable seat and subjected to bumps and sways. Not only that but for part of the time he would be in darkness. To minimise the discomfort some passengers split such long journeys, permitting themselves an overnight stay at an inn along the route.

These breaks must have been more than welcome, especially for the driver, guard and outside passengers; all of whom were exposed to wind, rain, sleet or snow in addition to the shaking and rolling inevitable on any wheeled vehicle of the period. Often the innkeepers were also the Deputy Postmasters, for it was to their advantage to attract trade via the coaches. In theory they knew exactly what time the coach was due and so were ready to supply any meals required. The

menu was probably somewhat limited since there was not much time for preparation; it would most likely have included such dishes as green pea soup, potted
venison or some fine sausages. There would be China tea to drink or, after the
1830s, Indian tea. For a stronger taste there was punch made of claret and brandy
with various herbs to taste.[94] Beer would have been on tap.

The inns were known for the little tricks they used to ensure a maximum profit
from the coaching trade. Since the stop was short, if the food and drink was slow
in coming then the passengers had little time to eat or drink and any leftovers
went to the staff. Since passengers had paid for it when ordering, this was a bonus
for the innkeeper and it was well known that bills were 'adjusted' to the passengers'
apparent ability to pay. The accommodation for those who stayed overnight was
often far from luxurious and Charles Dickens writes of fleas being one particular
problem. Many of those who listed the joys of coach journeys were often writing
some time after the trip, and nostalgia and time inevitably softened the picture.[95]

At the end of the rest period the horn was blown, this was to warn passengers
that time was up and that they should board the coach. It is certain that not
everybody would have been inclined to rush out to remount, but every minute's
delay meant an extra minute the driver had to make up – or else there would be
trouble explaining the lateness. Some idea of the difficulty that the guard had
in coaxing the passengers back into the coach can be gained from a note by the
Postmaster General. Mr Freeling was told to speak to Mr Hasker about the coach
being delayed half an hour by passengers drinking tea at Malton in January 1793.[96]

By the early nineteenth century the Post Office had outgrown its old premises at
Lombard Street and plans were made for new premises at St Martin's-le-Grand. The
new building, designed by the famous architect Smirke, was completed in 1829.

There are anecdotes which indicate that the drivers were not at all inclined to wait for latecomers, and there is no doubt that on occasions some tardy passengers were left behind. There were other reasons for the delay of a coach, one such occured in Liverpool in May 1794 when the Hull coach was held up by a Naval Press Gang looking for seamen to serve in the Navy. The word 'affray' was used by Hasker, which suggests things may have become a little rough. Hasker planned to write to the Liverpool Deputy Postmaster with a request that he contact the Mayor, and to ask that the Royal Navy lieutenant be told that 'such a molestation may not happen again.'[97]

There were also many temptations likely to cause a delay of which alcohol was one. Drink and drunkenness were serious problems for the Post Office, many guards and drivers seem to have been keen, dedicated tipplers. There are frequent references to intoxicated staff and warnings about stopping at alehouses on the excuse of watering horses, all contractors were warned:

General Post Office
1800
Sir
Stopping at alehouses on the road between stage and stage under pretence of watering horses, but in reality to drink, have been found very detrimental to the service. I have, in conjunction with many principal mail coach contractors, determined to annihilate so shameful a practice, and I have my lords The Postmaster General's commands to find the enclosed letter to all the guards, and this to you, desiring you will immediately give full directions to your coachmen not to go into, or even stop at such houses – it is only done (under pretence of necessity) to carry on bad commerce to the injury of yourselves, by illegal practices of taking up passengers and parcels which are never accounted for.
I am
Sir, your most obedient servant
T. Hasker[98]

On 18 August 1802 he repeated the substance of this letter, 'in consequence of recent circumstances, particularly the Bristol Mail Coach horse running from the Magpye, Hounslow Heath, with the coach, while the servants were in the Alehouse drinking.'[99] Sadly, the guards seem to have been the hardest drinkers and a number are listed as having been discharged for drunkenness. The driver was sometimes held responsible for any delay, and on 18 July 1814 Thomas Williams, driver of the Carmarthen mail coach, appeared before a Justice of the Peace of Brecon and Carmarthen and on the evidence of the guard, Thomas Hart, was fined £5 for not keeping to time as ordered by various laws.[100]

Another factor which had an enormous effect on the journey was the weather, and during the summer the coachmen generally had less trouble in keeping to the timetable. Autumn and winter could be far more difficult, as the weather deteriorated timings became more difficult to meet. In town, with all the coal-burning fires, industry and oil lamps, fogs were not uncommon. On 5 January 1791 there were payments to an I. Tomas for flambeaux to light the Exeter coach in foggy weather by walking ahead carrying the burning torches.[101] There are similar references on other occasions.

Heavy rain, swollen rivers and melting snow could all contribute to flooding, and, in addition to the inconvenience and mud, could place the coach and passengers in great danger. It was in such situations that many of the guards showed just how dedicated they were. In January 1795 Hasker wrote to the Postmaster General to ask if he might reward some of those who had shown great bravery; like John Rees, guard from Swansea to Bristol who went through floods up to his shoulders. Hasker suggested that a guinea would be appropriate, whilst Thomas Sweatman of the Chester mail had to fix harness during flooding, for this bravery he was rewarded with ten shillings and sixpence.[102] In fact, Hasker thought seventy of the guards warranted a reward, for they had risked their lives during the floods and snow, thus he sought permission to pay out a total of £51.[103]

Although rare there were fatal accidents, one such occurred on 25 October 1808. As the Glasgow to Carlyle coach was crossing a bridge the arch gave way, depositing coach, horses, passengers, driver and guard into the flood. Two of the horses were killed, the others were injured and the coach suffered serious damage, the Post Office paid the owner, Mr James Rae, £73-10-0 compensation. Tragically the driver, Mr Cooper, was killed and his widow was granted £21 for her sad loss.[104] On 23 October 1829 the Gloucester to Stroud coach overturned and the coachman was killed.[105]

Heavy snowfalls were always a serious hazard as the icy roads made it difficult for the horses to keep their feet and deeper drifts simply halted the coach. According to Mallet,[106] one trick to improve the grip was to pack the hooves with soft soap to prevent the snow being compacted into ice. A heavy fall of snow could bring the entire postal system to an almost complete stop. Coaches simply came to a halt as the depth of snow proved too great for the horses to push through. In such an event the driver or guard often asked farmers to loan them a couple of their horses to pull the coach free.

Payment was authorised on 26 February 1791 for, 'R. Briscoe for 2 waggon horses to help the Exeter coach out of snow 6/3.'[107] This document lists a series of payments incurred by accidents in the 1790s and authorised by Hasker, including such incidents as:

January 21 1789; to chairmen for stopping Exeter coach in St James St when driver and guard were 'shook from their seats' and for assisting in mending harness 3s (15p)

Following his printed 'Instructions to the Guards', this one has taken two horses from the coach team to make his way to the next Post Office with the post bags. He takes his blunderbuss for protection. (Detail from a painting)

> August 10; to T. Robertson for medicines and bleeding J. Denys Portsmouth guard who was hurted by a fall from the mail coach £2-3 (£2.15).

Some simple steps could be taken to reduce the problems caused by snow and ice. Johnson, together with the Surveyor and Superintendent, sent a notice to the contractors complaining that they, or their servants, had not roughened the horses' shoes, which would help them keep their feet and so avoid injuries and delays.[108]

If no other way could be found then there was a procedure set down authorising the guard to hire extra horses to help the teams. These were small, blue-covered notebooks known as 'Snow Books', in which the guard was required to enter full details of any extra horses and where and when they were used. A number of them – dating from January and February 1838 – are preserved in the archives and the pages are divided into columns. The typical headings include Date, From what place, to what place, no. of miles, by whom supplied and whether leaders or otherwise, reason and by guards order or not. The guard had to sign the entry, could add any remarks and the Post Office would only pay those accounts with a signature.[109]

The archives also include the plans for simple snow-ploughs, the planks fastened together to form a wedge shape, which was then to be pulled or pushed through the snow clearing a path for the coach.[110] Some of the ideas were considered worthy of a test, and there is some correspondence about one, with contradictory accounts. On 23 December 1814 Hasker suggested to Freeling that a copy of the plan for a simple plough should be sent to all Postmasters. This was done[111] – with further correspondence indicating that it was used right up to the 1840s. It was apparently the brainchild of a Norwegian; Captain Mariboe.[112] There is some controversy about its effectiveness, as one letter from Dublin said it was a complete failure and that the wood and iron should be sold as scrap, which would probably realise half the purchase price of £10. Louis, writing in 1838, disagreed, he claimed that it had been used quite effectively at South Shields over twenty-five years ago. He also thought that its components of wood and iron would only sell at half the original price, saying the wood was only fit for firewood.[113]

In January 1814 some particularly heavy blizzards did indeed bring about an almost total breakdown of the system, and some towns received no mail for days. When a coach was firmly snowed in and all attempts – even using extra horses – to move it had failed, it was the guard's duty to make every effort to get the mail pouches through to the next post. In these circumstances the guard was instructed to take one or two of the coach horses and make his own way to the next post, leaving the coach and passengers. As indicated above, many of the guards made heroic efforts to do just that. The guard from Shaftesbury once arrived on horseback at a post and was so cold that he had to be lifted from the saddle and put to bed.[114] The records give no indication as to what happened to the abandoned passengers and driver. Presumably they staggered through the snowdrifts until they found shelter. Such bad weather not only caused delays but threw the entire system into confusion. On 27 April 1799 Hasker issued a circular saying that several coaches were missing from as far back as 1 February, he asked for details of any spare patent coaches lying about and their condition. He wanted to know whether they were in a barn, field yard or coach house, what condition were they in and did they have a complete set of seats, rugs and windows?[115]

Coaches were not where they should have been, guards were so stranded that even when coaches were available they sometimes had no guard. It is no wonder that Hasker, writing on 30 April 1814, explains that the guards' wages were higher than usual; so many guards had been isolated away from their coaches that it was necessary to find willing substitutes. However, those who volunteered thought 1s 6d a day was meagre recompense for the danger and discomfort involved, the Postmasters had to negotiate special rates and some claimed as much as five shillings a day. Hasker thought that in the circumstances it should be paid, and the Postmaster General agreed.[116] These temporary guards were issued with a lock for the box and a horn, both of which were demanded back when their duty ended.[117]

The *Instructions to the Guards* set down in detail the procedure to be followed when there was a conventional problem like a broken wheel, an overturned coach or a broken harness. The instructions were different for coaches on their way to London to those going out of London. Basically the guard was under a strong directive to get the mailbags through to the next post, some made Herculean efforts to do just that. Thomas Hasker, writing in the 1790s, states that if the accident occurred on a coach on its way to London then the guard was to hire a chaise and proceed with the mail and passengers to the next stage. (See Appendix V.) The owner of the chaise would be paid 3p a mile for its use. If this was not possible then he was to take one of the coach horses and ride with the mail to the next stage, or if there was a lot of mail he was to take two horses, using one as a packhorse.[118]

No journey was without danger, and whilst accidents were not common they did happen, and the guard himself was often a casualty. As pointed out above, the Postmaster General usually approved payment to surgeons and apothecaries for their treatment of the injured. In the sad event of death, either a pension or a lump sum was forthcoming. Sometimes the accident was due to bad driving, as on 10 March 1837 when the London to Pool coach did not arrive until 8 p.m. There was a serious accident four miles from Farnham when the mail coach passed *The Royal William* coach destined for Southampton. There was a violent contact and guard, coachman and one outside passenger were thrown off, the coach chassis was damaged and three horses were set free. The guard, Black, was severely stunned and thought one or more wheels had gone over him, but the passenger was only bruised and the other coachman was unhurt. When Black recovered he took the pouches and got various chaises from Farnham to London. Black reported that the coachman could drive well when he wanted to but that he was not happy to ride behind him. Louis thought the contractor should discharge him at once but Lichfield was of the opinion that an inspector should check up, while the coachman should not only be dismissed but be taken before a magistrate as well.

Some accidents were remarkable in that passengers survived without injury from what appeared to be a very serious crash. In March 1837 the Pembroke coach arrived at Hobbs Point at 8 p.m., as the guard delivered the Irish mail and left the office he saw the horses run away. The driver was on the ground and grabbed for the reins but failed. The lead horses did a sharp turn which snapped the pole of the coach, the poles then ran on 'with great fury' over the pier and rolled over a sloping rock face of about twenty feet. The two women passengers inside the coach were – amazingly – unhurt. The guard got the horse and rode with the mail to Pembroke. He then returned to the scene of the accident to find the coach with a broken pole, damaged panel and broken springs. The coachman's box was smashed but was eventually repaired. An official *Overturn* was filled out, the Inspector thought the horses had been frightened by the sudden light from the opening of the office door and that the driver and guard were blameless.[119]

Coaches were liable to overturn and such accidents were frequent. The Post Office had a form for recording details of all such accidents under the various headings.[120] Rough roads, top-heavy loading of luggage on top of the coach, bad driving or a collision could all result in the coach ending up on its side. A letter of 5 June 1794, dealing with an overturn which left one dead, claims that it was caused by too much weight on the roof of the coach. The contractor said that the coach on the York run had a larger post box than usual, the coach was consequently of heavier construction which tired the horses and meant extra horses were needed. On the last load the weight was 517lbs (258kg) and it had been as high as 525lbs (263kg). The extra weight could cause a side tilt as the coach rode a slope.[121] The Exeter mail overturned on Bagshot Heath – on a broad road on a moonlit night – because of a drunken coachman. Two passengers, Mr and Mrs Anthony, were in the coach and the wife dislocated her shoulder and was badly bruised. The guard, W. Roe, showed her little sympathy and 'was brutal in the greatest degree' while she was in pain. He was obviously a shady character for he, along with others, was dismissed for swindling the proprietors of nearly £100, for this a public prosecution was recommended.[122]

Some accidents were caused by sabotage, for at the time there were strong political feelings about turnpikes, enclosures and industrialisation. Sometimes the coaches were targeted:

General Post Office
26 February 1811

Whereas some malicious persons did on the night of Sunday the 17th Instant willfully place a large tree across the centre of the turnpike-road between Lemming Inn and Borough bridge whereby the mail-coach was overturned, part of the carriage broke and the coachman and guard hurt.
In order to bring the offenders to Justice His Majesty's Postmaster-General hereby offer a reward of FIFTY POUNDS To be paid upon conviction

By command of the Postmaster- General
F. Freeling[123]

Some accidents were blamed on bad driving and the driver of the mail coach could even be charged with murder. On 14 September 1796 William Clark, the driver of the Newmarket coach, was charged with the murder of a child by running over him in Bishopgate Street on 16 August. After hearing the evidence, especially testimony that the guard had blown his horn[124], Clark was found not guilty. Similarly Joseph Akerman, driver of the Bath mail coach, was charged with the murder of a John Southcombe on 22 October 1815. It seems that on this occasion there were three coaches, one behind the other,

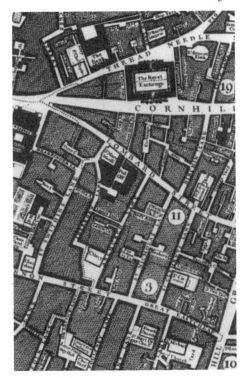 

Above left: Detail from Roque's 1746 map of London, clearly showing the Post Office and its environs.

Above right: John Townshend, one of the best known Bow Street Runners, who helped with Post Office investigations.

with Exeter and Worcester in front and Bath behind. The Bath coach hit a cart and Southcombe was thrown into the road and run over by the coach. The evidence suggested that the cart may have swerved into the coach, and again the verdict was not guilty.[125] Some accidents were due to poor driving; in March 1837 the London to Southampton coach overturned and the coachman, guard and one outside passenger were thrown off, in the event the driver was blamed.[126]

Bolting horses were always a serious problem and in October 1794 a coachman was killed and the guard rewarded for his gallantry in stopping the horses.[127] Falls were not uncommon, which is hardly surprising considering the situation of the guard perched at the back of the coach. Many illustrations show him holding on to what appears to be a strap fixed to the top of the coach. In September 1790 a surgeon was paid for attending to a guard on the Manchester route who fell from his coach.[128] In June 1791 a surgeon was paid £6-7-6 (£6.37) for treating Alexander Young – the Norwich guard – for a 'scull (sic) fractured by a fall.'[129] Accidents were not limited to country roads, seventeen shillings (85p) were

MAIL COACHES.

/3.(

PASSENGERS' LUGGAGE.

Memoranda.

NO Luggage can be allowed on the Roof which interferes with the proper packing and safety of any Sacks of Letters which the Mails are obliged to carry there.

No Luggage to be placed on the Roof till after the Boot is full, and then only that which belongs to Passengers.

No more than three Articles, being Portmanteaus or Carpet Bags, are, on any pretence, to be allowed, whether they be large or small; and the largest Portmanteau is not to exceed 2 feet 4 inches in length, and 1 foot 6 inches in height. They are never to be placed on each other. By Portmanteau is meant, any article made of or covered with Leather or Hair, and of course all Boxes of other Materials, Bundles, Baskets, &c. are to be rejected.

The Portmanteaus are to be fastened at one end to the Seat-Irons, and a Staple will be placed on each side the Coach, for one Strap to go over and further secure them.

~~Fastened with their tarrauleen or their tarrawes byput inside, except with the Chairment of all the other Passengers.~~

GENERAL POST-OFFICE,   CHARLES JOHNSON,
    December, 1828.   *Surveyor and Superintendent.*

Late luggage specification, including the definition of a portmanteau. (PO 10/6 153)

allocated for expenses for attendance at an inquest into the overturning of the Chester coach – which resulted in one death[130] – at Saint Bartholomew's Hospital in London.

The most bizarre cause of delay was that which happened to the Exeter mail coach on the night of 26 October 1817. As the coach neared the Pheasant Inn at Winterslow the outside leader horse was attacked by a lioness. The animal had escaped from a travelling wild animal caravan on its way to a fair at Salisbury and was harried by a large mastiff. The lioness left the horse and turned on the dog, killed it, but was then chased and cornered in a small grain store and recaptured. The horse was quite seriously wounded and, according to the report in *Truman's Exeter Flying Post*, was not expected to survive, but surprisingly the horse seems to have recovered and continued working. It is perhaps of interest that Joseph Pike – the guard – seems to have made no effort to use his firearms to drive off the animal. The menagerie itself benefited from the event, for its advertising now featured the famous lioness.

The Turnpike Acts included a concession which allowed two to six dogs through without payment. Small tradesmen, pedlars and hawkers naturally took advantage and carried their stock in small carts drawn by a team of dogs. Sometimes coach horses were startled by the dogs and shied away, causing an accident. In August 1837 a meeting of the Turnpike Trustees of Leicester heard a report on the accident sustained by the London to Manchester coach, which was upset on 30 July between Derby and Leicester. The horses took fright at a dog team which upset the coach and led to several passengers being injured, the coachman fatally. The number of these dog carts was increasing and this was not the only accident. Lord Russell thought legal advice should be sought to see if any action could be taken by the office. The answer was that they were legal and action could only be taken if the dogs were negligent or savage.[131] Dog carts were officially banned within fifteen miles of Charing Cross in 1840 and a total ban was proclaimed in 1855, resulting in a massive cull of the dogs.[132]

When the coach reached its destination it became accepted custom that the driver and guard would be tipped. In addition to their fixed wages the guard and coachman did quite well through tips from both passengers, and perhaps the Postmasters on their routes. On 13 October 1796 Hasker received a letter from a traveller, J. Davis, who complained that he had been obliged to give fees to two coachmen between Exeter and Taunton and another coachman and guard between Taunton and Bath. Hasker replied on the same day, saying that no coachman or guard was allowed to claim 'Vails as a right', but that the custom had developed of giving a shilling to the guard and coachman at 'the end of the ground.' This was a courtesy and not a duty. If no money was forthcoming then they might solicit a tip, but no more, and if the drive was less than thirty miles then they should count themselves satisfied with 6 pence from each passenger. In this particular case the driver apparently did better than the guard who, 'might add to his abusive language of which I understand he is apt to use too much.' Hasker suspended the guard and called him to London to promise better behaviour in future and, if Mr Davis wished, to make a personal apology.[133]

The tipping problem persisted, and on 14 November 1825 Freeling wrote in his Order Book about passengers tipping the guard and coachman, but stressed that they must not aggressively solicit tips. Hasker specifically forbade such ideas.[134] According to Harper (*op. cit.*) the collecting of tips was known as capping, as the coachman went round with his hat to collect the money. The amount of tips obviously varied from route to route, and guards on lesser runs made much smaller incomes from tips. By the 1830s this was officially recognised and it was the practice that when a guard on a well-paid route left, the post was offered to guards of good reputation. The same notice from Hasker warned the guards about attempts to make a little extra cash on the side by carrying unauthorised letters or packages, anybody found doing so would be sacked. It was known that many guards could make several pounds a week in addition to their wages by some recognised 'fiddles', such as 'shouldering' when a passenger paid for a short journey of which the proprietors knew nothing. The fare was often split between the guard and driver on these occasions.

Aside from guarding the mail, inspecting the coach, reins and passengers, blowing his horn, assisting the coachman and collecting and delivering the bags there were still other duties for the guard. It must be remembered that from 1793 to 1815 the Napoleonic Wars were raging, and very much affected life in the country, and as a result the guards were given extra orders. One unusual responsibility was to watch out for escaped prisoners-of-war. Large numbers of French prisoners-of-war were housed in Great Britain and many French officers were allowed a degree of freedom if they gave their parole. This was a solemn promise that they would not attempt to escape. Such was the code of honour of the period that in general the parole held, but of course there were a few who broke it. To escape they needed to get to the coast, which could well mean taking a coach trip at some point. In December 1811 a letter from the Transport Board asked all guards to be on the alert for any such parole breakers. In 1812 Freeling circulated all Postmasters and guards seeking their support. He suggested that they look out for foreigners, who were supposed be in possession of a passport from the Transport Board or Alien Office, if they had one they were to be checked for any signs of alteration, erasures or over-writing, especially so if these were in a foreign hand. If they had any suspicions then the person was to be detained, if they were then found to be an escapee then there was a ten guinea reward. This would also be available to any guard who made a capture. However, since the guard could not stop to deal with the matter they were to give the details to the proprietor or the Postmaster.[135] This procedure was a little less drastic than that reported by one writer, who claimed the guards had permission to shoot any such unfortunate.

Inevitably the guards did not always live up to the high ideals expected of them, and there were one or two instances recorded in the archives of alleged misbehaviour. In July 1808 a solicitor reported a complaint brought by Christiana Simpson against Joseph Sayer – the Leeds mail guard – for a violent assault, he recommended that Sayer be prosecuted. However, on 3 November a letter was received from Messrs Townend and Oldfield of York, stating that the woman 'was persuaded to accept a pecuniary satisfaction of the guard.'[136] It was not only the guards who sometimes lapsed and James Dunn, a coachman driving between Abergavenny and Llandveby (?), was dismissed but then petitioned for reinstatement. Mr Freeling wrote to the Postmaster General:

> I presume that their Lordships cannot fail to approve of Mr Hasker's act in having obtained the dismissal of the driver, and that there are no good reasons assigned for his reinstatement. A coachman who gets drunk, sleeps on his box, and is insolent to the officer who urges him not to harm the public service by unnecessary delays, ought not to experience any favor (sic) whatever.

The Postmaster added a note; 'This man certainly deserves no favour.'[137]

When he reached the end of his stage the guard passed over the time bill and timepiece, as has been mentioned the guards were not always as careful as they should have been at this point. What happened to his firearms is unclear, but it seems likely that each pair of pistols and blunderbusses were personal issue, so it is almost certain that he took them with him. As soon as his return coach arrived he checked the coach and then mounted-up and set off to his home base. As seen above, on reaching London the bags were loaded into a small cart and taken off to Lombard Street offices, he was then free to go off-duty after reporting any problems and handing in the duly completed time bill.

Despite the hardships the guards endured they seem to have been a dedicated group, and the few surviving lists suggest most stayed in their job for many years. Their wage may have been fairly small, and when new recruits worked as stand-ins – during bad weather or the like – the newcomers often demanded, and got, a much higher rate. Later on there was considerable discussion over a proposal to put the guards on a fixed wage and stop the practice of collecting tips. The response was mixed, for those guards on the few remaining busy routes saw that their earnings were likely to fall and so were not always keen on the change. Those guards on routes being undercut by the railways, who had seen the number of passengers steadily diminishing, were in favour. In April 1840 guards expressed the wish to remain on the old rates rather than the Treasury ones on offer.[138]

What little evidence the archives offer seems to indicate that some, if not all, of the guards worked on a daily basis. However, some arrangements presumably existed to give them some time off. What is made clear is that they worked hard, suffered some considerable physical discomfort and were susceptible to all human weaknesses. Each journey was, to use the old cliché, a challenge, with the possibility of accident, death, injury or a handsome tip at the end.

THE ROADS

On paper Palmer's proposals offered every hope of a speedier, safer postal service. However there was one potentially serious handicap and it fell largely outside the control of the mail office; the roads of Britain. Even with the best planning, the best horses and the finest coaches, if the roads were poor then the viability of his plans had to be in doubt. The condition of Britain's eighteenth-century roads was varied; ranging from the London to Bath road, rated first class in contemporary terms, to some that were almost impassable, even in good weather. Those in Ireland were generally thought to be the worst. Among the correspondence dealing with disputes over payment is a statement of the situation by W.H. Bourne, which mentions the poor condition of Irish roads prior to 1791. It says that detours were inevitable in Ireland and that they caused delays, in one place it needed two men carrying long poles to prod and explore the ground in order to get the coach safely along a causeway over a morass flooded by the River Shannon.[1] Scotland was also poorly served, except for a military network of roads generated by General Wade during the Jacobite rebellions of the early eighteenth century.

The main cause of the poor condition of the roads was the lack of any central planning. In order to maintain anything approaching a reliable national road system there has to be a common plan. From the time the Romans left the country there had been no overall authority. When the Romans came to England in AD 43 they found some well-established, ancient roads that they developed. By AD 95 they had a very extensive and wide-ranging road system in place. The roads were planned and built to last, with the most important ones made up of as many as five layers of material. These military roads were given very firm foundations, they were at least 14ft (4.2m) wide and had a gravel surface and a ditch on either side. The roads and bridges were regularly inspected and they were maintained with money from Imperial funds.

The main Imperial roads radiated from a milestone set at the centre of Rome, the milestone bore the name of the important cities of the Empire together with their distance in miles from the capital. Each of these main roads was under the control of a keeper and there was an overall commissioner to supervise them.

To the Mail Guards.

(CIRCULAR.)

GENERAL POST OFFICE,
December 5th, 1811.

SIR,

AT this Season, and particularly this Year, when in consequence of the warm Autumn, and wet Weather, the Horses are very weak, and Roads very heavy, it is incumbent on you to use every possible exertion at Changing Places, and where Stoppages are made at Post Offices or otherwise; so that if even a Minute can be saved in changing Horses, or going to and from the Offices, or where the Coachmen may necessarily stop, (for they must not be permitted to stop otherwise) by these and such Exertions (the Means of obtaining which occur every Journey) it is expected the Mails will be kept more regular to Time than they have been for some Days past.—On any Occurrence where you cannot keep Time, you are expected to write me Particulars.

I am,

Yours, &c.

T. HASKER.

The difficulties of winter travel are clear in this circular, which stresses the need to make every effort to keep to the timetable. (PO 10/6, no.73)

The Romans were familiar with staging, for there was an organised system of mail routes in Italy. This had first been set up during the Republic and was completed during the reign of the Emperor Augustus.

Such was the skill of the Roman road builders that their roads remained in use for centuries, largely because they had all the characteristics of a good road. They were built on a firm foundation, were well drained and had hardwearing surfaces. When the legions left Britain in the fifth century all central control ended, and from then until the nineteenth and twentieth centuries roads were under local control, as many still are. Standards were set by the local authorities, but road repairs were generally considered to be of low priority and for long periods there was virtually no road maintenance. Some roads leading to places of pilgrimage like Canterbury were reasonably well maintained to ensure the steady flow of pilgrims.

During the early Middle Ages the responsibility for maintaining the roads lay with the Lord of the Manor. Bridges were also a local responsibility, but some were associated with the church and were therefore a little better cared for than others. This connection was largely lost with the dissolution of the monasteries in Tudor times, an event which meant roads were even more neglected. During earlier times the condition of roads and bridges were a matter of minor importance to the majority of the population. Travel was very limited and, in general, was restricted to the main roads.

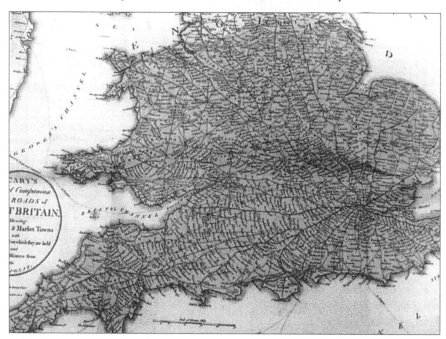

Two Hundred Pounds Reward.

4%4

GENERAL POST OFFICE,
Tuesday 3d July, 1798.

THE Post-Boy carrying the Mail from Bromley to Seven Oaks last Night was stopt about Two Miles from Farnborough, between the Hours of Ten and Eleven o'Clock, by a single Highwayman, who presented a Horse Pistol and demanded the Mail, which the Boy gave him. He offered the Robber Half a Guinea, but he declined taking it.

The Robber is described to be a Young Man, Middle Size, had on a Drab coloured Great Coat, and rode a Horse with a White Face. The same Man, as supposed, passed through the Turnpike Gate at Pratt's Bottom, towards Riverhead, on Horseback, about Three o'Clock in the Afternoon, returned about Seven in the Evening, and asked his Way to Croydon: He had a Pair of small Saddle Bags, and had the Appearance of a London Rider in the Opinion of the Turnpike-man.

The Bags taken away are,

Seven Oaks,	Battle,
Tunbridge,	Rye,
Lamberhurst,	Hastings.

Whoever shall apprehend and convict, or cause to be apprehended and convicted, the Person who committed this Robbery, will be entitled to a Reward of TWO HUNDRED POUNDS, over and above the Reward of FORTY POUNDS given by Act of Parliament for apprehending Highwaymen: Or if any Person, whether an Accomplice in the Robbery, or knowing thereof, shall surrender himself and make Discovery, whereby the Person who committed the same may be apprehended and brought to Justice, such Discoverer will be entitled to the same Reward of TWO HUNDRED POUNDS, and will also receive His Majesty's most gracious Pardon.

By Command of the Postmaster-General,

FRANCIS FREELING.
SECRETARY.

Above: A section of one of Carey's road maps. This gives some idea of the enormous growth in the number of mail and stagecoach routes in use prior to the development of the railways.

Left: The usual amount offered by the Post Office for the conviction of robbers was £200, a substantial sum at the time. (PO 107/36)

Opposite: One of Carey's maps showing the various turnpike trusts around London in July 1790. The number of turnpikes steadily increased during the eighteenth and early nineteenth centuries, and lingered on until well into the latter century.

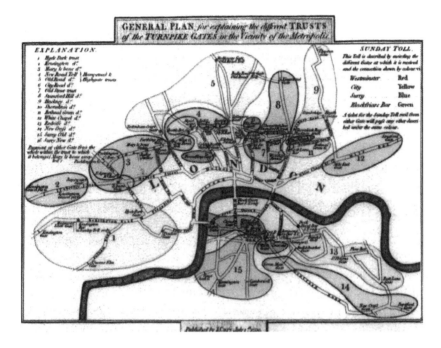

The minor roads were less used and probably deteriorated faster. Some form of local tax – or toll – to raise money for their care was very occasionally instituted by the lord or governing body, but in reality this was a rare occurrence. The travels of the King and nobles visiting their scattered estates meant that some roads were better cared for than others. As commerce developed, trade fairs became established and the number of pilgrimages increased, there were obviously more people on the move.

By the sixteenth century contemporary accounts suggest that the roads were at their worst, and indeed many were impassable in winter. Accidents and long delays were commonplace, and people only undertook any journey when there was no alternative. Matters became so bad that eventually Parliament was forced to take action in an attempt to improve the situation. In 1555 Parliament passed an Act (2&3 Philip and Mary c8) which placed responsibility for maintaining the roads firmly on the parish. The local community as a whole became duty-bound to contribute time and labour to the maintenance of the roads within their boundaries, the amount of time and effort demanded was determined by how much land each individual owned. Those with land worth £50 were obliged to provide a horse, cart and two men, and every member of the parish was ordered to work for four days a year on the roads and bridges.

One unfortunate parishioner was elected to supervise the work and became known as the Surveyor of Highways – or some similar title. He was ordered to carry out a survey of all the parish roads and note any faults, which he would then announce publicly in church. Once reported, the law stipulated that the faults had to be repaired within thirty days, failure to do so obliged the surveyor to have the work done and any costs were charged to the parish. The money came from the parish community chest, into which went all the fines levied by the Manorial court. There is no doubt that, despite a good deal of public grumbling, the Act brought about some improvement.

The Act was modified in 1563 to become the Statute for Mending of Highways, and the statutory labour period was extended from four to six days a year. Probably of more importance was the fact that the local justices of the peace were granted the power to levy quite hefty fines on any parish which failed to carry out their obligations. Since few, if any, of the Surveyors had any technical knowledge, the repairs tended to be somewhat basic – ruts and potholes were filled in with any material available and the surface was flattened. However, by the 1580s specialist workmen were being used to work on the roads. In a proclamation of 1586 for regulating London wages, the paver was reckoned to earn 9p a day plus food and drink whilst a common labourer was valued at 5p a day plus food and drink. The basic road was 'soft surfaced', but this was not too important since wheeled traffic was relatively uncommon, although hoofed traffic did cause some damage.

By the seventeenth century increased trade and commerce placed greater pressure on the parishes to keep the roads in good condition. By now there was also a 'Surveyor of the Highways to the King', and James I's travels around the country ensured that those counties through which he passed were reminded of their obligations. In 1622 the Home Counties were told that their roads were greatly decayed and that they should take immediate action to improve matters. Despite all these and other pressures there appears to have been little real improvement, with local surveyors claiming that they could not do their job, as the parishes would not pay their dues. The parishes blamed the poor state of the roads on the damage caused by the increasing number of heavy, four-wheeled carts using them.

Increased powers were given to the King's surveyor, and he tackled some of the recalcitrant local surveyors and did generate some improvements. However, the English Civil Wars (1642 – 1649) meant that roads were once again neglected, but in 1650 it was decided to take action. In 1652 two commissioners were appointed to prepare Ordinances to tackle the problems, and in 1654 they produced 'An Ordinance for Better Amending and Keeping in Repair the Common Highwaies within this Nation.' Henceforth, in every parish two of the wealthier members were to be elected as surveyors. If no person was qualified then other local officials, the Overseers of the Poor, had to do the job or pay a fine of £10. Within ten days of their appointment they were to survey the entire parish, draw up lists of repairs or pay a fine of ten pounds. More importantly, they were given the right to decide on whether a local tax to raise the money to pay for the repairs should be established. Limitations were placed on the use of heavy wagons, and the sum effect of the law was a big improvement in the state of the roads.

After the Restoration of Charles II in 1660 a new man, Andrew Lawrence, was sworn in as 'Surveyor-General of the Highways and Guide of Ways, Bridges, Gates Causeis and Passages.' The growing attention to improving the roads led, in 1662, to another Act which authorised the levying of a tax — not to exceed 6 pence in the pound — to cover the cost of repairs. The pattern was now set and there was a small but steady improvement to the roads. It became increasingly common for the parish to pay the fine, this was so that the surveyor could hire workers to carry out the repairs rather than use the statutory local labour. This change led to the growth of a new trade, the 'paviour' — or road worker — whose standard of work was usually far better than that of reluctant parishioners.

One general complaint of parishes along main routes, and one with some justification, was that they were obliged to take responsibility for repairs that were mostly caused by passing — and not local — traffic. The passing traffic was not obliged to make any contribution towards the costs borne by the parish. One obvious solution was to impose a tax on all the users of the roads, and in 1663 the Turnpike Act was enacted. Despite initial unpopularity the idea was gradually accepted, and it was decided that the number of turnpikes would be increased at an enormous rate. The idea had merit, but it was soon to be somewhat perverted. There was a growing emphasis on the financial side of the turnpikes, for some trustees saw that there was money to be made, and more and more turnpikes were established with this feature in mind. Later on, many of the trusts found themselves in financial difficulty, having borrowed money in expectation of a bigger income than that which was generated.

During the seventeenth century there was a steady growth in the number of wheeled wagons, and their great weight increased the damage to the roads. There was much discussion about the ideal width of tyres and whether two wheels were better than four. This increase in numbers was not only in commercial vehicles, but also in personal use as coaches became more popular. In London there was a great increase in the number of hackney carriages, which were used more and more for short, local journeys, so much so that restrictions on their numbers were introduced. However, the increase in carriage traffic was limited by the state of the roads, and often conditions were still so bad that it was usually much quicker and safer to go on horseback.

The introduction of turnpikes gathered pace in the eighteenth century, the number eventually reached around 1,100 and covered some 23,000 miles of road. Each new turnpike required legislation before it could be set up and authority was usually granted for a period of twenty-one years. At their quarterly sessions the local justices were allowed to authorise bodies of trustees to supervise the erection, at certain points on the road, of a form of gate through which few were allowed unless they paid a fee. Many of the trustees were often uninterested and took little part in the functioning of the trust. The surveyor was the important officer, and he was supposed to inspect the road and report to the trustees on what repairs were needed. There were graduated rates of toll; with those on foot passing freely and heavy wagons paying the most. The income from these tolls would go towards the maintenance of the roads. Setting up a turnpike imposed costs on the trustees, for pivoted gates were obviously needed as well as someone to look after them. As the road was in use for twenty-four hours a day, that attendant had to be on site for the whole period. This meant accommodation was needed and so small tollhouses were built by the gate. Some of these keepers kept a firearm handy, and there are accounts of those trying to dodge payment being fired on.

The turnpikes proliferated during the eighteenth century, then in 1755 a General Turnpike Act was passed. This made turnpikes compulsory where they were needed, although it seems that this rule was not applied countrywide. One problem was meeting the definition of 'where they were needed'; within the organisation there was no system of accounting, and as the proportion of income that went on the road was arbitrary the trustees could dispose of the income more or less as they wished. The cost of the toll was not fixed, but generally the price was one penny for a horse, rising to 6 pence for carts, while those on foot and some privileged travellers passed through for nothing.

To the Mail Guards.

(CIRCULAR.)

GENERAL POST OFFICE,
December 5th, 1811.

SIR,

AT this Season, and particularly this Year, when in consequence of the warm Autumn, and wet Weather, the Horses are very weak, and Roads very heavy, it is incumbent on you to use every possible exertion at Changing Places, and where Stoppages are made at Post Offices or otherwise; so that if even a Minute can be saved in changing Horses, or going to and from the Offices, or where the Coachmen may necessarily stop, (for they must not be permitted to stop otherwise) by these and such Exertions (the Means of obtaining which occur every Journey) it is expected the Mails will be kept more regular to Time than they have been for some Days past.—On any Occurrence where you cannot keep Time, you are expected to write me Particulars.

I am,

Yours, &c.

T. HASKER.

Another of Hasker's exhortations to the guards to make every effort – despite adverse conditions – to keep to their time bills. (PO 10/6/73)

From 1784 mail coaches did not have to pay tolls; this was not popular with the trustees who saw a potential income denied in a perfectly legal fashion. This toll exemption seems not to have applied uniformly in Scotland, where the mail coaches were passed through without delay, they were then recorded and a bill submitted. The legal position of the Post Office over charges levied at turnpikes was open to debate, and over the years several cases went to court. The question was not so much about the coaches but rather the mail itself, the exemption did not apply if the mail coach was not carrying mail. In 1837 Freeling was advised that tolls were not payable on hired chaises or extra horses when they were employed in bad weather. Despite the defects in the system the Turnpike trusts did effect some improvement in the condition of the roads.

Turnpikes were, mostly, limited to the major routes and minor side roads, those in towns remained in a terrible condition. Equally, the turnpikes did provoke quite a lot of opposition; sabotage and minor riots were not uncommon and the tearing down of a turnpike was made a capital offence. One way of expressing resentment was to block the roads with any large object, and at night the coach lamps were unlikely to illuminate the obstacle until the coach was practically on it. The mail coaches suffered on a number of occasions from small barricades on the road, at these times horses, coach and passengers were at risk from these potential death traps. The Post Office regularly offered cash rewards for information, but never with a great deal of success. The majority of cases occurred early in the nineteenth century and one such case, recorded in 1820, involved two large wagon wheels, followed half a mile further on by two gates and a thirty-foot tree placed on the road. The driver and guard must have been very alert, very observant or perhaps just very lucky, for the coach was not halted or overturned. The Office offered a £20 reward for information on this one.[2] This amount seems to have been the standard rate, for it was offered in June 1804 for information about a gate left on the turnpike road near Welwyn Green.[3] In February 1811 the saboteurs were more successful in their efforts:

General Post Office

26 February 1811
Whereas some malicious persons did on the night of Sunday the 17th Instant willfully place a large tree across the centre of the turnpike-road between Leeming Inn and Borough bridge whereby the mail-coach was overturned, part of the carriage broke and the coachman and guard hurt.
In order to bring the offenders to Justice His Majesty's Postmaster-General hereby offer a reward of FIFTY POUNDS to be paid upon conviction.

By command of the Postmaster-General
F. Freeling,
Secretary.[4]

Fifty Pounds
REWARD.

WHEREAS on the Night of Saturday the 28th Instant, about Eleven o'Clock, the Postman conveying the MAIL between *Whitehaven* and *Cockermouth*, was Fired at with a Gun loaden with Shot, at or near the Foot of Winscales Brow, by some Person or Persons unknown, with an apparent Intent to *Rob the Mail*, by which he was Wounded in the Head and Face.

NOTICE is hereby Given,

THAT whoever shall Apprehend and Convict, or cause to be Apprehended and Convicted, the Person or Persons who committed this Outrage, will be entitled to a REWARD of FIFTY POUNDS; or if an Accomplice in the Transaction will surrender himself and make discovery, whereby the Person who committed the same may be Apprehended and brought to Justice, such Discoverer will be

ENTITLED TO THE SAID

REWARD of 50 POUNDS
AND WILL ALSO RECEIVE

His Majesty's Most Gracious Pardon.

WILLIAM HODGSON,
Surveyor General Post Office.

POST OFFICE, COCKERMOUTH,
30th NOVEMBER, 1812.

BAILEY, Printer, COCKERMOUTH.

Reward offered for help with an attempted robbery in November 1812. It was probably on a rider since it just mentions 'postman'. It is offering a pardon to an accomplice if he comes forward to name the villain. (PO 107/52)

The same sum was offered in May 1812 when eleven gates were placed on the turnpike road between Burton and Kendal, all of which were spotted and avoided.[5]

In the 1830s and early 1840s there was a very serious outbreak of anti-turnpike rioting in Wales. By then the mail coaches were in decline, although the Irish mail was still using this route but, judging by the archives, the mail seems not to have been much affected by these riots. They came to be known as the 'Rebecca riots', although quite why is much debated. Many of those taking part wore women's clothes as a disguise, one leading character was addressed as Becca, and there was also a connection made with a biblical verse which mentioned Rebecca and referred to gates.

Despite the improvement brought about by the turnpikes the roads remained largely quite poor. The archives contain a number of reports about problems encountered by the mail coaches. A note of March 1795 commented that the roads were improving but that there were still too many deep holes forcing the driver to slow down which was causing accidents. The York coach, going down from Huntingdon, was so severely jarred that it was reported that, 'both coachman and guard chucked from their seat.'[6] Another report said that the guard was standing blowing his horn when the coach hit a bad patch and that he was shaken off in mid-blast.

Engraving of the trial run from London to Bristol in August 1784. It is an ordinary stagecoach with four passengers – one is possibly Bonnor. The guard carries one blunderbuss with another slung on a cross belt.

The intended speed of a ride in 1827 was 7mph, but many failed to reach that figure. Indeed a survey was made of those at 6mph and a few made only 5mph. Whilst there were other factors, bad roads figure in several explanations of these figures.[7]

When a stretch of road became too bad the office would usually contact the parish, remind them of their duty and request some repair work. If this approach failed to bring about the desired effect then the surveyors would recommend going to the law and forcing some action. On one occasion surveyors inspected Stratford Bridge from both the Essex and Suffolk sides but could get no agreement on the matter of repairs, so it was decided that the solicitor should write to them threatening that if the parish did not take action immediately they would be indicted before the court.[8]

As late as August 1837 the road between Alfreton and Chesterfield was in such a dangerous condition that the office solicitor was instructed to complain to the clerk of the local trust.[9] On 29 April 1838 a letter from guard Wm (?)Aldis reported that, when the coach was going from Sutton to Lynn on Friday the seventeenth of that month, the pavement near Sutton Bridge gate was in a very bad state. There was a heap of dirt on the side of the road, and as the front wheels of the coach went over it the coachman was jerked off. Both wheels passed over him and broke several of his ribs. The guard left him at Sutton where he 'now lay very bad', and the guard went on to Lynn with the coach. The driver complained about the horses to the horse keeper, saying that these were horses of Mr Coates about whom complaints had previously been made. On 5 May there was a report from the inspector – Mr Akers – in which he said that the horses were not too bad, he rather implied that the coachman may not have been in full control. The left ribs of the driver were broken but he appeared to be 'cheerly'.[10]

Many of the accidents that befell the guards were the result of being thrown or jerked from the coach as the wheels hit a particularly deep rut or wide hole. The Postmaster General paid the surgeons and apothecaries for their treatment of the injured guards. One archive[11] lists the payments made by Hasker for debts incurred as a result of the weather or accidents, several feature guards;

July 16th 1788 paid J. Edward surgeon for treating Lewis Williams guard of Newmarket coach whose leg was much bruised in fall from coach 19/6.

7th September 1790 paid to Mr Laycock surgeon for medicine & c administered to Wm. York guard of Manchester coach hurt in fall from coach £0-11-4.
12th June 1791 attendance to Alex Young Norwich mail guard who had his scull fractured by a fall £6-7-6.

13th June 1791 to R.E. Mason for the eating washing & c of the above Alex young before he was able to be removed £2-2-10.

10th August 1791 to T. Robertson for medicines and bleeding J. Denys Portsmouth guard who was hurted (sic) by a fall from the mail coach £2-3.

Extract from a Snow Book for January and February 1838, showing an extra horse authorised by the guard Greatheart. (10/101)

The Napoleonic Wars raged for more than twenty years and many French prisoners-of-war were lodged in Britain; the guards were encouraged to watch out for escapees. (PO 10/6 75)

(CIRCULAR.)

GENERAL POST-OFFICE,
January 20, 1812.

- SIR,

IT being supposed that Prisoners of War when breaking their Parole of Honor are in the habit of escaping in Mail Coaches, I am commanded by my Lords the Postmaster General to desire that you will question any suspicious Foreigner travelling by the Coach to which you are Guard, and give information to the Proprietor or Postmaster at the first Town at which you arrive.

Prisoners of War have Passports from the Transport Board or Alien Office, which they are bound to produce on being demanded, but any Document purporting to be a Passport is of no validity if filled up on erasures or in a Foreign Hand; if the Parties cannot produce a correct Passport from the above-named Offices, it may reasonably be concluded that they have broken their Parole, and those apprehending them will be allowed the usual Reward of TEN GUINEAS each.

As the Service will not admit your stopping on the Road to take such suspected Foreigners before a Magistrate, it must be done by the Proprietor or Postmaster, to whom as before stated, you must give Information of your suspicions, and acquaint me with the Circumstance that I may lay it before my Lords the Postmaster General.

I am,

SIR,

Yours, &c.

T. HASKER.

In December 1824 Lord Chichester requested a list of the trusts upon the North Road, there were eight and were separated by distances of three-and-a-quarter miles and twenty-one miles respectively. The report speaks of hills and flooding problems and remarks that the hill road leading into Grantham is, 'much cut down but in a bad state to travel now and beyond Grantham is Gonersby (?) Hill which, after all, will perhaps be avoided by another route.' There are other comments on bad patches.[12]

Around the middle of the century there were signs of a new approach to the roads and their condition, strangely enough one of the first to point the way was the blind John Metcalfe, 'blind Jack' of Knaresborough. John Metcalfe was a remarkable man who refused to let his disability stop him from trying anything. In 1765 an Act was passed authorising a turnpike between Harrogate and Boroughbridge, Metcalfe somehow persuaded the contractor to let him make three miles of the road. Under his supervision it was built both efficiently and well, so much so that he was then asked to undertake similar jobs, including building bridges.

In Ireland steps to improving the state of the roads were in hand, and the Statute of Labour, which forced parishioners to work on the roads, was abolished. In 1798 an Act modified the turnpikes. Under the Act three directors were elected to run the trust rather than the entire group, so making for an improvement in efficiency. In 1838 there were more complaints about the bad state of Irish roads, despite these problems the Board of Works disclaimed all responsibility and did nothing. Two surviving time bills for the Limerick and Cork coach along with the associated vehicles – coach 108 with timepiece 57 and coach 54 with timepiece 45 – have entries explaining that their late arrival was due to the hills, flooding and general poor condition of the roads.[13]

It was in Scotland that the transformation of road construction began. Various legal changes were made to the way in which the trusts were organised, and in 1803 Commissioners were appointed with the power to fund half the cost of road improvement, with the other half to be provided by the landowners. A year before a general survey of Scottish roads had been undertaken by Thomas Telford (1757-1834), and he was now put in charge of the new construction programme.

Telford, the son of a shepherd in Eskdale, was determined to improve his lot, and after serving an apprenticeship as a stonemason he went to Edinburgh. Impressing people with his ability and skill he was eventually appointed as County Surveyor for Shropshire in 1786, where he developed his skill in architecture and bridge building. In 1793 he worked for the Ellesmere Canal Company and gained national recognition for his use of modern methods and outstanding aptitude. In 1803 he was put in charge of the Scottish road programme, under his command the system was revolutionised and bridges and canals were developed. Traffic increased and there was great economic growth, emphasising to the rest of the country how the condition of the roads had an enormous impact on many aspects of their lives. Telford understood, like the Romans, the importance of a good foundation to a road, and he had the surface slightly cambered so that water drained off to the side instead of lying in puddles. His roads were wide and had a three layered base; the bottom was seven inches thick and hand set, the middle was another seven inch layer of broken stones and there was a top two inch layer of gravel or broken stone. The Post Office called upon him in 1825 to produce a report on mail roads through South Wales.[14]

With the example of Scotland before them the public was now more ready to support reform. In 1806 The Chairman of the Board of Agriculture, Sir John Sinclair, introduced a bill for the complete reform of road infrastructure. The public were invited to submit comments, ideas and plans for improvements, and among those offered was a lengthy one by a Scot, John Macadam (1756-1836). His paper impressed Sir John and he had it published as part of a commission report. Macadam had gained experience in America, and when he came back to Scotland after the War of Independence he became a turnpike trustee, involved with the management of roads. One of his basic ideas was to reverse the normal line of argument about road building. Much time and discussion had been spent on debating whether wide wheels were better than narrow, whether two wheels were better than four. He argued the opposite way, instead of adapting traffic to the road adapt the road to the traffic, roads could be made to cope with any type of wheel. Another of his basic beliefs was that road building was best done by men who understood the trade and knew what they were doing.

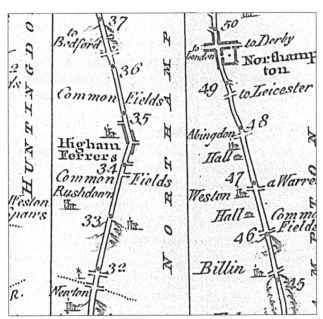

In October 1812 the Leeds coach was robbed near Higham Ferrers. Lavender, a Bow Street Runner, was involved in tracking down the notorious criminal responsible, Huffey White. (PO 10/6/70)

In 1816 he became General Surveyor of the Roads but, although the title is impressive he was only in charge of the roads and turnpikes in the Bristol Area. Even so, his work and the resulting improvement he brought about meant he acquired a fine reputation and his influence spread. One big change he introduced was the idea that the road surface was not worn away, but rather dispersed. Like Telford, he was positive about a good base and his system favoured a basic foundation of an eight inch layer of stones, each of which was to be not more than two or three inches in diameter. On top of this went a layer two inches thick, with some smaller stones to fill the gaps. The Post Office was well aware of the work of these experts, and in August 1829 Charles Johnson – writing from York – commented that the road between Sunderland and York needed the attention of Telford and Macadam.[15] There was an exchange of correspondence concerning road improvements and costs between Freeling and Macadam from 1818-1826.[16]

The improvement in roads in England, Scotland and Wales generated demand for some improvement in Ireland, this was speeded by the Parliamentary Union of 1801 which led to an increasing volume of communication. Telford had been asked to carry out a survey, with the basic idea of creating a good run of 194 miles between Shrewsbury and Holyhead. It was a formidable task, for the environment was very rugged, necessitating much blasting and building of bridges. Under Telford's control the plan was pushed through, with such an emphasis on safety that the public was both greatly impressed and reassured. It is perhaps rather ironic that there should have been this great improvement in road building just when the railways were making them far less important. The turnpike's importance had been decreasing steadily, in fact there were now so many and they were so far in debt that the system was drowning itself. They were gradually reduced in number as contracts were not renewed, but it was not until 1895 that the last turnpike, on the Anglesey and Holyhead road, was closed.

The importance of the roads had always been obvious, even more so when the mail coaches started to run. Post boys and carts might be slow, but there would be times when they were more successful in making a run than the coach – which was far more likely to be bogged down. As the system expanded and more and more routes were set up, the Mail Coach Office planners needed to know which routes had greater potential than others. They also had to know how the system was working, and for this information they relied on a small, dedicated band of employees – the surveyors. Although from Tudor times there were men who were *de facto* surveyors, it was with the Act of 1711 that the post was really recognised. Nevertheless, it was not until 1715 that six surveyors were appointed.

The Postmaster General wrote on 25 May 1715 to the Treasury, pointing out that supervision of the Deputy Postmasters was very slack and that they had the ability to make decisions irrespective of any central control. They also feared, quite rightly, that much mail was being dealt with unofficially, depriving them of income and that the privilege of franking was much abused. They asked therefore that the Treasury authorise them to appoint six officials at 20s a day each, they were intended to take one area of the country, check for any fraud and generally tighten control, to this the Treasury agreed.

From 1715 to the early 1780s the surveyors played an important role in tight-ening Allen's grip on the post. They visited their Deputy Postmasters at regular intervals, checking on the system and attempting to reduce the various malprac-tices indulged in by them and the post boys. The surveyors were important officers and no doubt earned their money, but it was the advent of Palmer that enhanced their status. As the men personally familiar with the different areas and personnel, it was to them that Todd turned when asked to comment on Palmer's reform.

As seen above, the response of all three was most unfriendly and, as Palmer commented, they proved that his system could not possibly work. Some of their objections were valid ones, but many were based on a state of mind resistant to innovation. One suggestion that provoked a particularly strong response was that which advocated forming a committee of local dignitaries that would offer sug-gestions for improving the service. The surveyors were indignant that it could even be suggested they were not the best qualified men to decide on what was best for the mail. If Bonnor is to be believed then the surveyor Allen was collabo-rating with Todd in his schemes to delay the implementation of the mail coach plan. The surveyors probably saw Palmer as a well-meaning but ignorant meddler in matters he did not understand. However, the animosity seems to have eventu-ally faded and, according to Foxell[17], a mutually enjoyable meal was held at the Inland office, with Palmer and Bonnor invited as honoured guests.

Stage-Coach Act

By 30th. Geo. 3d. Ch. 36.

THE Driver of any Coach, Chaife, or other Carriage, of the like Sort, drawn by 3 or more Horfes, travelling for Hire, admitting more than one Perfon on the Box befide himfelf, and 4 on the Roof; and if drawn by lefs than 3 Horfes, more than one Perfon on the Box and 3 on the Roof; is liable to the Penalty of 5s. for every Perfon above the number fo limited, to be Paid to the Collector of the Tolls at every Gate through which he Paffes; and fuch Driver attempting to evade the Act by fetting down or taking up Paffengers, to be imprifon'd not more than one Mouth, nor lefs than 14 Days.

Penalties to be recovered as Turnpike Tolls are.

The Name of the Proprietor to be painted on each Door, except Mail-Coaches.

The Driver not to permit any perfon to Drive without the Confent of the Paffengers within, nor quit his Box without reafonable Occafion, nor longer than fuch Occafion may require, and if by furioufly Driving, or by any act of Negligence or Mifconduct, he fhall overturn the Carriage or in any other manner endanger the Perfons, or property of the Paffengers, or Owners of the Carriage, he fhall for every Offence forfeit not more than 5l, nor lefs than 40s.

The perfon acting as Guard to any fuch Carriage, firing off his Arms, while the Coach is going on the Road, or going through, or ftanding in a Town, otherwife than for the Defence of fuch Coach, fhall for every Offence forfeit 10s.

Half of the two laft mentioned penalties to go to the Informer, the other half to the furveyors of the Highways.

If the Driver neglects to obey the Juftice's fummons, or cannot be found, the Owner of the Carriage to be anfwerable.

The Stage Coach Act of 1790 contained several clauses that applied specifically to the mail coaches.

With Palmer established in post he divided the country into six districts, each under the control of a surveyor on a salary of £100 per annum, plus a guinea a day travelling allowance. Much of the surveyors' time was taken up with their 'riding work', where they visited and checked on the local Deputy Postmasters. Carteret, when writing to the Treasury, justified Palmer's request for increased staff by commenting that many of the past problems in the Post Office were due to having only three surveyors to cover the whole system – including over 700 deputies. Under the Palmer system surveyors would reside in their districts and were to keep a full diary of riding work.[18] The posts were approved and confirmed on 15 March 1787, with the six named as Hodgson, Wilkinson, Lott, Woodcock, Saverland and Western. Five of the English surveyors, along with one Scottish and two deputy superintendants (sic), were each allocated a guard, 'which is occasionally employed by them as a servant.' They also acted as supernumerary guard when any of the others upon the road were taken ill. On 17 October 1792 the Postmaster General wrote to the Treasury outlining the arrangement. They did not want to deprive their men of any of the advantage that they had enjoyed for some time, especially as, 'our surveyors are discharging their duty with great attention and assiduity.' However, the Postmaster General said that they had no authority to pay this allowance of 10s 6d a week which:

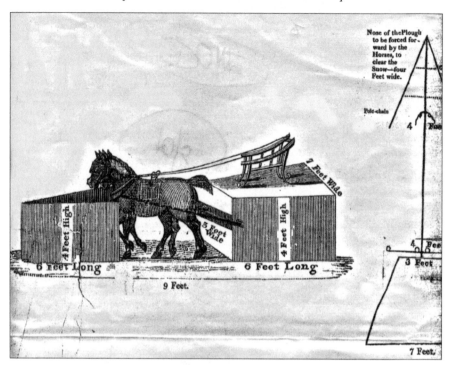

Floods and snow were the two main problems for coaches and there were various schemes to overcome the snow. Most consisted of plans for some form of horse-powered plough. The records show that some were used, although their efficiency was disputed. (PO 10/232)

...with a uniform amounts to about 30 guineas per annum for each, or 230 guineas a year for 8 guards. We request your Lordships permission for our continuing this expense.[19]

Hasker also drew attention to the set up, but the outcome is unclear since the records, so far, have not provided us with an answer. The Surveyors kept their diaries and submitted them monthly, although in the early days Hasker liked to see them weekly in order to assess the new routes. The Postmaster General was in favour of extensive diaries, and in August 1790 he expressed the firm opinion that 'a riding work book setting out work of each deputy, places he goes and what distance and at what price is indispensably necessary.'[20] Whilst no diary appears to have survived, a number of their later returns remain – including a group for 1826. (See p100).

When the Surveyor Hodgson wrote in asking that these trips and diaries be dropped on account of his ill-health and the fact that they involved so much work, the Postmaster General was quite curt in his reply, 'one man's indolence and ill-health was no reason to drop an agreed term.'[21] The Postmaster General was soon

on Hodgson's case again, this time over his very high expenditure on chaises –
because his health did not allow him to ride a horse. He demanded a medical cer-
tificate from a respectable medical man to say that Hodgson was indeed incapable
of horse riding (*ibid*). Shortly after, in December 1792, the Postmaster General
entered in his report:

> …tell the Comp. Gl that Mr Pitt spoke to their Lordships again upon the sub-
> ject of the Surveyors Journals yesterday that he expressed his opinion of their
> utility and necessity in the strongest terms, and that he has ordered the PMG to
> give this long and full notice viz that if they are not ready and delivered into the
> Board by the 5th of April next whoever is deficient will infallibly be dismissed
> therefore the Compl Genl will give notice to all the surveyors that they may
> know finally and decidedly what to expect.

The Surveyors were generally consulted on matters of policy, as can be seen in
this discussion about arming the riders. In 1832 a summary of office staff and job
descriptions was drawn up and the Surveyors duties listed:

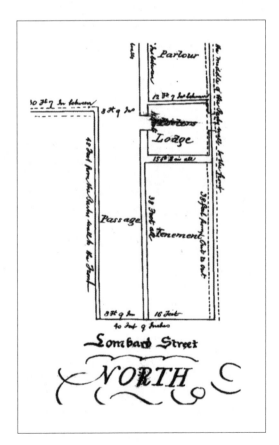

Details of the Mail Coach Office
as given in the auction sale
catalogue of 1831. (PO 91/12)

Part of the façade of
the Lombard Street
office, *c.*1800.

An internal view of
the sorting office.
(PO 46)

The Surveyors are selected from the most important officers of the department,
they are required to visit frequently the post offices in their respective districts
for the purpose of inspecting the mode in which the Deputy Postmasters
perform their business-they take charge of offices which become vacant and
instruct all Deputy Postmasters in the discharge of their duty they make contracts for the conveyance of the mails other than be Mail Coaches and maintain
proper discipline in the Horse and Foot posts.

They were also expected to suggest any improvements and keep the Board fully
informed.[22]

A few mail routes had to cross rivers, which obviously involved the use of ferries, the guards would have to accompany the mail on what were often rather wet crossings. The charges for crossing in such vessels were a matter of negotiation. One occasion was reported in April 1838 between the Post Office and the proprietors of a ferry across the Severn River, who demanded £100 to transport guard and mail. The Post Office replied with an offer of £36-10-0 (£36.50p), this was dismissed out of hand but a generous counter-offer of £60 was quickly made. Back came the mail with an improved offer of £40, which was also rejected at which point negotiations stalled. The Post Office made a final offer of £50, which was finally accepted and a deal was struck with the Bristol to Carmarthen mail. In September passengers on the Bristol and Liverpool runs complained that they were being ferried across the Severn in open boats. They got a good soaking and vowed that they would never travel that route again.[23] The same file contains several other letters concerning the use of ferries and steam boats, mainly complaints over a variety of matters.

In the mid-nineteenth century the Post Office underwent great changes; railways superseded coaches, postage stamps, pillar boxes and all manner of technology was incorporated into the system. In 1855 the Postmaster General, the Duke of Argyle, had 'A Circular to Surveyors' issued, in which their duties were detailed. It placed on them responsibility for the efficient organisation of the Post Office. It was a daunting task when the system was expanding so quickly and in so many directions, the number of surveyors was increased and some assistance was given. In the 1930s there was a move to decentralise the organisation and give some to the provinces, thus the position of surveyor mutated into the Regional Director.

Obviously the early surveyors had to travel quite a lot, and whilst much of it was done on horseback for the longer distances they used coaches. In the early days they were permitted free travel, but this made the contractors unhappy as they had lost a paying passenger. It was not only the surveyors that claimed the right to free travel, which only exacerbated the problem. Not unnaturally the contractors complained, and on 24 August 1792 a message for the Postmaster General settled the matter. It was pointed out that covering so much ground by horseback would prove to be too slow, for the surveyors were all-important. They had been travelling by coach, which represented a loss to the contractor of 4p a mile, while other officers were claiming free travel without any justification. The decision was reached that in future all surveyors would pay their fares in full, with the exception of Freeling and his two deputies, Wilson and Woolmer, and that the Treasury would be asked to approve the extra cost – reckoned to be about £150-£200.[24]

As the contractors were paid by the mile it was important that the office should know exactly the distance covered by their routes, indeed the surveyors were sometimes called upon to measure them. For this a 'waywiser' or large wheel

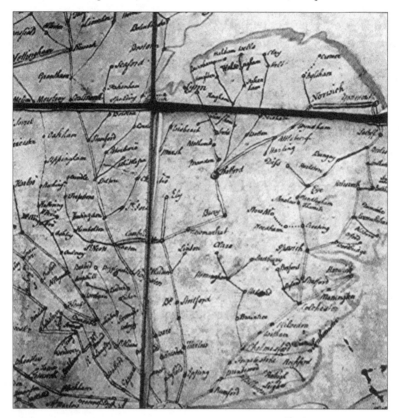

Section of the compiled map of mail coach routes. It was probably made up by Hasker and was referred to by the Postmaster General. (PO 96/21/pt1/fol 9)

was used, on which the number of revolutions was recorded and converted into distances. The surveyors did some measuring, and in April 1794 the Postmaster General authorised the purchase of a good wheel for each of the surveyors. He also thought it might be a good idea to carry out a full survey, but if Hasker thought that some of the existing measures were accurate then he was to use his discretion.[25] It was agreed that a full survey should be made, and the well-known cartographer John Carey (1754-1835) was asked to undertake the task. He was to be paid 6 pence a mile, the total bill would be £75 for 3,000 miles.[26] Not surprisingly, the check revealed some differences. The run from York to London was reported in January 1794 to be 196 miles, whereas the contractors were only paid for 193.[27]

The routes were all carefully surveyed and measured, and the routes were often tried out before a run was established. The archives include many detailed route maps, but one of particular interest is to be found in Post 61, part 2, fol.9. It is made up of a series of postcard-sized pieces of paper stuck onto a sheet of material – probably linen. It covers England and Wales, all the posts are labelled in script and the entire map gives the appearance of having been compiled in quite a piecemeal fashion. It could well be the map cited in Post 42/9 p 40, this refers to Mr Hasker, on 2 April 1792, being asked to complete, as quickly as possible, the manuscript map that he showed Lord Walsingham.

Carey's work was comprehensive and accurate, and there was to be some legal squabbling over the ownership of the rights to use it. On 18 July 1799 Carey sought permission to publicly declare that he was officially Surveyor to the Roads to The General Post Office. In fact he was only acting as such and had used the title without authority, Freeling had to report that there was no record of him being appointed to the position. The Postmasters General said that they could not agree to Carey's request as there was no record of it, however, they would state that nobody had been appointed to the post. This included Mr Coltman, who was apparently also attempting to lay claim to the title.[28]

There were further problems to come, Carey asked for legal clarification over the question of the publication of his maps, which he had made under the direction of the General Post Office. He said that permission was given as long as the price was kept as low as possible and control of the profits was ceded to him. Now a new edition of the standard reference work on the roads of the kingdom; *Paterson's Roads*[29], was in hand, and there was a question about passing over Carey's maps for publication. The Post Office Solicitors were consulted and they stated that the copyright of the maps lay with Carey and that the Post Office had his permission to publish them.[30] Carey continued to work for the Post Office, as is shown in the entry for Messrs I. & G. Carey for supplying maps and measuring roads from March 1833 to 31 December 1836.[31]

As the Post Office and other commercial enterprises developed there was a greatly increased amount of wheeled traffic using the roads, the growth of the railways led directly to growth in the roads, for the two systems were complementary. This increased traffic led to developments in road building, in general standards improved considerably but it was a two-sided problem. As roads improved so traffic increased, this increased wear and tear and meant the road surfaces suffered, which in turn led to more repairs and more development. The process continues today as motorways are constantly repaired and upgraded. Even the worst of modern roads would no doubt appear to the coach driver on his stage or mail coach as being absolutely first class.

8

THE COACH

From antiquity right up to the nineteenth century, the horse and its near relatives were the prime carriers in Europe. Horseback was the usual mode of personal travel and for transporting goods there was a line of packhorses or mules. Wagons were used for goods and chariots were used for war, while passenger coaches only made a relatively late appearance. Its development in the United Kingdom lagged behind that of the Continent, where from quite an early date they were in common use among the aristocracy. By the fifteenth century wagons were being modified to carry passengers as well as goods. There was the two-wheeler, drawn usually by one horse harnessed between a pair of shafts and the more stable, but slower, four-wheeler drawn by a team of two or more horses or oxen. On the larger coaches the horses were attached to the wagon or carriage by leather harness made up of various straps, chains and collars. Some form of covering was fitted over the body of the vehicle to provide shelter from the elements and primitive seating was added. By the second half of the sixteenth century passenger coaches were in fairly common use.

In the United Kingdom they were still regarded as being suspiciously effete, but in 1564 the coachman to Elizabeth I imported one. This gave them some social credibility and they gradually became accepted as a normal means of travelling. From then on ownership of a coach became far more socially acceptable, and by the mid-seventeenth century most English families of quality owned at least one. There was a growing custom for anybody with social pretensions to possess a coach as a status symbol, and Samuel Pepys was delighted when he purchased his first.[1] The majority were four-wheeled and they were manufactured in a variety of designs, all with different names.[2] Not only had the private use of coaches become far more widespread, but from about 1640 the commercial stage-coach was a common sight on the roads. They connected London to most of the important towns throughout the country and more and more people used them. Around this period the design of the coach was improved, features like windows were added and by the 1660s coaches were no longer a novelty. The social status of their owners was emphasised by carved decoration and gilding that became so excessive that legal restrictions were placed on them.

GENERAL POST-OFFICE,
December 12th 1816.

THE Guards are directed to pay every attention in Chaining the Wheel as the Coach goes down those Hills which require the use of the Chain: Also to have the Time-Bill dated by the Postmasters at such Places as are mentioned in the Bill, except in the middle of the Night.

THOs. HASKER.

Guards were not always as conscientious as they should have been, and consequently Hasker often had to remind them of their duties. Going downhill could be hazardous if the braking effect of the chain was absent. (PO 10/6, no. 110)

By the eighteenth century wagons and coaches were commonplace and the commercial stagecoach was flourishing. Well-defined routes traversed the country picking up and delivering both passengers and parcels at various inns along the way. However, they were still forbidden from carrying the mail for that was a royal monopoly. Details of fares and routes of the stagecoaches were advertised in directories and newspapers, as commerce and industry developed so the number of both passengers and routes increased. Businessmen like Palmer would have been fairly regular users of the stagecoach, and they cannot have failed to notice how much quicker they were than the mail carts and riders. It needed someone like Palmer to make the connection between mail and coach. While many privately owned coaches and some Post Office vehicles were drawn by two horses, the greater weight of the stage and mail coaches meant that most were drawn by a team of four horses. In bad weather – or on difficult terrain – as many as six horses were used.

The coach was, in a way, two separate items – the chassis with the wheels and the cabin to hold the passengers. Since the wheels were solid rimmed there was no softening of the bumps and thumps as the coach trundled along the roads. To prevent these impacts being passed directly to the passenger some sort of shock absorber was used. In the early days this took the form of large leather straps which were strung from front to back of the chassis to support the cabin. The pliability of the leather absorbed some of the impact – making for a slightly less bumpy ride – but there was still a drawback in that the cabin, being rather suspended in mid-air, was inclined to swing and tip which caused some unfortunate travellers to suffer a form of motion sickness. These straps were replaced from around 1805 with steel springs of various designs, these were more effective shock absorbers but they still imparted that swinging motion. Mathew Boulton, a renowned engineer and metal worker from Birmingham, when travelling in 1798 complained of being seriously upset after a coach journey. He was told by the innkeeper's wife – somewhat unhelpfully – that many passengers suffered in the same way.

In 1784, when the first mail coach ran between London and Bristol, an ordinary stagecoach was used although, in the interests of speed, it can be assumed that a lightweight model was chosen. Assuming that the engraving (see page 187) depicting the first run is accurate, the coach had a front bench for the driver and the guard – who were to be seated above a large storage space. At the rear is a box, later to become the mail box, and some luggage is stored on the roof. Inside the cabin, which is secured by straps, four passengers are seated. From the comments he made it is possible that Bonnor was one of them. For much of the early period the majority of mail coaches carried four inside and one outside passenger, although later on there were larger ones capable of taking many more. Most commercial stagecoaches always carried several passengers, with their luggage carried on the roof. In order to encourage contractors to participate in the conveyance of the mail, not only were they paid for transporting the mail but they were also given permission to carry paying passengers.

A.D. 1786 . . . . N° 1574.

Wheel Carriages.

BESANT'S SPECIFICATION.

TO ALL TO WHOM THESE PRESENTS SHALL COME, I, JOHN BESANT, of London, Engineer, send greeting.

WHEREAS His most Excellent Majesty King George the Third, by His Letters Patent under the Great Seal of Great Britain, bearing date the
5 Twenty-ninth day of November, in the twenty-seventh year of His reign, did give unto me, the said John Besant, His special licence that I, the said John Besant, during the term of years therein expressed, should and lawfully might make, use, exercise, and vend, within England, Wales, and Town of Berwick-upon-Tweed, my Invention of "CERTAIN IMPROVEMENTS OF
10 WHEEL CARRIAGES, BY MEANS OF WHICH THEY ARE LESS LIABLE TO OVERTURN, WILL FOLLOW WITH LESS DRAFT, GO DOWN HILL WITHOUT DISTRESSING THE HORSES, AND HAVE LESS FRICTION ON THE AXLETREE THAN ANY NOW IN USE;" in which said Letters Patent is contained a proviso obliging me, the said John Besant, under my hand and seal, to cause a particular description of the nature of my
15 said Invention, and how the same is to be performed, to be inrolled in His Majestie's High Court of Chancery within one calendar month next after the date of the said recited Letters Patent, as in and by the same, relation being thereunto had, may more fully and at large appear.

NOW KNOW YE, that in compliance with the said proviso, I, the said
20 John Besant, do hereby declare that my said Invention of Certain Improvements on Wheel Carriages by means of which they are Less Liable to Overturn, will Follow with Less Draft, go Down Hill without Distressing the Horses, and have Less Friction on the Axletree than any now in Use, is and are described

The first page of Besant's coach patent of 1786 detailing his self-acting brake, a feature which was not utilised by the Post Office. It was the hub fitting that was of most practical use.

Model of the
first mail coach
as shown in the
engraving on
p. 187, the seat for
the guard appears
to be lacking.
(Permission
of Bath Postal
Museum)

Conventional stagecoaches were used for the first year or two of the mail coach era, but from 1786 there was a gradual change to more appropriate coaches. The basic mail coach was composed of three parts; the front section with small wheels, the driver's seat and a storage space. The rear section was similar; it had larger wheels, the guard's seat and, most importantly, the mail box with a strong lock (the front and back wheeled structures were joined by a substantial bar, the perch). The box was fairly large and officially was used to carry only the mail bags and certain permitted items, mostly official materials. These permitted items were specified in a circular of 22 January 1813, it stated that nothing was to go into the box except:

> ...mail or items relating there to. These articles are materials for repairs of Mail
> Coaches passing between the Manufactory in London and Mr Vidler's Country
> Shops or work-men; lamps, new or repaired, Bye bags on their way to the Post
> Offices, Fire Arms, Guards New uniforms or other official articles necessary for
> the service.[3]

Steering the coach was achieved by allowing the front wheel assembly to pivot, but it was essential that it did not turn too far in either direction or it would stop rotating, act as a brake and overturn the coach. The wheels had to clear the body of the coach as they pivoted, and to prevent them striking the sides their diameter was deliberately made to be less than that of the rear ones; 42in (105cm) and 54in (135cm).

As the mail service expanded it became obvious that the ordinary coaches were less than ideal. Their heavy usage and speed over rough roads was enough to expose any weakness in construction and materials, the need for better, custom-built vehicles became apparent. John Besant, a coachbuilder of Millbank,

Westminster and Henley-on-Thames was granted a patent, number 1574, on 29 November 1786. His coach design offered improvements to the standard coach and attracted the attention of the Post Office. Besant claimed that his patent:

> ...by means of which they (wheeled carriages) are less liable to overturn, will follow with less draft, go down hill without distressing the horses, and have less friction on the axletree than any now in use.

Ironically, a main feature of his patent was a strap which operated automatically and applied a braking effect on the back wheels as a coach went down a hill. However, this idea was not adopted by the Post Office, who continued to use the old system. As a coach was descending the combined weight of the coach, passengers and luggage was pressing forward against the horses, at this point the guard dismounted and applied the breeching. Attached to the coach by a length of chain was a scoop-shaped metal shoe which was placed under the back wheel, effectively stopping it from turning and so slowing the coach. In 1816 Hasker thought it wise to remind the guards of the importance of breeching, pointing out that several accidents had been caused by the lack of it. There had been a major accident in March 1795 but no details were given[4], given these warnings the guards were to ensure that the horses did not go without breeching.[5]

Besant's patent also offered a means of attaching the passenger cabin to the main chassis, he claimed this made for smoother travel and would, 'only set the body down on its bottom between the fore and aft wheels when they lay flat on the ground.' In this case he was presumably talking about what would happen if the coach was involved in an accident.

One of the most important and practical ideas in his patent was an improved means of attaching wheels to the axles. The system commonly in use at the time was to drive a stout wedge through the axle on the outside of the hub of the wheel. To reduce friction between the wedge and the rotating hub a wooden disc was placed between the pin and the hub of the wheel. The wedge, subject to friction and stress, was vulnerable; if it sheered or broke then the chances were that the wheel would slide off the axle and probably overturn the coach. Besant's coach wheel was held more firmly in place by a neat arrangement of bolts and plates which considerably improved safety.

Besant took out another patent – number 1767 – in July 1790. This was for a series of multi-wheeled carriages with greatly improved suspension. One design was for a mobile home which would have a fire and:

> ...two or three apartments, so that a family of fifteen or twenty by sleeping by turns, may travel for months or years without leaving the carriage.

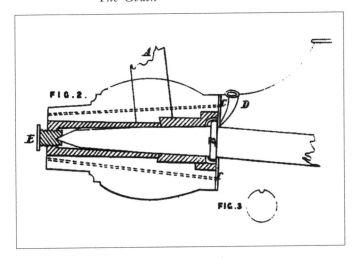

Detail of hub fitting from Besant's patent. This was much more secure than the earlier wedge fitting.

The designs were ingenious but not popular and few, if any, of these later specially designed coaches were made, certainly not by the Post Office.

Since there had been a number of breakdowns with the ordinary coaches, Besant's design appealed to Palmer and Bonnor and negotiations between them commenced. However, at the time Palmer was working in Paris negotiating an agreement with the French on a mutual postage system. This left Bonnor to deal with the matter and it seems that the decision to adopt Besant's design was primarily taken by him, but certainly with Palmer's agreement. Agreement was reached, and in 1786 the decision was made that in future Besant's patent coach would become the official mail coach. The contractors were told that they would be allowed to use only the new coach. Although the decision to adopt the patent coach had been made, no contracts between the Post Office and the manufacturers, Vidler and Besant, were signed. Whether this was a deliberate policy on the part of Palmer or just bureaucratic inefficiency is not clear, but the unfortunate effect was to create confusion later.

There the matter remained until 1791 when Vidler, the main coach maker, began making requests for a contract, something which he did not have at the time. Several years had elapsed since the original decision about Besant's coach, and those Post Office staff involved were a little unsure as to exactly what had been agreed. In order to clarify matters officials were questioned, documents were sorted out and on 26 July 1791 a corpus of information was assembled.[6] In a statement by Besant, dated 8 November 1786, he told of how he had invented a coach and made a prototype for the Post Office. He had agreed that he would supply nobody else for a year without an order from Palmer, in effect giving the Post a monopoly. Another document of the same date was from Bonnor, agreeing to the arrangement on Palmer's behalf and stating that the cost of the coach was to be decided by an independent assessor.

Time bill for the London to Liverpool run in January 1827, showing short breaks and very tight timing. (PO 10 /203)

Another document from Bonnor, dated 16 November, asked Besant for another six coaches. In December a report from the Post Office stated that Besant's coaches had been tested on the 'worst roads', they had performed very well and were much lighter than others. The letter went on to contain a dire warning, saying that in future all contractors were to use only this coach, and that if they refused then this letter was to count as their notice. They would have to pay the coach maker a fee of 2½ pence a mile, this price did not even include lamps, harness or extra items and they were to keep the coach in good repair. The Postmaster General issued a circular, saying that letters had been late because of coach break-downs, this was due to the poor workmanship and inferior materials used in their manufacture, whereas the new coaches were a great improvement.[7]

An agreement of 1787 between Palmer and Besant said that contractors had to use Bezant's (sic) coach for a period of fourteen years, Besant was to supply and repair such coaches as required while contractors would pay Besant 1¼d a mile. The guards were to check and report on coaches and Besant was to be given at least twelve months' notice to end the contract. Palmer had to pay over all moneys received from contractors for three months as compensation, if there were problems then arbitration would be sought.

There is also a copy of a 1788 agreement between Palmer and Besant to supply coaches for the conveyance of letters and parcels, subject to the orders which then list the details quoted above. In another agreement Besant was forbidden to build coaches for any other company unless Palmer gave his written permission. If Besant did supply any coaches to outsiders then they had to post a bond of £500, further they were not to be used to carry people and if the company eventually wanted to dispose of them then they had to give Palmer first refusal. Palmer would ensure that all contractors used Besant coaches and would pay him for the carriage, or use thereof, with a fair price to be assessed. Besant could build coaches on this principle for those not employed in stagecoach business, but if Palmer did not order carriages from Besant he would be free of constraint. Besant gave a bond of £500 as surety and Palmer did the same.

A long-term contract had been drawn up between the Mail Coach Office and Besant. The contract was for thirty years, a very long commitment:

London March 22nd 1788
I do hereby Promise to deliver to the contractors for the conveyance of his Majesty's mails to and from London and Pool on or before 29th day of March 1788 three new coaches made upon my patent principle and according to the orders of the Surveyor & Comptroller General of the Post Office the said coaches or a like number to be reserved for the entire use of the said contractors for the performance of the said duty and for the conveyance of passengers and parcels & agreeable to such directions as may from time to time be issued by or under the authority of the said Surveyor and Comptroller General proper coach houses cleaning & c to be provided and done at the expense of the said contractors and the coaches kept in thorough and constant repair by me and to remain the joint property of the several said contractors until the expiration of the period for which they may now or at any future date engage by draft or otherwise to pay for the use of the same at the stipulated rate of two pence half-penny per mile or five farthings per mile each way after which the said coaches are to become my property again

Signed for self & co John Besant
Witnessed Bonnor.[8]

The agreement makes clear that the user was leasing the coach and paying the maker a hiring price, whilst the Post Office was paying the contractor a fixed fee to carry the mail. Any passenger's fares or payment for private collection and delivery of parcels made the contractor extra profit. Against this income the contractor had to supply the drivers and horses – the number of which could run into hundreds – and the cost of stabling and fodder.[9]

Also included is an agreement dated 9 August 1788 between Besant, now of Millbank Row, and William Graves of Holborn – an innholder. It was stated that overturns, accidents and poor maintenance were delaying the mail, in response it was agreed that when a better coach became available it would quickly become

standard and all coaches would have to use it. Besant now had a virtual monopoly
on the supply – for Palmer – of as many coaches as were required. Besant subsequently ordered five coaches to travel from Pool and London and all places
inbetween, he accepted the conditions of the agreement and would be paid 5
farthings a mile on a quarterly basis, details of other financial arrangements are
given but those outlined above comprise the main body of the agreement. Costs
of repair were excluded, as was the supply of lamps, light bars or glasses – all
quite fragile – while the cost of supplying coach houses when not in use was
not included either. Proper cleaning or costs incurred due to wear and tear were
also excluded, but these costs would be paid by Graves. If he failed to perform
adequately then Besant would do the work and charge Graves. If Besant or his
workers had to visit somewhere for repairs then they would travel for free. The
contract was to hold for as long as they were employed by the Post Office, in the
event of difficulties then Besant and Graves were to nominate an arbitrator to settle matters. It was signed and sealed by Besant.[10]

Among the papers submitted by Vidler on 26 July 1792 – in support of his
claim for a binding contract – were several statements from Besant, who was then
listed as living at Henley-on-Thames. These papers stated that in November 1786
he had agreed to furnish his patent coach and deliver 150 of them, however the
costs were high. When Vidler joined the system he had expected that the contractors would be purchasing the coaches, not leasing them. He also complained that
because the office demanded that a number of spare coaches be kept in readiness
these were often left exposed to the weather, their condition consequently suffered.[11]

According to the correspondence of 11 January 1793 Besant was first employed
in November 1786 to build patent coaches for the office. On 30 May 1787 Palmer
wrote to a Mr Wilson saying that the coaches would be supplied by Bezant(sic)
and would cost the contractors 2½d a mile to hire. Sometime in 1787 more articles of agreement were prepared between Palmer and Besant, but dates were not
filled in and they were never signed, sealed or confirmed. Starting in 1787 the
contract was to run for fourteen years and no other coaches were to be used,
this was on the assumption that Besant would supply a sufficient number and
keep them in good repair. There was a clause stipulating that after the end of the
first year Palmer could put an end to the agreement, there would be a twelve
month notice period and he would pay £3 for each coach.[12] All the supplied
correspondence confirmed beyond any doubt that Palmer and Bonnor had made
a firm agreement with Besant, but for unknown reasons this had never been
formalised.

On 19 November 1792, as the Postmaster General prepared to draw up a
contract to remedy the situation with Vidler, it became obvious that there was
a problem. The wording of the proposed contract spoke of a previous contract
between Palmer and Besant, but it was now known this had never been endorsed

and so was legally invalid. Mr Freeling pointed out that as far as he recalled Palmer had not even promised to endorse it. This was not the only problem, since the original agreement stated that a payment of 2½p was due to the contractors, the solicitor (Parkin) now found that some were running at 3d a mile.[13]

When Besant died in 1791 Vidler then bought out his partners. He then supplied the coaches on the same conditions as he had previously. However, he was now sole owner of the patent coach design, having inherited the un-endorsed contract.[14] In July 1793 there was more correspondence about the contract situation, Vidler claimed that when he first became involved he had expected his commitment to be a few hundred pounds and not the £30,000 it had now risen to. Initially he was asked to advance only £550, it turned out that he needed more cash and so Bonnor became a partner on a payment of £500. However, as he was barred – because of his official position – he had to turn over his share to Mr Willson who helped with a large sum. Willson then passed his share back to Bonnor, who wanted Vidler to take it. Vidler claimed that as the original contract had not been signed he had no official status and thus wanted some kind of security. Vidler reiterated that Palmer, in about 1786, had signed a contract with John Besant to convey mail by coaches, furthermore no other coaches were to be used for fourteen years.[15]

A copy of the unconfirmed agreement between Palmer and Besant, dated 16 November 1786, states that 120 coaches were to be built each year from that date. The agreement continues:

> And it is hereby agreed that the several guards to the different coaches shall be strictly injoined and required to inspect the state and condition of the coaches at each stage or places whereas horses shall be changed and make regular returns thereof to General Post Office for the information of the Postmaster General and of said John Vidler --- and in case of any defect or accident to state the particulars thereof and the time place and real cause of such accident or defect with the number of passengers in and upon the coach and likewise that the guards be strictly injoined that they do not permit on any account more than the stipulated number of passengers to travel in or upon any of their coaches.[16]

There was an exemption clause about the patent coach, it stated that:

> …it may be lawful to and for the Postmaster General for the time being at all times during the continuance of this contract to permit the several persons who may contract with government for carrying the mails on any roads within great Britain where the patent coaches are not at present used or established to use or employ any coaches or carriages whatsoever (not being the patent mail coaches) for carrying such mails any thing therein before contained to the contrary notwithstanding.[17]

A NEAT MEETING.   A MUFFISH MEETING.

According to the author of *Old Coachman's Chatter* the body language of the coachman, along with his use of the whip and reins, could let other drivers know his feelings.

On 10 May 1793 Vidler asked that he be granted a contract for the rest of the fourteen years, although Freeling did not like the idea of committing the office to him for so long a period. The Postmaster General, Thomas Lord Walsingham and Philip Earl of Chesterfield, suggested that a contract be drawn up for fourteen years from 10 October, this would serve to regularise a very muddled situation but it would still be based on the original agreement. On 4 May 1793 the Treasury approved the agreement and it was signed on 10 May 1793, the completed version runs to five large handwritten sheets. It accepted that in 1786 Palmer had made an agreement with *Bezant* (sic), this agreement stated that his coaches had exclusive rights to transport the mail for a period of fourteen years. The Postmaster General had received the approval of the Treasury, and from 10 October – subject to Vidler supplying the coaches – he would collect 1¼ penny for each mile and keep the coaches in perfect and complete repair.[18]

In the archives there is a typical contract, dated 20 June 1793 it was made on 17 June 1793 between Wilson (sic) of Lad Lane, London (Innholder) and John Dover of the City of Bath, Coachmaker:[19]

Wilson (sic) and to transport every day his Majesties mail of letters from London to Bristol and Bristol to London in present patent coaches in use or in such as the Postmaster General shall decide and all other bags of bye and cross road letters or of any other description that may be delivered to them and that they will pay quarterly 1 penny farthing a mile to and from the places and will build the coaches or carriages and must keep to hours specified. Promise to stop coaches and coachmen stopping at alehouse on the pretence of watering the horses between the places where horse are changed and all other stoppages except those allowed on the time bill unless accident or roads impassable. They are to excite guards and horse keepers coachmen and other servants ready and active attention to job and they will discharge any who fail. If any signatory is bankrupt etc and Postmaster General has to take over then they will retain money they should have paid. Not to use any other coaches without Postmaster General's permission and to experiment and if they use other coaches they must conform in measure etc to current. If no passengers that is not to be used as an excuse for not running the mail. Must not use a mail coach bearing 'usual inscriptions and the distinctions peculiar to the mail coach' not be used for any other purpose. Contractors to supply 'dry and fit coach horses' at stages set by Superintendent and if accident happens they must take the coach to stage point. Superintendent and deputies to travel free. No coach to travel without 'a screw wrench a hammer a cord and chain'. No driver shall be put on to drive a single stage only at the desire of any contractor under any pretence whatever except in illness or accident The Postmaster General will decide on stage to be driven and they are not to run horses for any distance that requires them to be watered except at stages. Inn keepers where coach stops for break are not to delay it longer than time allowed and servants not to ask passengers to get out where this is not allowed in time bills. Contractor to fit lamps approved by Postmaster General. They are to make every effort to promote service and keep all rules and they are responsible for any costs caused by their neglect. The Postmaster General will pay contractors quarterly 1 penny a mile to and from destination except for deduction of one pound per cent as at present and that ' a guard to the said mail coach shall be furnished paid clothed and armed at the expense of the revenue of the Post Office to protect the said mail and carriage throughout the whole of the journey by night and day'. The Postmaster General will pay and discharge all turnpike tolls and dues and other tolls wherewith the coaches and horses shall as may by law be charged or to which they may be liable. They may carry one passenger on the coach box and no more. Agreed contract will run to Lady Day 1794 and from thence for and during and until three moths notice of quitting by either party. Then clause agreeing and signature of Walsingham and Chesterfield witnessed by Hasker.[20]

(NB. Wilson is the most common spelling in the contract.)

Although it was agreed that the Besant patent coach was the official vehicle of the Post Office, it is apparent from the archives that changes were made to the basic design and that Vidler was instructed to carry them out. These changes exposed him to some financial uncertainty. On 23 December 1803 he wrote to Hasker stating his case. Commenting that three months ago he had received an order to build a coach to a new design he said it was, 'now at work on Leeds road and which seems to please everybody but myself.' He would be happy if he could supply more of this coach at the same price, but whilst he states that he is able to use all the parts on the same scale for the current coaches, if new ones were required then the situation would change. It was also suggested that horizontal springs be used on the coaches rather than elliptical ones.[21]

Up until this point Vidler had submitted to many of the demands made upon him. However, this time it was against his interests, and although he had modified several patent coaches he was not sure they would stand the shock of overturning quite as well as the old ones. This would mean that they would cost more to repair. He had put one on the Southampton Road and two on the Manchester Road, there were twelve more intended for the Post Office's exclusive use and another one in the process of construction. However, before he went any further he pointed out that expenses were very high on men and materials, and despite their lordships having given an extra £1,250 per annum in taxes, the total cost of repairs and maintenance on their large premises kept increasing. Each coach alteration cost about £33 – or £528 for sixteen coaches. Vidler's fleet numbered 120, the alteration of which would come to a total cost of £3,690.

GENERAL POST-OFFICE,
January 11, 1812.

SIR,

IT being an object with the Government to discover such Prisoners of War, *breaking their Parole,* as may travel by Mail Coaches, I am commanded by the Post-Master General specially to desire that, as far as may lie in your Power, you will aid and assist the Mail Coach Contractors at your Town, and the Guards, in the object above mentioned.

he several Contractors and Guards have proper Orders upon this Subject, and whenever you are applied to by either or both, particularly by the *latter,* for any necessary Co-operation and Assistance, you are hereby enjoined to render the same with energy and dispatch.

I am,

Your assured Friend,

FRANCIS FREELING,
Secretary.

Notice circulated by Freeling to all Postmasters, requesting help in the capture of any escaped prisoners-of-war. (PO 10/6/74)

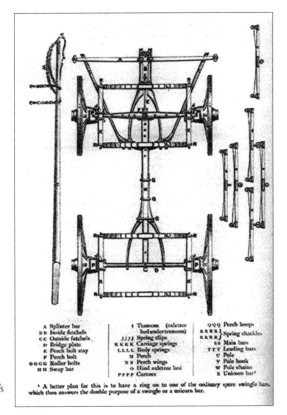

A Splinter bar	I Transom (axletree	QQQ Perch hoops
B B Inside futchels	bed under transom)	R R R R Spring shackles
C C Outside futchels	J J J J Spring clips	R R R R
D Bridge plate	K K K K Carriage springs	S S Main bars
E Perch bolt stay	L L L L Body springs	T T T Leading bars
F Perch bolt	M Perch	U Pole
G G G G Roller bolts	N N Perch wings	V Pole hook
H H Sway bar	O Hind axletree bed	W Pole chains
	P P P P Cartoux	X Unicorn bar[1]

[1] A better plan for this is to have a ring on to one of the ordinary spare swingle bars, which then answers the double purpose of a swingle or a unicorn bar.

The chassis of a mail coach along with various poles and bars, as depicted in Capt. Malet's book, *Annals of the Road*.

Vidler asked for clear instructions over the sort of coach he was to provide, he also requested guidance as to the specifications for the coach for His Majesty's birthday. He was forced to ask for help, and pointed out that he had signed the contract in 1793 for fourteen years – in fact he believed it had been drawn-up as far back as 1787. However, the economic conditions of the time did not help his business, and for more than two years he got little more than 5 or 6 per cent, which obliged him to give up all other concerns:

> By the third year by systemizing every part of the coach to scale and my coach manufactory regulated I for one year saw myself as I thought beginning to reap the harvest of my labours but immediately afterwards an advance took place beyond all computation. Materials, wages etcetera continued to rise until peace[22] nor did the high price then diminish only on a few articles but the renewal of war increased them beyond all examples and they are now nearly double what they were in 1787 when the contract was drawn though not signed.

Had he not:

THE COACHMAN.

He will bear you easily, and reins well.
(TWELFTH NIGHT.

This nineteenth-century engraving of a coachman gives him a somewhat sinister look, but as he is holding only one set of reins he could not have been on a mail coach. Interestingly it shows that the habit of chewing something is long-established.

...formed my materials to a regular scale and obtain apprentices & c I should not be able to proceed at all for journeymen get such astonishing wages from governments at barracks & c that many of the artisans ask nearly double the price for piece work and my very labourers in general half as much more for the same work than was formerly given. This being a fact and I hope admitted it must appear that without any alterations to the coaches even with the addition of the £1,250 per annum I much fear I shall not be able to proceed to the end of my contract how then can I alter my plan either to make new coaches on the horizontal springs or to alter the mail coaches at the expense of £33- each to make them nearly to that plan.

Here is another unforeseen grievance I have to state the luxury of the times in coaching has gone rapidly. Mail coaches long bore the Bill which put all the coach masters to their metal to outdo them if possible and when opposition started instead of giving £70 per coach as they did 10 years ago they now give £120-£130 or even £140 and I have been informed they have gone to £150 part for increased expense and part for improvements & ornaments that everything may appear in style with the best finishing & varnish can equal to gentlemen's carriages This I have long seen with much concern but I cannot afford to vie with them, my coaches are full as good or better than they ever were. I have further to observe the mail boxes are more than twice as large as they were at first – and even some of the contractors make continual attempts to carry baggage on the roof & outside passengers all of which add to the increase of wear & tear, the contractors formerly complained of paying me 2d a mile and that they could get it done cheaper but they are now in the habit of charging one another 3½ d and 4 d per mile and this when they live on the middle of the road all, this plainly shows the increase on coachmakers work- I therefore appeal to you in writing as I have often done by words to assist me in stating it to their lordships the Postmaster General.

I am dr sir,

Your most hblr Set J Vidler. [23]

On 21 January 1804 Hasker wrote to the Postmaster General forwarding Vidler's letter, he added that he had been checking on his claims, looking at the various papers and was now in a position to offer some proposals on how to deal with the rising costs. He pointed out that stagecoaches could carry many passengers whilst the mail coach contractors were limited to five – four inside and one on the roof. He suggested that to even things up there should be a tax on the number of stage-coach passengers. The cost was to range from 2d a mile – with four inside and three outside – to 3d a mile for more than six inside and five outside. A child car-ried on the lap would not be counted. Next he suggested a change in the design of the mail coach so that it could carry two or three outside passengers. He also proposed that coaches be built to a new plan and suggested that the coachman's boot and mail boot at the back of the coach be united. They could then lie on the horizontal springs between the perch, axletree and satchels, this would work up to a maximum weight of 17 hundredweight. [24] He thought the use of steel springs would make for a more comfortable ride for the passengers. It was agreed that a meeting of the Board be held to decide on these and other suggestions, this was duly arranged for 14 February 1804. [25]

Agreement was reached on the tax on stagecoach seats and it was decided that the Treasury would be approached. It was felt that it would help contrac-tors if they were allowed an extra passenger, it would also give the Post Office a reason to withdraw the extra penny they had been paying them – so saving £6,000 a year. The Postmaster General raised the point that the extra passen-gers might well slow down the coach. They were assured that the new design would make sure this couldn't happen. They asked whether the extra springs might lead to more breakdowns, but they were told that the new design was just as safe as the old system. The next problem they raised was the danger of the outside passengers uniting to assault the guard, it was agreed that this was possible but extremely unlikely, inside passengers would have to be part of any such plot if it were to be executed. If the Post Office offered an extra penny a mile would this be considered reasonable? They were assured that this increase, plus the projected growth in passenger numbers, would please the contractors.

If Vidler was allowed to build the newly designed coach – and the extra one penny a mile was paid – could they then save the £1,250 they had paid to Vidler? It was claimed that if Vidler did not build the new coach then he would need subsidising annually, as the prices of the various materials to be used in the coaches had risen by 30 per cent, 50 per cent or even 100 per cent, in particular the cost of labour had risen substantially. In view of the wide variety of theories offered the Postmaster General agreed that new coaches could be tried out on one or two roads, if they proved satisfactory then all coaches would be modified to take an extra outside fare. The contractors would pay 3 pence instead of 2 to Vidler.[26]

Not every user was happy with Besant's patent coach, over the succeeding years there would be frequent complaints and requests for permission to use another model.[27] In April 1792 a petition was raised with the support of about a hundred partners, they were protesting at the price which had been paid for the coach and its construction – which they blamed for the death of their horses. When one ran his own coach before Besant's was officially adopted Hasker thought it to be a superior model; it never overturned, was always full and attracted no complaints. He and his partners would save about £300 a year if they used them. As such they offered to pay Mr Bonnor £200 a year if they could run their own coaches and claimed that five non-patent coaches were already running on bye roads.[28]

The Bristol mail coach passing by Hyde Park Corner. It was here that the thief Thomas left the coach.

Typical eighteenth-century inn with galleries and open yard for the coaches. This one stood near the site of the new post office at St Martin's-le-Grand.

There was some correspondence in April 1793 between Lord Walsingham and a Mr A. Walker – who appears to have been something of a coach expert. Mr Walker stated that he had viewed Vidler's coaches from skeleton to finish, he did not think that they could be any lighter in view of the hard use they were expected to endure. He said he saw a number of improvements; in particular the design of the wheel would prevent them coming off the axle. The box and guard were situated over the large wheels, these overrode obstacles very easily but Mr Walker suggested that the springs would not be the best for the passengers. In the circumstances their strength and elasticity was the best possible, Mr Walker thought the coach could not be any lighter but was still too high. Outlining how he gained his expertise, he recounts how he came from York in four days with his wife, three children, a maid servant and lots of luggage. He did fifty miles a day, despite which the horse was as fresh at the end as it was when it started, this was with a wagon built to Walker's design. It was great for the country but less so for London and so he broke it up, something he regretted greatly. He also expressed sorrow for the post horses which were hacked to death pulling coaches which were too heavy. Despite his comments, he feared that the London coach makers were very formidable and that he did not have the temerity to break in on them.[29] Walker also opined that the perch was unnecessary on four-wheel coaches and that removing it would reduce weight.

Detail from the painting on p230, showing one method of suspending the guard's coaching horn.

One problem that was to bedevil the relationship between office, contractor and coach maker was that of maintenance. In a report by Hasker of 5 May 1793 he stated that the patent coach was first used by the Post in the Spring of 1787, about a year later the roads were thick with patent coaches. One employee was deputed to go round to the inns and check the condition of the coaches, any in need of attention were to be sent to the manufactory. However, this system was not very reliable, sometimes coaches went out without the bearing areas being well greased. The lack of grease allowed the friction on the wheels to build up until the heat was such that some hubs would catch fire, 'seldom a day passed a coach did not fire and generally without being washed or cleaned.' As a result, Palmer ordered that all coaches were to be taken daily to the manufactory for inspection and such attention as was required, but this was expensive for the contractors and they could not always be relied on. Besant agreed to do the job, collect the coaches, and take them to the factory. He estimated that on average each of the fourteen London coaches would need to be driven two and a half miles to the manufactory and the same distance back to the starting point. This amounted to five miles for each, or seventy miles in total. Besant thought eight horses would be enough, but this number proved to be insufficient and in practice ten or twelve were needed. As the number of routes grew Palmer ordered spare coaches on to the road, he said that London arrivals were not to go out the day after their arrival which would allow a day or two for repair.

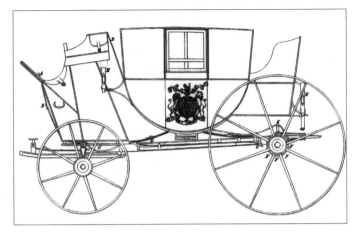

Besant's patent coach which became the standard vehicle; it was modified and manufactured for many years by Vidler.

This meant the number of coaches required almost doubled, Hasker reported that Palmer often said an amount of one shilling a day was reasonable.

A contract was arranged for spring 1788 and this date was confirmed by the Post Office Solicitor, who reported that he had met Bonnor around this time at Palmer's request to draw up contracts.[30] He submitted a similar report to the Postmaster General.[31] Furthermore, Hasker thought Besant was to be paid and he was told to get contractors to agree to it. The contractors were to pay for the greasing and maintenance, however, only three or four would and many others refused point-blank. In 1791 Palmer told Besant that the debt was so large he should write it off, except for the previous year,[32] surprisingly he seems to have done this.

This problem was to trouble the Mail Coach Office for some considerable time, Vidler justifiably claimed that the collecting, cleaning and maintaining of the coaches cost him time and money for which he received no recompense. The contractors claimed that they were paying Vidler a hiring charge for the coaches and did not see why they should pay any more for the maintenance. Both sides had a case, and the problem was worsened by the unsigned Palmer/Besant contracts. In the original clauses of Besant/Graves contract (see above) it had said that the hiring fee did not cover maintenance, but as these contracts were of no legal value they were irrelevant. There was also the problem that those contractors based outside London did not always have to pay. Hasker, in one report thinks 'end', i.e. terminating in London, contractors would pay if ordered to and middle contractors must also pay their share. He sounded a note of caution, saying that such a:

> …wet winter as the last, dreadful roads, horses dear beyond any former prices, provender never remembered so expensive, notwithstanding which the contractors are in general in good humour and five years being elapsed without being

able to get payment I think it my duty to submit to your Lordships whether it would be proper or advisable to put them out of temper with the business by desiring them to pay what in fact they had not agreed to.

All means were tried to persuade contractors to pay, one or two did without too much enthusiasm, and that number did eventually grow. As Hasker pointed out, they probably would pay if they were ordered to do so, but at the moment they were reasonably happy and such an order would not help matters. In the meantime Vidler was losing money and had been for years. In May 1797 Vidler submitted a long report to the Postmaster General, accompanied by supporting documents and accounts, setting out his memory of the history of the deal over the coaches. He said that he, John Besant and John Brooks, his late partners, had undertook in November 1786 – in agreement with the Comptroller General – to supply as many patent coaches as were required. There were now about 150 coaches in the hands of the contractors. He pointed out that alterations had been requested and that this had involved him in some considerable expense, he had also had to restrict production of other coaches. Further he had been forced to answer prejudicial comments, Brooks had been inefficient and Vidler had bought his share of Besant's patent for £1,000 in August 1787.

Vidler was now in financial difficulty and hoped that the Postmaster General would be able to support him. He said that under the original arrangement with him and Besant the contractors were to buy the coaches at a fair price, allowing a fair profit to him which would be better than the:

> ...risk and disadvantage which necessarily clogs the business by the alteration adopted in the mode of payment and less objectionable than the payment of so much a mile.

He added that the reason for introducing the payment for mileage was to ensure repairs which, if the contractors had owned the coaches, might not have been carried out.

Vidler said that despite claims his prices were too high he had been able to expand the manufactory and hold stocks of the various items required for maintaining the coaches. These had to be kept at sites not under his direct control and he had been forced to pay the workmen well to ensure good service. If the business were to close then Vidler would lose £20,000. Costs had risen; as Palmer insisted on a number of spare coaches being put into service, these were committed to the contractors, some of which had been standing for weeks in their yards with no shelter. Consequently they had suffered almost as much damage as the regular working coaches. He pointed out that under the original agreement he was responsible for repairing damage caused by wear and tear, but he was not responsible for collecting the coaches, taking them to the manufactory and greasing and so on. He stated that the contractors were to pay for damage and repairs incurred for reasons other than normal wear and tear. The contractors refused to pay for the service, and for 1790 and 1791 the amount due was £1,676 14s. He gave a list of the amount due from each contractor – numbering thirteen. He also suffered other losses due to the withdrawing of several runs and had to repurchase the Dover mail for £63, this had been seized by Officers of His Majesty's Customs because the guard was carrying manufactured goods. He begged their Lordships to protect him from ruin and prayed that they would continue to support him. He pointed out, as an extra pressure, that if he went under then the Post Office and mail would be seriously harmed which would lead to industry and commerce being greatly inconvenienced.

Vidler sent a letter on 13 August 1792, asking the Postmaster General to press the contractors who owed him £1,600. These monies were due for maintenance, and as he was in financial difficulty he would be obliged to sue if they did not pay. On 17 August Parkin, the solicitor, said that Vidler had no claim on the office. The Postmaster General could recommend that the contractors pay or alternatively he could accept arbitration, but it was down to Vidler himself if he chose to take legal action

Vidler acquiesced to the idea of arbitration but requested the chance to explain his situation personally before he formally agreed. Come 10 October 1792 and Vidler was upset that Hasker was to delay issuing applications to contractors to pay until after Christmas. This would push up Vidler's debt to £2,400, as two years' worth of accounts would be due on 5 January 1793. He said Palmer had promised that all debts would be cleared, Vidler received this assurance the day before he purchased Bonnor's share of the patent.[33]

A study by the solicitors and Hasker found that most of the maintenance was done in London, but some was still done in other towns. Vidler claimed that he had put £30,000 into his position and could only carry on because Sir Benjamin Hammett was helping, even with this help he could not go on much longer, Hammett had advanced £14,000 to Vidler. If he failed then the whole mail coach system would be deranged, in such a scenario it would be difficult to get anyone to take on a venture so expensive, so new and so experimental. On 27 September 1793 the Postmaster General sought permission to take on the charge, he would pay Vidler one shilling a day for examining, oiling and greasing. The pay would be sixpence for drawing coaches to Westminster and 6 pence for bringing them back, this arrangement to run from 5 January 1792. These costs amounted to a projected £584 per annum on sixteen coaches and 2 pence a day in London, exclusive of oiling and the associated costs. Approval was finally given in November and this long-running problem was put to rest, with the office paying Vidler an agreed sum for doing the job.[34]

Internal view of the Post Office in the late eighteenth century. The courtyard would normally be crowded with customers and staff. (PO PE 086)

Maintenance was obviously vital – accidents were costly and upset both contractors and the public. One of the most dangerous accidents that could befall a coach was being overturned. The cause could be an unexpected projection in the road, a clip from a passing vehicle, a broken or detached wheel or an abrupt turn. A number are listed in the archives and on occasion they resulted in a fatality. Each was investigated by an Inspector of Mail Coaches, and in the 1830s there was a standard form to be completed. A typical one deals with a coach overturning on the Pool to London run on 10 March 1837.[35] There had been a crash with the *Royal William* stagecoach, partly due to the fact the nearside lamp on the mail coach was out and that the *Royal William* driver did not see the mail in time to pull up. There were a series of questions on the form designed to identify the exact location, the cause of the crash, condition of the horses and the harness, whether the driver and guard were sober, injuries and any complaints about guard and driver, damage to the coach and finally what had happened to the bags of mail. In this particular accident both driver and guard were 'much hurt, no bones broken.' The harness was very important, since a broken strap could lead to problems with the horses.

The guard was supposed to check the state of the harness, when there was a problem he was to report it and the contractor would remedy the matter. In October 1792 Hasker was told to keep at least half a dozen reins by him, so that if a serious problem arose then the coach need not be delayed by sending for replacements. Should the contractor refuse to supply replacements then Hasker was to send him a set of reins and deduct the cost from the contractor's account.[36]

The fee to lease the coach did not include harness or reins and lamps were also excluded, even though they were vital items. Much of the driving was done in darkness, and it must be remembered that once the coach left urban areas street lighting was minimal while country roads were totally dark. The mail coaches had lights – usually four – but they were oil lamps and the light could hardly have been very bright, it is a tribute to the skill of the drivers that they were able to handle their teams and keep accidents to such a minimum. Hasker sent a note to the staff telling them of a Miles Patent coach lamp, designed to prevent oil spill by sealing it in. He stated that the reflectors were to be bright and that the lamps should be kept upright. He passed on the instructions on how to service the lamp,[37] there was also discussion on the best position for the lamps on coaches and on the issue of whether placing lamps so far forward as the footboard and throwing the rays between the horses was better than at the sides.[38] This position was more dangerous for the lamp, but Lord Beaulieu had experimented and Hasker had the opportunity to go and look at his Lordship's coach in Dover Street.[39] Hasker obviously had a strong belief in the quality of the coach lamps, for on 3 August 1796 – in answer to a query from a guard – he wrote a letter to Baily, a guard himself:

…have you proper lamps for if you have the darkness of the night need never be hindrance to the safety of the coach traveling (sic).[40]

The hard life of a mail coach is reflected in some of the statistics. In 1790, during a single week as many as twenty-six springs were broken while fifty-three wheels were taken off. The chassis section had its problems, a particularly vulnerable section was the axletree, part of the front wheel assembly. On 4 September 1790 Hasker wrote to Vidler asking him to give orders that the axletrees be given close examination, as 'several has broke lately'. He mentioned that the Exeter coach had suffered a breakage on the previous Saturday, in fact it had been in 'a suspicious state' for some journeys.[41]

Despite the mail coach clearly approaching obsolence, tenders for new coaches were still being invited in the 1830s and 1840s. The country was divided into three areas, Southern, Midland and Northern, and each area called for a separate tender. The specifications were quite explicit, and despite protestations from the contractors that they were being run to ruin and bankruptcy, there were always a number of tenders. These calls for tenders marked the end of a long association, for Vidler broke away from the Post Office. There was a bitter quarrel over the terms of the termination of his contract, which was due to end on 5 January 1836 with a year's notice on either side. On 14 February Vidler wrote to the George Louis pointing out that his contract was nearing its end, he asked if it would be renewed as he needed to order materials. On 30 April he wrote again, saying that he had not had an answer to his earlier letter. He added that he had cut the charges for oiling and greasing and that this had cost him £1,800. The costs that he, his father and his brother had taken on were substantial and demonstrated their commitment to the production of good coaches. On 16 May 1835 Louis passed on Vidler's letter, saying that there was no doubt that the coaches were 'as safe as any vehicles that run.' Inspectors reported that breakdowns due to inferior materials happened very, very rarely. He added that it was only fair a decision be taken soon, the letter was sent to Freeling but a decision on it was further delayed by a change of administration – Lord Maryborough was no longer Postmaster General. Vidler received an offer to continue at nearly £1,800 a year less than he was then being paid, if the contract was given to some incompetent on account of these kind of offers then the office would be in trouble. Vidler wrote on 9 June 1835 to say that Mr La Boucher had called the previous day to suggest that Vidler extend his contract for six months from January 1836. Vidler replied on 9 June 1835, saying he could only extend the contract for twelve months – a shorter period would mean severe losses. He also wanted a twelve-month notice period if the contract was not to be renewed and to be notified if the contract was to be put out to public tender, this to give him the chance to prepare his application. On 27 June George Louis wrote, saying that Mr Peacock had drawn up a contract for the coaches which ran until 6 July 1835, he took it to Mr Clarke – Vidler's solicitor – who seemed to approve the terms. However, Vidler was out of town and would be asked to return early on Monday to meet at Clarke's office.[42]

On 1 July 1835 a report said that the Commissioners had considered the situation. As Vidler refused to sign the contract beyond 5 July – to which he had previously agreed – they recommended that notice be given to the public immediately that tenders were to be received for it. If Vidler submitted one they suggested that it not be accepted. Vidler wrote on 1 July 1835 to Louis, confirming that he would not sign any contract for less than twelve months and apologising if he had caused any offence. Louis replied to Vidler, asking him to reconsider and saying how sorry he would be if Vidler cut short such a long association with the Post Office. The letter was marked 'Private', presumably indicating that it was Louis' personal response. A meeting seems to have been arranged but Louis writes that:

> I waited till 3 o'clock but Vidler did not turn up as promised. Commissioners will now wait until 10 o'clock tomorrow for contract to be signed and executed before 11 at his office and there will be no further negotiation with Vidler after his extraordinary conduct in refusing to sign.

Louis wrote to Freeling on 2 July 1835, enclosing copies of his letters and saying that the department had tried to bring Vidler onboard. Despite all the efforts of the Post Office to persuade him to compromise he had refused. The outcome was that when tenders were called for Vidler was excluded.[43]

Eventually an appeal for tenders was put out giving the specification for the coaches:

General Specification of Mail Coaches and other particulars. (Rough draft)

Carriages to carry 4 inside and 3 or 4 outside passengers plus driver and a special seat for guard, mail box to be the largest possible, coaches to be uniform in construction so that parts are interchangeable, all materials to be the best for strength and comfort, seasoned wood and best iron springs of steel, axles upon approved principle (presumably meaning Besant's system). *Not to exceed 17¼ cwts but as light as is practical*, tenders will be received up to 1st Aug 1835 and coaches to be ready 5 Jan 1836.

The italicised section has been crossed out in pencil and replaced by, 'in to be as light as possible consistent with a due regard to the necessary degree of strength and safety the proposed weight to be included in the tender.'

Tenders will be received for pair horse mails as well as four, two horses to have special seat for guard and four outside and four inside passengers and same quality of materials, two horse not to exceed 12¼ cwt but to be as light as possible subject to strength and safety, contract to include oiling and greasing *in*

The records mention payments for men carrying burning torches to light the coach's way in heavy fog. (PO P9180)

A very rare Mail Coach ticket for a seat on the Glasgow-Edinburgh coach: price £1. (Permission of Bath Postal Museum)

pencil and the expense of drawing to and from office and coaches must be to approbation of PMG. The guards to inspect and report state and condition of coaches and he must not allow more than the correct number of passengers. Country to be divided into 3 areas and Postmaster General will require coaches to run at least 3,000 miles in Southern, 4,000 in Midland and 2,500 in Northern but he may require more. Map showing areas may be seen at Mail Coach Office.

A second draft appears later. The amendment mentioned above has been made and 'coaches' changed to 'carriages.' People had the opportunity to tender for more than one district while security would required for due performance. The Postmaster General was to define the roads to be used and there was a twelve month notice clause. It is dated 9 July 1835, with hand-written drafts for the later printed copy and signed 'Lichfield.' The detailed specification for the coach is set out, the coach is to, 'be painted with Royal arms names of the towns to which it visits number of passengers inside and outside and other details PMG may require.'[44]

On 1 August Vidler submitted tenders for all three districts from the mail coach factory. This was to cover 9,000 miles over seven years at 2½d a mile, but a note on the envelope from Lichfield said that Vidler was to be excluded. There was a meeting on 1 August to consider the tenders; Lines of Surrey was the cheapest but enquiries found that he was only a small business. It was decided to recommend Wright Horne of London and Williams of Bristol for Southern and Midland areas at 2d a double mile, Croall of Edinburgh and Wallace of Perth were jointly recommended for the North at 2d a double mile. The applicants were interviewed and asked about their securities.

Part of the written specification of the coach showing details of the driver's seat, at the bottom there is a sword case. Written about 1830, it lists every detail and measurement. (PO 10/109)

Seven-year contracts were drawn up on 1 January 1836 between the Postmaster General and John Croall – coach maker – of Edinburgh, and Patrick Wallace – coach maker – of Perth. The contract stipulated that they would construct, or have constructed, coaches ready by 5 January 1836 in sufficient number – with the necessary coach poles, horse cars, lamp irons, drag chains and iron shoes – to be used by contractors to carry mail for not more than 2,500 miles. They were to carry four inside passengers and such outside passengers as would be required, besides a driver and a guard. The guard would have a seat appropriated to him with a mail box of the largest possible dimensions, all to be standard so that they would be interchangeable with the other four horse coaches. They would be liable for all expenses in the event of breakdowns and the like, unless they were due to the carelessness of servants of Post Office. They were responsible for maintenance and paid one penny a mile both there and back. Mail guards were to inspect at every place where horses were regularly changed and they were to only allow the authorised number of passengers on the coach.[45]

All did not go smoothly, and there were complaints from petitioners on 25 June 1839 about the coaches supplied by John Croall. They were described as being imperfect, too heavy and of poor appearance. The wheels attracted criticism for not matching, some were of different dimensions and overall the vehicles were poorly maintained and often broke down.

George Stow apparently checked the coaches and admitted that there were grounds for complaint, but Croall improved and was told that he could continue – however, he was warned that if his standards slipped then action would have to be taken. Mr Woolmer was also called upon, he examined all the coaches and classified them as:

> 1st Class below 17 cwt. ; 2nd Class below 18 cwt.; 3rd Class don't exceed 19 cwt.; 4th Class not exceed 20 cwt.; 5th Class all coaches not weighed as at factory undergoing repair.

He said that they were dirty and did look too heavy, but a reprimand to the manufacturer seemed to bring about an improvement. In fact they were no heavier than the London coaches. Croall was under pressure, he had been unwell when he took on the contract and had used unseasoned wood for the coaches' manufacture. The sun had dried the wood out and caused problems. Woolmer said that they were shabby but big and passengers liked them. His recommendation was that Croall withdraw all coaches weighing more than 18 cwt, he should also withdraw others, clean them up and replace the worst examples. However, the inspector did not find any serious breakdowns apart from those caused by accidents.[46]

The same tendering procedure was repeated again in 1842, and either the staff were inveterate optimists or singularly ill-informed. By this time the railways were clearly taking over mail transport but the contracts were still to run for seven years. The terms were basically the same as in the 1830s, they specified:

> …best quality, two and four horses, springs of steel, best wood, greasing etc included, carriages as light as possible. Southern and Midland to run 3,000 miles and Northern 2,500, bonds required from contractors 12 months notice both ways.[47]

Eventually a choice was made and the whole procedure was repeated again in December of 1842. It is of interest to note that even at this late date, with the railways clearly in the ascendant, there were still several tenders.

In the archives there is a large parchment contract for the making of coaches for Midland & Southern district. Dated 29 December 1842 it is signed by the Rt Hon. William Baron Lowther – Postmaster General, Joseph Wright of Gough Street, Grays Inn Rd and Walter Williams of the City of Bristol coachbuilders. This contract was to provide a number of coaches sufficient for the

Mr Chaplin,
one of
the main
contractors to
the Post Office,
and the owner
of hundreds of
horses.

needs of the Midland & Southern district – the coaches were to be similar to those already in use by 6 January 1843. They were to be painted with the royal arms, the names of the towns which they visited, the number of passengers allowed in and out and any other details demanded by the Postmaster General. Steel springs were to be included along with space for four inside and up to eight outside passengers, plus driver and guard – who was to have a seat built for, and only for him – there was also to be space for a mail box of the largest dimensions possible. The Postmasters General were to pay 11/16 of a penny for every mile the mail was conveyed, it would be 9/16ths for every mile the coaches were carried by the railways in England with the same rate to be paid in Scotland.[48]

The Postmaster General stipulated that the coaches had to carry four passengers inside and a maximum of eight outside, there was to be a guard's seat, a mail box and they also required a bond of £2,000. The contract was to run for seven years. In December 1842 a contract for building coaches for the northern district was agreed between the Postmasters General on the one part and Patrick Wallace – coachbuilder – of Perth, and Jonathan Dunn and Thomas Rowland – coachbuilders – of Lancaster on the other. The coaches were to be ready by 6

January 1843 and it also mentions them being painted with the Royal Arms, the names of the towns to which they were to travel and the number of inside and outside passengers. There were to be both four and two wheel coaches, with the weight not to exceed 18 cwt and 12 cwt for pair coaches. They were to cover 250 miles a day while the Postmasters General could nominate people to examine the coaches; they were to pay 43/64ths of a penny for every mile travelled, 43/128ths of a penny for every mile travelled for maintenance and 43/128ths of a penny for each mile they were carried on an English railway. There was to be a similar arrangement for Scotland with guards to check at stages, they would operate on a seven year contract.[49]

Changes were at hand, and in 1839 contracts were invited for horse rides, mail carts, stagecoaches and omnibuses. No guard would be required if the mail was carried by stagecoach or omnibus. Details were listed under town rides (five), short rides (four), country rides (sixteen) branch country rides (ten) and early branch country rides (five):

> For conveying 2d post letter bags 2 September 1839 to be received by 10 October next to be from 5 April 1840 work to be performed by horse rides, mail carts, stagecoaches or omnibuses, three years contract on surety of £1,000.[50]

The coach was on its way out but the riders were still in action.

Coaching print entitled 'Waking Up', engraved by Charles Hunt after Charles Cooper Henderson, 1843. (Ack PO No 162)

Coaching print entitled 'Changing Horse', engraved by John Harris after Charles Cooper Henderson, 1843. (PO 159)

As the Post Office was not responsible for the horses – they were the concern of the contractor – there are relatively few references to them. Occasionally problems arose, such as the question of who was responsible for damage to the coaches caused by horses kicking out. On 7 May 1835 Louis wrote to Freeling, saying that he had written to the biggest horse contractors asking what the established practice was. He had received answers from Chapman, Sherman and Horne; they said that building contractors were not responsible for damage caused by vicious horse or unskilful driving.[51]

Baines (*op. cit.*), writing in 1895, said that Chaplin – the largest supplier – had owned some 1,200 horses in 1835, whilst at the same time Nelson of the Belle Sauvage had 400. The work was hard on the horses and they were generally replaced every three years. The most common breed to be used was apparently a half breed cob and cart horse.

There were other bones of contention, and a letter of 25 November 1842 sought guidance on who was responsible for providing coach houses for spare coaches and horses stationed at places outside London. Until then builders had accepted liability, but this time Croall was refusing and thus Stow sought to establish the position. The reply stated that whatever the superintendents decided, it was imperative that the horse contractors supply houses.[52]

One continuing discussion point over the mail coaches concerns the relevance of the numbers on the coaches, these numbers are shown on the vast majority of illustrations. There is, among some enthusiasts, the conviction that they are route numbers – rather like modern buses. As discussed above there is no evidence in the archives for this assumption, for at no time is there any reference to a route number. The runs are identified by the two termini of the coach, London and

Coaching print entitled 'All Right', engraved by John Harris after Charkas Cooper
Harrison, 1843. (PO 160)

York or Exeter and London to name but two examples. It is far more likely that
the numbers are solely for identification purposes, as is suggested by the listing of
coaches supplied by Dunn of Lancaster in 1848. The coaches are listed as serving
various routes, the numbers extend up to 364 while those numbered 265, 270,
271, 272, 276, and 278 are shown on a list as serving the Carlisle to Glasgow run.
Six coaches serving one route.[53]

A close examination of the many coaching paintings and engravings demon-
strates very clearly that a number will appear on the different coaches described
as being on a certain route. This evidence is not reliable, for some illustrators
changed details on different editions which means conclusions cannot be drawn
with certainty. It is also clear from the surviving time bills that a single coach did
not necessarily complete the full journey and that passengers changed coaches on
occasion. All the available evidence suggests that the numbers are sequential.

Despite all the detailed information supplied by the archives and near contemporary writers there are still some points about the coaches that are unclear. On
27 July 1796 Hasker answers a query by mentioning that the 'large key is for seats
within' and that the small key is for 'rumble tumble behind'.[54] There is nothing in
the coach specification (see Appendix 8) to identify what is meant by this. It may
be that the seats had a top flap which lifted to reveal a storage space below, and
this could have been locked by the 'large key', but the 'rumble tumble' remains a
mystery.

Another minor mystery about the coach is the sword case. This was a long narrow compartment with a sloping lid which lifted for access. It was fitted to the
back of the coach in front of the guard's seat and is detailed in the specification of
the coach (Appendix 8). It seems to be a nineteenth century addition, for illus-

trations of the earlier coaches do not appear to show it. Unfortunately it is not possible to be too specific, for coach illustrators are not the most accurate, especially those of the eighteenth century. References to the sword case in the archives are limited, apart from the accident in Sligo. Nobbs – the guard – mentions using it to store his blunderbuss, but common sense suggests that it would need to be in some cover, otherwise there would be a loaded firearm being shaken about in a wooden box, obviously a potential source of danger. Captain Malet said categorically that the pistols and blunderbuss were carried in the sword case, which again suggests that some sort of wrapping was used to prevent damage. He added that it was also used as a foot rest by the guard. One reasonable hypothesis is that it was introduced late in the eighteenth century when the Napoleonic Wars raged. The military and naval persons travelling with their swords may well have asked for a safe place to store the weapon during the journey, or maybe passengers expressed fear over having the swords inside the coach. So far no evidence to explain its adoption has been traced.

Another intriguing reference is to a very expensive model of the coach made by a Mr W.H. Harris in 1837 at a cost of £57-1-0, a cost well in excess of the usual coach.[55] There is no surviving record of what happened to this very expensive item, or indeed why it was made.

Despite the fact that hundreds of mail coaches were made, very few survive. In *Pickwick Papers* there is a passage which describes the sad fate of old coaches and details their skeletal remains. Fortunately there are a few survivors, these may still be seen on their rare outings at commemorations or festivals, and there is always the Christmas card!

THE END OF THE ROAD – THE COMING OF THE RAILWAY

Just as the delivery of the mail by coach in Britain reached a greater level of efficiency than most people had ever expected it was made redundant. From the beginning of the nineteenth century the railway; a fast, efficient and reliable means of transport, was developing at a great rate. One advantage that it offered was that once the track had been laid it was, barring natural disasters, no longer seriously affected by weather or topography. The advantages of fixed tracks were appreciated as early as the seventeenth century, and wooden wagon ways were in use in the collieries of northeast England as early as 1630. Trucks mounted on wooden 'rails' were moved by men or horses, and although speed may not have greatly increased bulk movements were made easier. One early difficulty was in ensuring that the wheels stayed on the rails, for they were very susceptible to slippage. A next step was to replace wooden rails with a more durable material, cast iron was used. To keep the wheels on the rails, in 1769 the Coalbrokedale Iron Works were using a special rail with a flange, a raised section of the track that engaged with the edge of the wheel to keep it in contact with the rail. This method was particularly demanding, in that the entire length of the track had to be fitted with the locating flange. The next big change happened in 1789, when the concept was changed and the flange on the rail was replaced by a flange on the rim of the wheels.

During the eighteenth century there had been much development in steam power and engines were made to operate lifting and pumping machines. One limitation of using steam at low pressure was that machines, by their very design, were generally rather large and heavy. Men of vision began to consider how this new source of power might be adapted, they saw using steam under high pressure as a potential means of improvement. There were several pioneers, but the one to whom most credit should go in the field of locomotives is probably the Cornishman Richard Trevithick (1771-1833).

Trevithick was familiar with the power of steam from the tin mines of Cornwall, where low-pressure steam engines were in common use. These machines were quite bulky and Trevithick conceived the idea that high pressure steam would give much better results. The engines themselves could be made smaller and would certainly be more efficient in terms of fuel and output. By 1797 Trevithick had designed and manufactured high pressure stationary steam engines. All that was needed to generate steam was fire and water, and as the engines were now fairly small it was possible to mount the mechanism on a moving base. Mount the steam engine on a wheeled base, convert the power of the steam to the task of turning the wheels and one had a locomotive. Trevithick saw that what was now wanted was a gear system to transfer the initial forward and backward movement into a wheel-turning system. He produced a steam carriage and demonstrated its power in 1801 by driving it up a hill before an astonished audience at a Christmas celebration. In 1802 he took out a patent on his design of high pressure steam engines, and in 1803 he built a second model; designed to run on a system of rails which demonstrated its power in London.

Another version of his locomotive was built at an ironworks in South Wales, and in February 1804 it clearly demonstrated its potential by winning a bet that it could pull a load of 10 tons of iron and seventy men along a track of ten miles. In 1808 he built a circular track in London near the present rail terminus of Euston and demonstrated his third model; named *Catch-me-who-can*. Trevithick rather lost interest in the theme of transport, mainly because the rails then in production proved to be too weak to support the weight of his machines, but his engine was still adapted to drive various farm machines and boats. Despite his great contribution to the development of railways Trevithick did not draw great benefits from his work and died a pauper's death. However, his work had demonstrated the possibilities of railways and others soon began experimenting and improving design.

As is so often the case, once the principle had been demonstrated development was accelerated. The early nineteenth century saw a growth of interest in the concept of railways. As early as 1801 an Act of Parliament granted permission to the Surrey Iron Railway Company to begin construction of a line from London to Portsmouth. The way forward was now seen by many engineers, experiments led to all manner of strange machines and real progress was made. After many years of discussion and controversy a line between Stockton and Darlington became operational in 1825, before long it was clear that steam locomotives were the way of the future. From the beginning locomotives were pulling loads of 80 tons at a speed of 15mph, almost double that of a good mail coach.

In the early days the railways were primarily used to transport goods and materials, the number of passengers also gradually increased as people found it a quick and – despite dire warnings about travelling at speed – safe means of travel. The line's engineer, George Stephenson (1781-1848), was gaining practical experience. When the construction of a line between Liverpool and Manchester began in 1821 he heard that it was planning to use horses for motive power. His enthusiasm and expertise persuaded the owner that a steam locomotive was what was needed. He designed the *Locomotion*, which on 27 September 1825 pulled a public passenger train with 450 people on board at a speed of 15mph (24 kph). When the line between Liverpool and Manchester was being built a competition was arranged, and a locomotive designed by George Stephenson – the famous *Rocket* – won by achieving a speed of 36mph (58kph), now four times as fast as the best mail coaches. On 15 September 1830 the Liverpool and Manchester line was formally opened, and it may be said that here the railway age really began. The financial success of the line soon persuaded other entrepreneurs to join the industry and there was a nationwide mania for new routes. The obvious outcome of the competition was a gradual taking-over of the mail by the railways. By the 1850s lines were spreading like a spider's web across the country. Between 1840 and 1850 the length of the national rail network increased from 1,497 to 6,084 miles.

Post Office officials were well aware that their hard-won speedy delivery system was being outstripped by these new locomotives and public and commercial pressure led to a gradual change from horse to steam. The changeover was obviously not without its problems as, after some sixty years, the Mail Coach Office still tended to think in terms of guards and mail boxes. The rail companies saw the carrying of mail as a profitable business, but compromise was still necessary to reach agreement. In 1833 the London and Birmingham Railway Act set down that the mail bags were to be accompanied by the guard, and that the Postmaster General had the power to order a box and seat:

> …under or near the same behind each of the said carriages for the exclusive conveyance of the said mail and bags of letters and the guard or person in care or charge thereof.

In 1838 the Government passed the Railways (conveyance of Mails) Act and the changeover from horse to steam was underway.

The systems most likely to be profitable were those lines which connected the main towns, cities and ports of the country, the same centres that had been catered for by the mail coaches. These routes were obviously more likely to attract freight and passengers for the rail magnates, and the corresponding coach routes were generally the first to suffer. At first there were attempts to integrate coach and rail; at some stations the coach would arrive to be loaded onto a flat truck and then taken to another station where it would be unloaded and continue as a horse-drawn coach. Timetables for London to Broxbourne, Hertford, Ware and Bishop's Stortford; dated 16 May 1842, distinguish between Coaches 'meeting the trains' and occasions when 'the following coaches are conveyed by the railway.' The latter list included Wisbech, Holt, Fakenham, Cambridge and several other destinations.[1]

At first the guard was seated at the back of the coach. The mail was then loaded on to the coach with him, where he sat exposed to the smoke, dust and cinders from the locomotive. It was not long before action was taken; on 26 July 1837 George Louis wrote to the Postmaster General saying that it was necessary to provide the guards on the Birmingham to Liverpool railway with 'shades' to protect their eyes from the 'sparks and cinders that fly from the chimney' of the engine. These – presumably protective – spectacles were supplied by a person residing in Birmingham, at a cost of 7s 6d (37.5p) a pair. Louis had purchased twelve pairs for £4 10s (£4.50). The guards would be responsible for their care and the spares would be kept in a tin.[2] It is not known what these spectacles were like, but at 7s 6d they seem very expensive. It was not only the guards who were at risk from cinders and sparks, and there were apparently one or two instances where the mail was set alight by sparks from the engine. On 10 October 1840 it was thought necessary to purchase, from a Mr B. Edington, 'for tarpaulins supplied for the protection from fire of the mail bags on the mail coaches sent by railways: £23-22-6.' These tarpaulins were to be used to both cover the bags and reduce the chances of accidental arson.[3]

The office structure was now reflecting the major changes outlined above, as shown by the Establishment Book for the late 1830s. The duty of the Surveyor and Superintendent of Mail Coaches – a position held from 1838 by George Stow – has an ink amendment inserting the phrase 'or by railway' when referring to the conveyance of the mail coaches. The staff comprised a senior clerk, a junior clerk, two senior, three junior and six railway clerks, seven inspectors and finally 277 guards.[4] This figure must include all those then working on the railway. With one inspector dealing exclusively with rail transport, as well as a number of clerks being specifically designated to work on the railway, the emphasis on the new form of transport was clearly growing. The railway companies were increasingly aware of their own potential, and in December 1837 The Grand Junction Railway informed the Office that it would not carry mail on the existing terms after 3 February 1838. The Office wasted no time, and on 28 December 1837 they signed a new agreement for trips to Birmingham, Manchester and Liverpool. The guard was to travel free of charge, and should the coach be late then the railway would organise a special steam locomotive.[5] There was apparently still a desire to achieve good results, and in May 1838 a letter was sent expressing their appreciation of the Inspectors' great efforts in transferring the mail to the London and Birmingham railway. One inspector had slept every night in a coach as there was no available accommodation.[6]

Legislation was soon in place to regularise the situation, and Act 1/2 Vic. Cxcvii, of 14 August 1838 set down that the Postmaster might require railway companies to take guards, other officers and coaches. This was modified in 1847 when a clause in a new Act allowed the mail to be sent without a mail guard, in effect transferring responsibility to the railways. All carriages reserved by the Post Office were to have the royal coat-of-arms painted on the side.[7]

In the records the signs of decay are clear, payments such as that on 5 January 1842 to Mr Wright for 'bringing sundry mail coaches to London £36-17-4', and that of 5 April 1842, '£15 Mr Wright the expense of bringing from York to London in June 1841 two Edinburgh mail coaches which had ceased running'[8] clearly indicate that the mail coaches were declining. One side effect of the closing of routes was that a surplus of coaches was building up, this in turn meant that fewer new coaches were required. The suppliers were bound by contract to the Post Office, and their trade was steadily diminishing in terms of both the amount of mail carried and the number of paying passengers. The contractors naturally sought permission to terminate the contract. On 28 November 1837 one wrote in to say that seventy-five miles of track on the London to Birmingham railway was to be opened in January 1838. This would kill their trade and so they would be grateful if they could terminate their contract. In this case the rail opening was delayed and the contractor – having received permission to terminate the contract – now asked if they could continue until February.[9]

Another market that was affected by the mechanisation was the horse trade, for contractors now wanted to dispose of surplus steeds as soon as possible. Each horse represented a trading loss as it had to be fed, groomed and stabled whilst it was no longer working. Their value was also falling, as the diminishing market failed to absorb the growing number being offered for sale. Adverts for auctions and other sales became more common, and many admitted that the sale was 'in consequence of coaches going per railway' when forty-nine horses and harnesses were offered (*The Times*, October 1838).

The incursions of the railway affected all branches of the Post Office's delivery system. In 1837 a list, 'of horse posts, foot messengers & C abolished on the opening of the railway communication between Birmingham and Liverpool' was drawn up. Thirteen Horse Posts, eight foot messengers and four miscellaneous characters, one a tollgate keeper, were listed. However, contained within it was another 'List of Horse posts, foot messengers, & c established in connection with the railway communication between London and Birmingham.' This consisted of eighteen Horse Posts, seven foot messengers and nine miscellaneous.[10] Presumably the end result was little more than relocation for most workers, and based on the numbers alone extra staff had to be employed.

New transport systems called for new methods, and the guards – who had become adept at tossing the mailbags through open windows at the various stages and snatching bags from outstretched hands and poles – now had to learn a new technique of exchanging bags. With the higher speeds and heavier bags in service a new changeover system was needed. The device used was basically a net and hook idea, the mail bag to be collected was hung from a pivotted arm by the side of the track. Projecting from the side of one of the coaches was a folding rope net, and as the train approached the pick-up point of the net was swung out from the side of the coach. The hanging bag of mail was scooped up by the net, which could then be pulled back into the coach. The reverse process was used to deliver the bags, they were swung out from the side of the coach and snatched by a net mounted by the side of the track.

The device was originally put forward and patented by a Nathaniel Worsdell, who in 1838 offered it to the Post Office. However, the price he asked for its use was much too high for the Postmaster General, who made a counter offer which the inventor rejected. The next step in the story involves some unscrupulous behaviour. An employee of the Post Office – named Dicker – was encouraged to modify the idea and his system was eventually adopted, although there were claims of a breech of patent. The archives contain several references to the erecting of this pick-up system, including:

> Messer Barrow and Turner for erecting the apparatus for exchanging mail bags at the several stations on the Birmingham Grand Junction Railway £454 -18 -6.[11]

Unlike the old coach guard, who might have had a second chance to leave or collect the bag, the new trains moved so fast that only one attempt was possible. The guards on the trains took a little while to master the new techniques, and on occasion either a pick-up or delivery was missed. In November 1839 this happened at Blisworth. The bag was hung up but the guard on the train forgot to put out the net. Peters, the guard, was suspended for two days and an entry made in his Black Book, but because of his previous good character no further action was taken. His excuse was that fog and steam had confused him, the locomotive pulling the train was a new one and had attained a higher speed than usual, this had caused his misjudgement of the time.[12]

The impact of the railway on the mail coaches was swift and severe, they hit the contractors hard and petitions and pleas for help soon reached the Post Office and Parliament. Early in 1840 a joint appeal by mail and stagecoach contractors pointed out how much the railways were affecting their trade, unless Parliament made some adjustments to taxes then they would simply collapse. There was also talk of allowing the mail coaches to carry parcels, which would undoubtedly hit the stagecoach trade. On 17 February 1840 the Treasury expressed their regret that they could not adjust matters, the public were benefiting from the new service and there would be no changes.[13]

Two documents make clear the drastic effect the railways were having on the mail coach system. Dated 12 January 1841, Post 30/35 is headed, 'A List of Mail Coaches which have been discontinued in consequence of the use of railways.' There are six listed for London, four for Birmingham and four for Liverpool reaching a grand total of thirty. This represented a distance of 2,811 miles 1 furlong. Accompanying it is another document headed, 'A List of mail Coaches which will in all probability cease in consequence of the use of the railway.' This lists nineteen routes, although in several cases only part of the run would cease, thus on the London to Devonport run only the section between London and Exeter is listed.

On 10 March 1840 a petition was addressed to Lord Lichfield from mail and stagecoach proprietors on the Great North Road. They accepted that some concessions had been made but pleaded for more help, they also highlighted another competitor – for untaxed steam vessels were apparently operating services along the coast and, without some more help, the proprietors were staring ruin in the face.[14] It seems that the warning of impending disaster was sometimes not given to contractors until shortly before it happened. It is obvious that plans would have to be made for the disposal of coaches, horses, fodder and drivers, and since the changeover was spreading across the country the demand for them would be getting progressively smaller. In March 1840 the Great Western Railway was planning to open a line to Reading, Bath and Bristol, with the mail to travel by train. The contractors were given fourteen days notice.[15] On 20 May 1840 the contractors for Sheffield and Derby were given twenty-eight days notice that they would no longer carry the mail and the North Midland Railway would take over.[16] A formal notice was issued on 22 September 1845 to end the London to Norwich coach mail service on 5 April 1846.[17]

Although demand was obviously diminishing, replacement and new model coaches would still be needed so not all coach building stopped. The coaches were to continue running on a gradually diminishing scale for some years. The situation of the manufacturers is clearly shown by a typical letter dated 23 November 1841 from Wright and Williams of Gough Street, Holborn. Their contract was due to expire in January 1843 and they needed to plan ahead as far as future materials were concerned, they wanted to know if they would get a contract. In support of their claim they pointed out their good past record, having supplied 140 coaches and carried out modifications at short notice – such as allowing for eight outside passengers instead of the usual three. The advent of the railways had led to a reduction in their mileage from between 11,000 and 12,000 miles of coverage to 7,000 miles. Some of their coaches were now at stations which were difficult to reach and service. They hoped that if tenders were sought for new coaches then some allowance could be made for all the losses that the firm had suffered. The Office replied that they were sorry but that the call for tenders for Midland & Southern Divisions would be announced on 3 December 1841.[18] This firm adapted to the changing market and their later adverts offered railway carriages as well as coaches.

There were other problems during this period of change, and Ireland in particular seems to have suffered. It was claimed on 10 June 1837 that the proposed new delivery to Dublin would arrive late in the evening, which would be useless, of the last 365 mails only 104 had (allegedly) arrived in time for the 3 p.m. delivery. The mail was dispatched from London at 8 a.m. and reached Dublin at

6.30 p.m. on what was a combined coach and rail journey.[19] There were other complaints at Birmingham on 20 November 1837 about the changeover of mail and passengers from coach to rail, but the office claimed that it could do little as it was down to the railway.[20] There were complaints from Scotland, with a printed petition from the Lord Provost Magistrates and Council of the City of Edinburgh on 20 January 1838. They were dissatisfied with the arrangement with the Grand Junction Railway, and they added that no extra horses were available when needed for difficult parts of the routes or when there was heavy rain. Louis replied that there were always extra horses if needed and that guards had been told to use them. Lord Litchfield also replied on 17 February; he agreed that although there was no contract with the railway company there was a clear understanding and agreement, he too said that horses were available if needed.[21]

Apart from the usual mail coaches there was now a demand for smaller ones that could carry mail from the train stations to the Post Office. On 21 May 1838 a contract was made with Vernon Abbott to convey mail and guards from Euston, Vauxhall and Paddington to the Office. He would supply carts, horses and drivers; who were not to be younger than twenty-one years of age. They were to maintain a speed of 8mph and would be under strict supervision from the Superintendent, they were subject to instant dismissal on his discretion.[22]

Whilst the railways made great progress in their takeover of the main mail routes the rural side was far less affected – and post boys and carts still played their part. On 8 September 1847 the Postmaster General – Clarincarde – made a contract with Thomas John Bolton of 32 Harrow Road, Marylebone, London. The contract was for the supply of horses, carts and wheeled carriages, riders, drivers, harnesses and other equipment, uniforms, hats and coats for riders of horses and drivers of carts, saddle bags, straps, and pouches for letters. The riders were to be a minimum of fourteen years of age and were to wear their uniform at all times, but it was to be surrendered if they left the job. The contract was to run for five years: Bolton would be paid tenpence three farthings per double mile in town and 9½ pence for country rides. The riders, carts and associated paraphernalia would collect and deliver the various mails from the London District to and from the main office at St Martin's-le-Grand.[23]

There was even talk of hiring extra guards when the various railway contracts came into operation on 9 June 1837. It was suggested that a minimum of thirty-one would be needed, all would be offered temporary employment on the understanding that if a permanent position became vacant then they would be appointed.[24] Some guards were made redundant and the general policy seems to have been last-in then first to go. In May 1848 permission was sought to remove twelve junior guards from the list. In 1848 an account details the Mail Guards whose services had been dispensed with. This was due to the reduction of the establishment's size, authorised by the Lords of the Treasury by a letter of 6 June 1848: to receive a gratuity Jon Paterson, Henry Jeffries, George Mills, Donald

Steward, Francis Hims, (?) Thomas Harrison, H(?) Carpenter and Charles Paul, £60 each.[25] The railway guards would now be responsible for the security of the mail. Some of the surplus guards might have been able to get positions as letter carriers in London, in which case they would not receive the gratuity.

This document is of particular interest; it lists the guards in order of seniority, details their dates of employment and whether they were engaged on coaches or railways and gives their total number as 213 (later amended to 215). The junior guards had only joined the mail coaches in 1840/41 and approval for their removal was given on 24 May. The total number employed on the railways far exceeds the number who still served on the coaches, almost all were paid a set salary – without the right to accept tips – as the number of passengers had fallen so much that the guards couldn't make a living wage.

One document[26] has a listing of the numbers of guards. It compares details of the service in 1838 and 1841 in terms of the number of guards and distances covered on both road and rail.

Great Britain
1838: 268 guards, 24 on railway, miles covered on roads 6,102,360, on rail 645,685
1841: 200 guards, 60 on railway, miles covered on roads 5,043,975, on rail 6,700,346

Ireland
1838: 79 guards, 4 on railway, miles covered on roads 1,747,985, miles covered on rail 30,660
1841: 74 guards, 3 on railway, miles covered on road 1,673,525, miles covered on rail 30,660

United Kingdom
1838: 347 guards, 28 on railway, miles covered on road 7,850,345, miles covered on rail 8,526,690
1841: 274 guards, 65 on railway, miles covered on road 6,717,501, miles covered on railway 1,687,030

It was during this period that the famous Railway Travelling Post Offices began, they were to remain in service – adapted to changing technology – for over a century. They were primarily sorting offices on wheels and did require some extra items in the early days. Messrs Miller & Sons supplied lamps and the like for the use of the Railway Travelling Post Office from May through to 31 December 1838 £44-11-9.[27]

Sadly, it was not long before the railways claimed their first victim from the mail guards. On 6 March 1840 Thomas Dougall was killed on the Newcastle and

Carlisle Railway when a line of coal trucks pushed the coach off the rails and he fell down an embankment. He had been a guard for thirty years and left a widow, Catherine, with eighteen children, four of whom were described as 'helpless.' The office was asked about a pension, they replied that there was no precedent but in view of the great hardship they would look for any fund that might be able to help. Unfortunately the archives do not give any further information.[28] Thomas Dougall was not the only casualty, indeed a guard was given £100 compensation – a year's salary – when he was so severely injured on the Dover railway that he was unable to work.[29]

Tragedy was not the only export from coach to rail, robbery was another. In January 1849 the Exeter mail left Plymouth at 6.35 p.m., reached Exeter at 9 p.m. and Bridgewater at 10.30 p.m. All the mail bags picked up en route were locked in a tender at the back of the Post Office carriage. The train continued on to Bristol, arriving seventy minutes later. It was here that the guards discovered the bags had been tampered with, some had been cut open and all the registered and banking letters were missing. All entrances and exits to the station were guarded, eventually two men were found in a first class coach adjoining the Post Office carriage together with some letters, a false moustache and a black crape mask. When examined, one of the men was found to have a piece of string stuck to his boot which was of the same type as that used to tie the sacks. Apparently they had left their carriage, crawled along the footboard on the outside and entered the postal tender. One of the men had served as a guard on the Great Western Railway and the other was Edward Nightingale, a horse trader from London. As the train approached Bristol station it had slowed down and they were able to jump off. They might have succeeded but the wife of one, in revenge for her brutal treatment, told the whole story and was at first not believed. After extensive enquiries by the police the villains were captured. The men were tried, found guilty and received a sentence of transportation.[30] (Another train, leaving London at 8.55 p.m. that night, was also robbed.)

By July 1850 the Post Office was dealing with quite a list of railways: London & North Western, Lancashire & Yorkshire, Chester & Holyhead, Midland, South Devon, Caledonian, Eastern Counties, York Newcastle & Berwick, Lancaster & Carlisle, Shropshire Union, Great Northern, Scottish Central, Norfolk, North British, York & North Midland, Edinburgh & Glasgow, Glasgow-Paisley-Greenock, London-Brighton & South Coast, Eastern Union, London & Blackwall, Newcastle upon Tyne & Carlisle, Manchester-Sheffield & Lincolnshire, Whitehaven Junction, Monkton & Darlington, Glasgow-Paisley & Kilmarnock, Glasgow-Dumfries & Carlisle and East Anglian. Some coaches were still running, a bill of £4,135-5-2 was run-up for the quarter ending 5 July 1850[31] and by the quarter ending in 5 October 1854 the business was still struggling on, horsing contractors were paid for mileage for the preceding three months.

One by one the routes were withdrawn, London to York ended in 1840 and London to Edinburgh in 1842. The capital's connections to Norwich and Newmarket stopped in 1846, that to Manchester in 1858, the Newcastle to Edinburgh service went in 1847 and that to Thurston survived until 1874.[32] The policy was quite clearly that the whole of the coach system should, and would, be transferred to rail as soon as possible. A circular to the Surveyors on 1 February 1847 stated that the:

> Post Office should be prepared to employ any new railway (if expedient to employ it at all) immediately on its opening.[33]

In August 1854, after some seventy years of operation, the Mail Coach Office became the Mail Office, which itself was abolished in 1869.[34] The end came on 1 August 1874 when the last coach from London arrived at Thurso. The mail coach, driver and guard were retired, to return only at festivals and parades, the post boys and riders gradually became telegraph boys and the increasingly familiar postman or woman. Palmer, Freeling, and particularly Hasker made their mark on British postal and social history, their influence lingers on and long may it do so.

ROYAL MAIL FIREARMS

Until the late nineteenth century all the firearms used by the Royal Mail were of the type known as flintlocks. They were loaded with a measure of gunpowder poured down the barrel – the amount was specified in the guards' instructions – and a lead ball, cast in a bullet mould, was pushed down to sit firmly on top of the powder charge. The gunpowder was ignited by a spark generated by the scraping of a wedge shaped piece of flint down a steel plate, the frizzen. These sparks fell into a small amount of powder placed in a pan set by the side of a touchhole, which had been drilled through the side of the barrel and connected to the main internal charge of powder. The flint was held between the jaws of the cock (or hammer), which was powered by a main spring to swing forward and generate the sparks.

Most of the coach weapons had a double safety system to prevent accidental discharge. If the cock was pulled back a certain distance to the half-cock position then pressure on the trigger would not fire the weapon. There was a second device, known as a safety catch or stop, which could be pushed forward to engage with the cock and lock it in the safe position. To fire the weapon the stop had to be pulled back and the cock pulled back to the full-cock position when pressure on the trigger allowed the cock to swing forward and generate the sparks. The guards were supposed to unload their weapons when they went off-duty.

It has already been pointed out in the chapter on the guard's equipment that many of the Post Office firearms have a number engraved on the barrel, and there has been much debate about its significance. The most common theory is that it matches a mail coach route number. The problem with this explanation is that there is no evidence to be found in the archives or other contemporary sources that the routes were ever designated by numbers. There is no doubt that the coaches were numbered, but again there is no evidence that these numbers had any significance other than simple identification. It is dangerous to base assumptions solely on contemporary or near contemporary illustrations, for the same subject was often reissued with minor changes and artistic licence can be quite a factor. However, pictures showing coaches described as being on different runs may be found with the same number. The impression gained from a close study of the many examples is that any coach could, in most cases, be used on any route. It was merely a matter of which coach was available for a particular journey. Some coaches had the name of their destinations painted on the side, many did not.

Only two gun makers, Mortimer and Harding, can be positively identified as being regular, or perhaps official, suppliers of arms to the Mail Coach Office. Their names and addresses are engraved on the barrels of the pistols and blunderbusses together with the number under discussion. Details of the makers' titles are well known and can be dated quite accurately, thus they can be used as a guide to dating the weapon. If the numbers are compared with the naming of the maker on the barrels then it becomes clear that the numbering is almost certainly sequential. This supposition is given some backing by the dates found on some of Harding's firearms, since generally the higher numbers match the later dates, e.g. the pistol with the highest number, 383, is dated 1840 – the latest date.

Mortimer traded under a variety of titles over the course of his career: H.W. Mortimer from 1782-1799, Mortimer & Co. from 1799-1806, Mortimer & Son from 1807-1812 and finally Mortimer (the son) from 1813-1816, at this point the firm ceased trading with the Post Office. In contrast Harding used only two trade names: J. Harding from 1816-1833 and J. Harding & Son from 1834 to 1843.

An examination of the listing below will show that the majority of numbered weapons match up with the appropriate trade name, but there are several anomalies. At times the gun maker's title indicates a much later date than the number or vice versa, e.g. Harding 61 and 68 clashes with the dates of the maker. Blunderbuss 369 was apparently supplied twenty years or so after the firm stopped dealing with the office.

There are a number of plausible explanations for these anomalies, but unfortunately there is not sufficient reliable evidence for assessing which is the most likely:

a) A simple mistake by the workman – possible but unlikely.

b) A renumbering of a later weapon replacing a lost one. It is clear from the archives that if a guard lost his pistol or blunderbuss he was expected to replace it. It is possible that the replacement might have been given the number of the weapon it was replacing but this is pure supposition. It is more than likely that the replacement item would have been ordered from the official supplier, which could explain why a Mortimer number might be on a Harding firearm or vice-versa.

c) The number on some has no real significance, it may just have been a deliberate attempt to suggest the piece was a Mail Office weapon and so increase its value on the antique market. It is a sad fact that false engraving has been added to pieces sold to collectors. Again it is impossible to say whether this is the case, but it is extremely unlikely.

Trade label from a pistol case by Mortimer & Son, the Post Office armourers from 1807-1812. The firm presumably did not consider it worthwhile announcing their connection with the Royal Mail. (R. Dale)

The flintlock of a guard's pistol by Harding & Son dated 1835, making it one of the last batches of weapons issued by this maker. The company's arrow mark is clear, as is the sliding bolt safety catch. (XII 8095 Courtesy of the Trustees Royal Armouries)

A few surviving Royal Mail pistols have the names of towns engraved on the barrel – in the Irish examples they are on the trigger guards – these are presumably the places between which the route operated. The distance between the two named places is fairly short, e.g. Norwich to Cromer, this could be taken to indicate that these were not carried on a coach but rather by a rider. There is no indication that the guards on the coaches exchanged pistols at the end of each ride, indeed the evidence suggests that the weapons were a personal issue retained by the guard. The named examples in the Royal Armouries collection are all dated 1835 and 1836, which may have some significance.

An attractive theory is that only those pistols and blunderbusses engraved at the muzzle with the appropriate legend were coaching weapons and that the others were carried by riders. Unfortunately, those examples in the Royal Armouries collection which have an engraved route all have the 'mail coach' legend around the muzzle, which rather weakens this theory. One could fall back on the 'false engraving' theory, but as these pieces have been in the collection for many years it is very unlikely that the engraving is a recent addition. It is possible that a close metallurgic examination of these weapons might be able to shed light on the matter, but to date no such tests have been made.

It is very sad to note that at one time Hasker listed the firearms and noted the person to whom they were issued. In a petition he said that 'seeing the fire arms for the guard properly disposed, whether in or out of use and kept clean and their numbers registered' was one of his many tasks, but there is no trace of any such record in the surviving archives.[1]

Those firearms engraved with the letters GPO or similar legends were supplied by Nock or Wilkinson to the Packet boats and are not mail coach weapons.

A HANDLIST OF POST OFFICE FIREARMS
IN THE ROYAL ARMOURIES COLLECTION

RA	No.	Type	Maker	No.	Date/ Remarks
XII	286	Blunderbuss	Rigby	–	
			Dublin Mail Guard No. 1 on barrel/Belfast & Derry 1		
XII	5589	Pistol	Mortimer & Co	11	–
XII	5591	Pistol	Mortimer	40	–
XII	8088	Pistol	Harding	60	–
XI	8094	Pistol	Harding	61	–
XII	8603	Blunderbuss	Mortimer & Son	68	–
XII	8083	Pistol	Mortimer	108	–
XII	4011	Pistol	Mortimer	111	–
XII	8096	Pistol	Mortimer	116	–
XII	1080	Pistol	Mortimer & Co	122	–
XII	3984	Pistol	Mortimer	132	–
XII	8092	Pistol	Mortimer & Son	148	–
XII	8089	Pistol	Harding & Son	162	–
XII	4861	Blunderbuss	Harding	230	–
XII	8090	Pistol	Mortimer & Son	249	–
XII	8061	Blunderbuss	Mortimer & Son	260	–
XII	8060	Blunderbuss	Mortimer & Son	263	–
XII	857	Pistol	Mortimer & Son	274	–
XII	8062	Blunderbuss	Harding	316	–
XII	8085	Pistol	Harding	321	–
XII	8087	Pistol	Harding	323	1835
XII	4862	Blunderbuss	Harding	328	–
XII	8084	Pistol	Harding	336	–
XII	5556	Pistol	Harding	339	1826

This engraving entitled 'The Exeter Coach' comes from *Stage Coach and Mail Days of Yore*. It shows a mail coach being halted at a toll gate, in fact they were excused all tolls and passed through without stopping.

XII	5583	Pistol	Harding & Son	360	1836
XII	4860	Blunderbuss	Harding & Son	361	1839
XII	855	Pistol	Harding & Son	369	–
XII	8604	Blunderbuss	Mortimer & Son	369	–
XII	856	Pistol	Harding & Son	374	1837
XII	8093	Pistol	Harding & Son	379	1837
XII	291	Blunderbuss	Harding & Son	286	–

UNNUMBERED EXAMPLES

XI	851	Pistol	Wilkinson	–	GPO on cap
XII	852	Pistol	Wilkinson	–	GPO on cap
XI	1865	Pistol	Harding & Son	–	Inspector/Foot?
XII	4858	Pistol	Harding & Son	–	1835 Norwich & Cromer
XII	4859	Pistol	Harding & Son	–	1835 Swansea & Merthyr
XII	5585	Pistol	Harding & Son	–	GPO on butt cap
XII	5593	Pistol	Tower	–	GPO
XII	8605	Blunderbuss	Mortimer & Son	–	–
XII	8606	Blunderbuss	Harding & Son	–	–
XI	8607	Blunderbuss	Harding	–	–
XI	8095	Pistol	Harding & Son	–	1836 Exeter & Budleigh Salterton

A sorting room at Lombard Street office with dozens of lamps or candles. This must have generated a very smoky atmosphere for the numerous sorters at work there. (PO PE 083)

EXAMPLES RECORDED IN PRIVATE COLLECTIONS OR OTHER MUSEUMS

Weapon	Maker	Number	Date/Details
Pistol	H.W. Mortimer	12	—
Blunderbuss	J. Harding	38	1834
Pistol	J. Harding	54	—
Pistol	J. Harding	55	—
Pistol	J. Harding & Son	60	—
Pistol	H.W. Mortimer	88	—
Blunderbuss	H.W. Mortimer	93	—
Pistol	H.W. Mortimer	101	—
Pistol	J. Harding & Son	101	—
Blunderbuss	H.W. Mortimer	104 ★	—
Pistol	H.W. Mortimer	104★	—
Blunderbuss	H.W. Mortimer	110	—
Blunderbuss	H.W. Mortimer	117	—
Pistol	J. Harding	119	—
Pistol	H.W. Mortimer	123	—

Typical bullet mould of the period and probably of the type issued to guards, however none has ever been identified as being a Post Office issue.

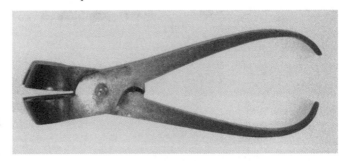

Detail of the engraved mail coach of the powder horn bearing a dedication. It was sold through a Sotheby's auction and may well be the only genuine Post Office example.

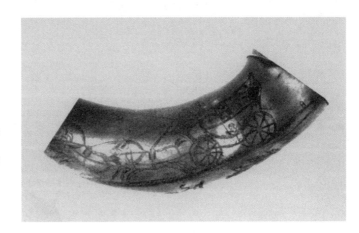

Pistol	H.W. Mortimer	126	—
Blunderbuss	H.W. Mortimer	140	—
Blunderbuss	H.W. Mortimer & Son	—	149
Pistol	H.W. Mortimer	150	—
Pistol	H.W. Mortimer	158 (2 recorded)	—
Pistol	H.W. Mortimer	161	—
Blunderbuss	H.W. Mortimer & Son	172	1808 Norwich and Cromer
Blunderbuss	J. Harding	205	—
Pistol	J. Harding	210	—
Pistol	H.W. Mortimer & Co	221	—
Pistol	H.W. Mortimer & Son	260	—
Pistol	H.W. Mortimer & Son	268	—
Blunderbuss	J. Harding	302	—
Pistol	J. Harding	303	—
Pistol	J. Harding	325	—
Blunderbuss	J. Harding	332	Stamford & Grantham★

Pistol	J. Harding	347	—
Pistol	J. Harding	359	1836
Pistol	J. Harding & Son	370	1837
Pistol	J. Harding & Son	377	1837
Pistol	J. Harding & Son	380	—
Pistol	J. Harding & Son	382	—
Pistol	J. Harding & Son	383	1840

*It seems unlikely that a rider would carry a blunderbuss, the references to 'riders' mention only pistols.

UNNUMBERED EXAMPLES

Weapon	Maker	Details
Pistol	J. Harding & Son	T
Pistol	J. Harding	W a pair
Pistol	J. Harding & Son	Caernarvon & Barmouth
Pistol	J. Harding & Son	Doncaster & Hull
Pistol	Goggin	Ashford & Wicklow (Irish)
		Post Rider No 1
Blunderbuss	Barbar London	With muzzle inscription
Blunderbuss	Goggin **	Mail Guard No.1
Blunderbuss	W. Mortimer***	York * Ric
Blunderbuss	H. Nock	—
Blunderbuss	Ketland	With muzzle inscription
Pistol	H. Nock	Butt cap General Post Office
Pistol	H. Nock	Butt cap General Post Office
		and sea service belthook

* Complete set at Edinburgh
** A recorded supplier of arms to the Irish Post Office
*** The only example of the legend appearing anywhere other than around the muzzle

END NOTES

INTRODUCTION

1.) Post 40/31, item 61g
2.) Post 42/16, p.10
3.) Post 9/9, p.157
4.) Post 1/11
5.) Post 1/11, p.228
6.) Post 9/9
7.) Post 42/75
8.) Post 42/15
9.) Post 42/29, p.31

CHAPTER ONE

1.) For a full description of the Roman systems see Beale.
2.) The Pony Express only functioned for about eighteen months but the journey
    of 1,800 miles (2,900 km) was accomplished in around ten days. There were
    approximately 157 stages, with riders changing horse several times between each stage.
3.) Beale, p.21
4.) 1681 Mr Richard Evans his bill for leathern bags from 3rd Sept 13th Oct 1681
    £4-2-0 (Post 2/1)
5.) Hughes and Larkin No.733
6.) idem 447
7.) Hughes and Larkin No.36
8.) idem p7

CHAPTER TWO

1.) See Joyce and Boyce
2.) Post 68/1.
3.) (Post 96/20, pt 3 fol. 47)
4.) (Post 10/200)
5.) (Post 1/11)

6.) (Post 96/20, pt 2)

7.) A diligence was a light coach and these are also referred to as chaise, carriage and machine.

8.) Franking was a system which allowed certain material to be carried by the Post Office without any charge; Members of Parliament were one group so privileged.

9.) (Post 1/11)

10.) (Post 96/20, pt 2 fol. 33)

11.) (Post 96/20, pt 2 fol. 33)

12.) For details of the event see Phillips

13.) (Post 96/20, pt 1 fol.19)

14. The Act 24 Geo III cap 37 introduced higher charges from 21st August 1784 unfortunately coinciding with the introduction of Palmer's plan

15.) (Post 10/200)

16.) (Post 10/200)

17.) (Post 1/13, p24)

18.) There is a simple clear resume of the details of appointment, salary and a list of his proposals contained in Appendices 2 and 3 of Palmer's Memorial Post 10/200.

19.) (Post 1/14)

19a.) (See Appendix 2 for listing)

20.) (Post 96/22, pt 1 fol. 6)

21.) (Post 10/27, p224)

22.) (Post 96/22, pt 1 fol.12)

23.) His petition (Post 96/22, pt 2 fol. 19). He says that when he comes to London:

> …instead of finding rest from the fatigues of the country business, he has greater labour and more anxiety to get the business to and keep it with that regularity he is desirous and which the Compt General expects,…

24.) (Post 1/15, p125)

25.) (Post 1/18, p137)

26.) (Post 35/10, p447)

27.) (Post 96/22, pt 1 fol 6)

28.) (Post 1/13, p108 /9)

29.) (Post 1/13, p108)

30.) (Post 1/17)

31.) (Post 96/20, pt 2 fol 38 and Post 96/21 pt I fol.2)

32.) (Post 96/20, pt 2 fol 35)

33.) (Post 96/22, pt1 fol 1)

34.) (post 96/22, pt1 fol 2)

35.) (Post 96/21, pt2 fol 9)

36.) (Post 1/14)

37.) (Post 10/201)

38.) (Post 96/17)

39.) (Post 42/16, p22)

40.) (Post 1/15)

41.) (Post 1/15, p129)

42.) (Post 1/15)

43.) (Post 42/29, p95, 98)

44.) The letters are given in full in the excellent book by Clear

45.) (Post 1/17)

46.) (Post 35/18)

47.) (Post 10/201)

CHAPTER THREE

1.) A Full and Impartial Account of all the Robberies committed by John Hawkins George Simpson, Wilson R., *c*. 1722 London 3rd edition

2.) (Post 10/9)

3.) Hanging in chains was abolished in July 1834 and public executions only stopped in 1868.

4.) (Post 10/9)

5.) The Act 7 GeoIII cap L stated that from 1 November 1767 anybody stealing any mail would, on conviction, 'suffer death as a felon without benefit of clergy.'

6.) A return to Parliament in May 1836 quotes some interesting statistics – in the five years prior to 1832 4,327 people were committed for burglary and house-breaking and forty-six were executed. Fourteen people were committed for letter stealing and one was executed. For arson 391 people were committed of which forty-two were executed, this made it the crime most likely to earn the death penalty. (Post 30/30/a)

7.) (Post 30/27)

8.) (Post 42/29)

9.) See *Post Office Notices extracted from the London Gazette 1666-1800*, Haslam D.G. and Moreton C. 1988. Also Oldham and British Post Office Notices, 1666-1899 and Vols 1-3 M.M. Raguin, published by the author in 1991.

10.) The Royal Mail its Curiosities and Romance, London, 1889.

11.) (Post 9/9)

12.) (Post 9/9)

13.) (Post 2/96)

14.) (Post 9/17)

15.) (Post 10/9)

16.) (Post 9/14)

17.) (Post 5/1)

18.) (Post 1/13)

19.) (Post 10/9, p66)

20.) Old Bailey Trials, t17820220-9.

21.) The Act 9 Anne cap X stated this clearly, although private business letters were exempted.

22.) (Post 40/87, p129)

23.) (Post 40/53, p87)

24.) (Post 96/20, pt 3 fol 47)

25.) (Post 1/11)

26.) (Post 1/11)

27.) (Post 96/20, pt 2)

28.) (Post 96/20, pt 2 fol 33)

29.) (Post 10/200, p35)

30.) *The History of the Post Office from its establishment down to 1836*, Joyce H, London Richard Bentley & Son, 1893.

31.) (Post 10/24, p114)

32.) (Post 10/2, p10)

33.) (Post 10/26)

34.) (Post 42/33, p152)

35.) (Post 42/33)

36.) (Post 35/6, p210).

37.) (Post 1/12)

38.) (Post 2/86)
39.) (Post 1/15)
40.) (Post 1/15, p112)
41.) (Post 2/83)
42.) (Post 2/84)
43.) (Post 2/86)
44.) (Post 10/33)
45.) (Post 42/30, p266)
46.) (Post 35/8, p29 & 67)
47.) (Post 10/27, p45)
48.) (Post 10/27)
49.) (Post 35/6)
50.) (Post 35/9)
51.) (Post 42/105, p482)
52.) (Post 35/10, p5)
53.) (Post 59/37, p32)
54.) (Post 10/27, p101)
55.) (Post 10/35, p260)
56.) (Post 35/12, p376)
57.) (Post 35/11, p223)
58.) (Post 10/26)
59.) (Post 35/24, p167)
60.) (Post 35/24, p167)
61.) (Post 10/26)
62.) (Post 42/18, p86)
63.) (Post 35/11, p397)
64.) (Post 10/35, p132)
65.) (Post 35/17)
66.) (Post 10/35)
67.) (Post 35/16)
68.) (Post 35/16)
69.) (Post 1/14, p228)
70.) (Post 10/35)
71.) (Post 96/22, fol 6)
72.) (Post 96/22, fol 6)
73.) (Post 30/9, appendix 4)
74.) See Appendices IV and V
75.) (Post 10/25)
76.) (Post 10/5)
77.) (Post 10/24; 10/113; 10/116)
78.) (Post 10/5)
79.) (Post 10/5, 47)
80.) (Post 10/5)
81.) (Post 10/6)
82.) (Post 10/27)
83.) (Post 10/26)
84.) (Post 42/ 76; 42/77)
85.) (Post 42/14)
86.) (Post 42/77)
87.) (Post 42/13, p150)
88.) (Post 31/14, p60)
89.) (Post 42/14)

90.) See Harper Vol II and Blew

91.) (Post 42/10, p3)

92.) (Post 35/10, p22)

93.) 11 May 1837, letter signed by Louis saying he had received approval for the procession to assemble in Lincolns Inn Field. There had been a slight change in the route in the previous year, now it would go out of St James's Square into George St and thence into Pall Mall and St James St instead of through King St into St James Sq. Afterwards it would proceed through Queen St, Long Acre, St Martins Lane, Trafalgar Sq., Whitehall, Horse Guards, St James Park, Stable Yard, Pall Mall to south eastern entrance. It was to continue through John St to St James Sq round the east and north sides of the square, by Lord Lichfield's House in the west side through
George (?). Next came Pall Mall, St James St, Piccadilly, Hyde Park, Cumberland Gate, Oxford St, Regent St, Waterloo Place, Pall Mall, Cockspur St, Charing Cross, Strand, Fleet St, Farringdon St, Skinner St, Newgate St, St Martin's-le-Grand into the north gate of Post Office Yard. (Post 10/48)

94.) The Coaching Age, Harris S, London, 1885

95.) Hone, in his Everyday Book, writing of 1822, tells us that George IV – who was born on 12 August 1762 – changed the celebration of his birthday to St. George's Day, April 23. 'According to custom,' said he:

…the mail-coaches go in procession from Milbank to Lombard Street. At about twelve o'clock, the horses belonging to the different mails, with entirely new harness, and the post-men and post-boys on horseback arrayed in scarlet coats and jackets, would go to Milbank and there dine; from thence the procession, being re-arranged, begins to march about five o'clock in the afternoon, headed by the General Post letter-carriers on horseback. The coaches follow them, filled with the wives and children, friends and relations of the guards and coachmen; while the post-boys, sounding their bugles and clacking their whips, bring up the rear. From the commencement of the procession, the bells of the neighbouring churches ring out merrily, and continue their rejoicing peals till it arrives at the Post-office again, from whence the coaches depart to the different parts of the country.
(Everyday Book 2 vols, Hone W, 1838.)

96.) (Post 6/28)

97.) (Post 6/29)

98.) (Post 6/29)

99.) (Post 35/2)

100.) If the Deputy Postmasters had been paying for five quarters then this suggests that the starting date must have been some time in 1788. This is another indication that the Post Office took over employment of the guard in this period.

101.) (Post 1/14)

102.) (Post 1/15)

103.) These 1791 payments for hats and uniforms could well be another pointer that the Post Office had taken over the employment of the guards.

104.) The pension terms, as stated in January 1807, were that a retiring officer should receive _ of his official income and ¾ if he had served thirty-five years or more. (Post 35/6)

105.) (Post 42/22)

106.) (Post 3/17)

107.) (Post 59/42)

108.) (Post 30/80B)

109.) (Post 35/9)
110.) (Post 10/68)
111.) (Post 30/33b)
112.) (Post 30/33B)
113.) (Post 42/22)
114.) (Post 42/34)
115.) (Post 42/22)
116.) (Post 10/8)
117.) (Post 35/2, p66)
118.) (Post 10/239)
119.) (Post 30/80B)
120.) (Post 9/22a)
121.) (Post 35/6, p27)
122.) (Post 96/22, pt 2)
123.) (Post 59/33)
124.) (Post 59/42)
125.) Old Coaching Days, Moses James Nobbs, London 1891. Born in Norwich in
      May 1817, Nobbs's father was a coachbuilder and worked in this trade until the
      age of nineteen. In 1836 he was a guard on both the London to Stroud and
      Peterborough to Hull routes. Later on he worked on the Portsmouth to Bristol
      run which involved a working day of 7 p.m. to 7 a.m. He tells of hardship in the
      snow, drunken coachmen falling into the road, some being killed when horses
      bolted and taking the coach on to Andover. In 1838 he moved to the Cheltenham
      to Aberystwyth run and stayed there until 1854. When that run ended in 1854 he
      transferred to the London to Exeter railway which ran from Paddington station, he
      remained there until 1861.

      On the Bristol to Portsmouth run in 1836 two men grabbed the lead horse, the
      coachman responded with his whip and Nobbs 'took the blunderbuss out of the
      sword case', fired it, and claimed it had 'hard kick'. No doubt it was loaded to the
      muzzle, as was usual with those weapons. This was in direct contradiction to the
      rules for guards, which specified that the weapons were to be unloaded after each
      run. Nobbs makes reference to guards earning up to £300 p.a., he also states that
      there were 365 guards in 1841 but by 1843 this number had been reduced to 327.

      The booklet also lists some notices, including one from Freeling dated 9
      February 1813. This notice gave the details of a notorious villain named Huffey
      White; he was a cabinet maker of London, thirty-five to thirty-six years old,
      approximately 5ft 9ins tall, of stoutish build, with thin legs, brown hair, broad or
      full forehead, pale complexion, light grey eyes, little eyebrows marked by small
      pox, large deep pits, turned-up nose, squeaky voice and a mild and quiet manner.
      He did time on the hulks and had returned ten years ago. Six years later he was
      sentenced at the Old Bailey to be transported for life but escaped. Twelve months
      later he was caught in Stockport and tried at Chester, he was sent back to hulks
      but again escaped. He robbed Paisley Union Bank, then went down to London;
      he was eventually caught in Surrey and convicted at Kingston Lent Assizes in 1811.
      Back he went to the hulks only for him to escape again. Travelling under his alias
      'Wallis' on the Shrewsbury coach with Robert Brady – or 'Oxford Bob' – on 29
      March 1813. He was seen with Richard Haywood wearing blue coat gilt buttons,
      white waistcoat blue pantaloons and a yellow belcher handkerchief about his neck.

CHAPTER FOUR

1.) (Post 1/11)
2.) (Post 200)
3.) (Post 2/84)
4.) See H.L. Blackmore
5.) See 'The Coach' chapter
6.) (Post 42/3)
7.) (Post 42/28)
8.) (Post 1/14)
9.) (Post 10/26)
10.) (Post 42/3)
11.) (Post 1/14)
12.) (Post 35/6)
13.) From correspondence from a family descendant.
14.) (Post 42/100, letter 229)
15.) From correspondence from a family descendant.
16.) There is a reference to a T.Harding supplying staves, but no indication of whether there was any family connection. (Post 5/1)
17.) From the collection of R. Dale.
18.) (Post 10/6)
19.) (Post 96/22, pt 2 fol 49)
20.) (Post 10/6)
21.) (Post 10/151)
22.) Calderwood is listed by Carey as having a shop in Dublin from 1815-1860.
23.) (Post 10/151)
24.) Whilst it does not prove anything, it is of interest to note that none of the apparent routes engraved on the three coaching pistols appear in these lists, e.g. Norwich & Cromer (Post 40/324, fol.181)
25.) (Post 40/324 -313)
26.) (Post 10/9)
27.) (Post 6/17)
28.) (Post 6/29)
29.) Short guns probably refers to a coaching carbine, which was simply a reduced in size version of a conventional flintlock musket, often finely decorated and designed to be carried on a coaching journey.
30.) See above for evidence that this was probably John Carter.
31.) (Post 42/3)
32.) (Post 5/1)
33.) (Post 10/291)
34.) (Post 42/13, p 136)
35.) A note by Hasker detailing his jobs mentions a book listing the weapons, timepieces, uniforms and to whom each was issued – alas this has not survived. (Post 96/22, pt 2 fol 12)
36.) (Post 42/34)
37.) (Post 10/291)
38.) (Post 42/34)
39.) (Post 10/5)
40.) (Post 10/6)
41.) (Post 35/3)
42.) (Post 42/31, p84)

43.) (Post 10/24)

44.) For discussion of the firearms see Appendix Firearms

45.) (Post 10/24)

46.) (Post 42/33)

47.) (Post 42/33)

48.) (Post 10/26)

49.) (Post 10/26)

50.) The architectural plans for Lombard Street Office show two vaults that may have been at this site, but on this date the records state that a room in Sherborne Lane was being rented.

51.) The report of 1814 (Post 91/12) says that 'A room for the firearms is engaged in Sherborne Lane there not being a place to be obtained in the office for this purpose.'

52.) (Post 42/104)

53.) (Post 35/11)

54.) (Post 6/16)

55.) (Post 35/16)

56.) (Post 6/32)

57.) (Post 35/26)

58.) (Post 9/17)

59.) (Post 6/4 and 10/26)

60.) (Post 6/4)

61.) (Post 5/3)

62.) (Post 10/6)

63.) (Post 10/53)

64.) Road Scrapings, Coaches and Coaching, Haworth M.E. (Captain), London, 1882.

65.) (Post 1/4)

66.) (Post 5/5)

67.) (Post 6/31)

68.) (Post 6/31)

69.) (Post 6/31)

70.) (Post 6/31)

71.) (Post 5/5, p76)

72.) (Post 9/17)

73.) (Post 9/17)

74.) (Post 9/17)

75.) (Post 6/30)

76.) (Post 96/22, pt 2 fol 49)

77.) (Post 42/30)

78.) (Post 35/10, p180)

79.) (Post 42/12, p138)

80.) (Post 10/24)

81.) (Post 10/26)

82.) (Post 1/4)

83.) (Post 1/14)

84.) (Post 10/27, p300)

85.) (Post 10/112)

86.) (Post 1/14)

87.) (Post 4/24)

88.) (Post 6/6)

89.) (Post 6/14)

90.) (Post 6/14)

91.) (Post 6/16)

92.) (Post 35/8, p363)

93.) (Post 6/18)

94.) (Post 6/33)

95.) (Post 10/27)

96.) (Post 6/5)

97.) (Post 6/34, p256)

98.) (Post 9/9)

99.) (Post 6/31 and 6/32)

100.) Annals of the Road, Captain Malet, London, 1876

101.) Old Coaching Days, Harris S., London, 1882

102.) Illustration in Heritage Archives

103.) (Post 10/26, p54)

104.) (Post 10/65)

105.) (Post 10/27)

106.) (Post 10/5)

107.) The Proceedings of the Old Bailey t17960914

108.) (Post 10/26)

109.) (Post 35/3)

110.) *The King's Post*, Tombs R.C., London, 1905

111.) In the directories of this date a J. Turner is recorded at this address for one year only, for similar dates at 84 Leadenhall Street a pianoforte maker and musical instrument warehouse is listed.

112.) (Post 10/6)

113.) (Post 10/26)

114.) (Post 42/20)

115.) (Post 42/2, p48)

116.) (Post 42/9)

117.) (Post 6/11)

118.) (Post 6/27)

119.) (Post 6/17)

120.) (Post 61/1)

121.) (Post 42/104, p382)

122.) (Post 61/1)

123.) (Post 10/27)

124.) (Post 2/60)

125.) (Post 5/7)

126.) (Post 5/1)

127.) (Post 61/1)

128.) (Post 10/24)

129.) (Post 42/114, p294)

130.) (Post 42/5)

131.) (Post 42/12)

132.) Harper

133.) (Post 9/17)

CHAPTER FIVE

1.) (Post 1/18, p142)

2.) (Post 10/27, p51)

3.) (Post 10/8)
4.) (Post 42/75, 76B)
5.) (Post 42/15 p142)
6.) (Post 10/8)
7.) (Post 42/13)
8.) (Post 42/15)
9.) (Post 41/18)
10.) (Post 10/8, vol.1)
11.) (Post 10/8)
12.) A farthing was a quarter of one old penny
13.) (Post 42/34)
14.) (Post 10/6, vol 1)
15.) (Post 10/8, vol 1)
16.) (Post 40/31, p238-240)
17.) (Post 35/2)
18.) (Post 35/2)
19.) (Post 30/3)
20.) (Post 10/8, vol 1)
21.) (Post 35/3, p298/9)
22.) (Post 10/8, vol 1)
23.) (Post 10/8)
24.) (Post 42/114)
25.) (Post 5/2)
26.) (Post 5/2)
27.) (Post 10/8)
28.) Arms and Uniforms of the Napoleonic Wars, Funcken L and F, London, 1973.
29.) (Post 10/193)
30.) (Post 10/174)

CHAPTER SIX

1.) (Post 42/16, p84)
2.) (Post 42/30)
3.) (Post 35/3, p239)
4.) (Post 1/14)
5.) (Post 96/21, pt 1 fol 19)
6.) (Post 1/14)
7.) (Post 2/85)
8.) (Post 2/86)
9.) (Post 96/21, pt 1 fol. 9)
10.) (Post 42/16, p89)
11.) The firm were listed as Engine Manufacturers and located at 165 Great Surrey Street, Blackfriars. (Post 6/19, p207).
12.) (Post 1/10)
13.) (Post 1/10)
14.) (Post 91/12)
15.) (Post 91/12)
16.) (Post 6/23)
17.) (Post 6/22)
18.) (Post 6/35)

19.) Quoted in His Majesty's Mails, Levins W.

20.) (Post 2/65)

21.) (Post 2/83)

22.) (Post 59/26)

23.) (Post 1/11)

24.) (Post 42/7, p15)

25.) (Post 9/37)

26.) (Post 91/12)

27.) (Post 91/1).

28.) (Post 6/30, p311)

29.) This was C.L. Hoggart, auctioneer, of 62 Old Broad Street (P.O. Directory)

30.) This could well be the room referred to as being used by the guards when they reported for duty, alternatively it could be the room used by Mr Broadrib, the official armourer. (Post 91/12)

31.) (Post 68/95)

32.) (Post 2/1)

33.) A maile was a type of leather container.

34.) (Post 9/9, p22)

35.) (Post 5/1)

36.) The instructions to Guards (1829) (Post 6/18).

37.) Trial reference tl-7810425-67

38.) (Post 9/12)

39.) (Post 6/4)

40.) (Post 5/1)

41.) This document includes a long report on the supply and costing of these post bags. (Post 62/10)

42.) (Post 42/14, p10)

43.) (Post 10/27)

44.) (Post 10/6)

45.) Case reference ti7950416-53

46.) (Post 10/26)

47.) (Post 10/116)

48.) Proceedings of the Old Bailey t17810425-67, also see Post 1/11.

49.) (Post 1/11 and 10/2)

50.) (Post 42/10, p20)

51.) (Post 42/30 p76)

52.) The English mail coach---de Quincy.

53.) (Post 10/6)

54.) (Post 10/5)

55.) (Post 10/5)

56.) (Post 42/24)

57.) The Mail Coach from Confessions

58.) (Post 42/14)

59.) (Post 10/24, p37)

60.) (Post 91/12)

61.) (Post 91/12)

62.) (Post 91/12)

63.) (Post 10/25)

64.) (Post 10/25, p15)

65.) (Post 10/25, p20-22)

66.) (Post 42/22, p122)

67.) In September 1829, coinciding with the new Post Office, the Metropolitan Police were officially established and were known as the New Police.

68.) (Post 35/16, p454-455)
69.) (Post 10/26)
70.) (Post 35/5)
71.) (Post 10/108)
72.) (Post 10/100)
73.) (Post 42/30)
74.) (Post 10/247)
75.) (Post 10/245)
76.) (Post 42/10, May 1792)
77.) (Post 42/30)
78.) (Post 42/9)
79.) (Post 10/27, p53)
80.) (Post 10/5)
81.) (Post 10/25)
82.) (Post 10/65, p199)
83.) (Post 30/31)
84.) (Post 35/8, p256)
85.) This sentence was the traditional one when a defendant was found guilty of an offence considered so trivial as to merit only a nominal punishment.
86.) (Post 10/135)
87.) (Post 10/27, p160)
88.) (Post 10/6)
89.) (Post 42/10)
90.) (Post 10/6)
91.) (Post 10/203)
92.) (Post 10/168)
93.) (Post 10/203)
94.) Georgian Cookery, Stead J., Swindon 2003.
95.) For details of the coaching inns see Hanson, The Coaching Life
96.) (Post 42/14)
97.) (Post 10/26)
98.) (Post 10/5; 6)
99.) (Post 10/5)
100.) (Post 10/6)
101.) (Post 10/239)
102.) (Post 10/26)
103.) (Post 6/4)
104.) (Post 6/14)
105.) (Post 35/16)
106.) Malet (*op. cit.*)
107.) (Post 10/239)
108.) (Post 10/5 - 3)
109.) (Post 10/101)
110.) (Post 10/5)
111.) (Post 30/35d)
112.) (Post 10/164)
113.) (Post 10/164)
114.) (Post 30/9b)
115.) (Post 10/5;24)
116.) (Post 30/9b)
117.) (Post 10/50)

118.) (Post 10/5)
119.) (Post 10/52)
120.) (Post 10/40)
121.) (Post 10/239)
122.) (Post 35/9)
123.) (Post 10/6)
124.) Old Bailey Trial t17960914-22
125.) Old Bailey Trial t18150111-41
126.) (Post 10/40)
127.) (Post 10/26)
128.) (Post 10/239)
129.) (Post 10/236)
130.) (Post 10/239)
131.) (Post 30/35d)
132.) See *All Heaven in a Rage*, Turner, E.S. London, 1964. For £535-19-6 p.a. he would supply and maintain in good repair. He would supply leather bags and canvas wallets for inland foreign West Indies office letter carriers and inland letters and will rivet brass labels on and supplying them on proper rings and straps 890 of them and Hurst will take on present bags as stock and this will result in big saving.
133.) (Post 10/27)
134.) (Post 10/6, p127)
135.) (Post 10/6)
136.) (Post 35/6)
137.) (Post 35/6)
138.) (Post 10/126)

CHAPTER SEVEN

1.) (Post 10/18)
2.) (Post 10/6)
3.) (Post 10/5)
4.) (Post 10/286 /6)
5.) (Post 10/6)
6.) (Post 10/26)
7.) (Post 10/258)
8.) (Post 10/26, p135)
9.) (Post 35/24, p370)
10.) (Post 10/102)
11.) (Post 10/239)
12.) (Post 10/254)
13.) (Post 10/165)
14.) (Post 10/30)
15.) (Post 10/280)
16.) (Post 10/28)
17.) Quoted in *Monarchs of all they Surveyed*
18.) (Post 1/13)
19.) (Post 1/16, p202)
20.) (Post 42/1)
21.) (Post 42/29, p10/11)
22.) (Post 59/37, p10)

23.) (Post 10/111)

24.) (Post 1/16)

25.) (Post 42/34, p34)

26.) (Post 42/9, p40)

27.) (Post 10/24, p145)

28.) (Post 35/2, p164/165)

29.) This was the standard reference and ran to numerous editions. It listed the main routes and gave its details. It often included a potted history or points of interest, the times of mail coaches and the size of populations.

30.) (Post 10/286)

31.) (Post 6/29, p217)

CHAPTER EIGHT

1.) He agreed a price on 24 October of £53, plus more when it was finished. He was thrilled with his first ride on 2 December 1668.

2.) There is some confusion over the naming of the coaches, with the same vehicle often being known by several titles. The terms coach, chaise and diligence seem to have been almost interchangeable in Post Office records. Other four-wheeled coaches were the landau, sociable and the Berlin.

3.) (Post 10/5, p83)

4.) (Post 10/26)

5.) (Post 10/5)

6.) (Post 10/264)

7.) (Post 10/264)

8.) (Post 10/231)

9.) (Post 10/264)

10.) (Post 10/264)

11.) (Post 10/264)

12.) (Post 10/24)

13.) (Post 10/8)

14.) (Post 10/26, p89)

15.) (Post 10/263/.264/.265)

16.) (Post 10/264)

17.) (Post 10/4)

18.) (Post 10/264)

19.) (Post 10/251)

20.) (Post 10/251)

21.) (Post 10/10)

22.) This was the peace of Amiens, which was little more that a short truce in the Napoleonic wars, it was signed on 27 March 1802 and lasted only fourteen months

23.) (Post 10/10)

24.) A hundredweight was 112 pounds and twenty or 2,240 pounds made one ton. – a hundredweight was roughly equivalent to 56 kilos

25.) (Post 10/10)

26.) (Post 10/4)

27.) (Post 10/248)

28.) (Post 10/248)

29.) (Post 10/250)

30.) (Post 10/24)

31.) (Post 10/3)
32.) (Post 10/24)
33.) (Post 10/263-5 and 1/176)
34.) (Post 1/17, p31)
35.) (Post 10/40)
36.) (Post 42/12)
37.) (Post 10/5 n 9)
38.) (Post 10/24, p136)
39.) (Post 42/21, p104)
40.) (Post 10/27, p104)
41.) (Post 10/27, p144)
42.) (Post 10/34)
43.) (Post 10/34, pt1)
44.) (Post 10/90)
45.) (Post 10/15)
46.) (Post 10/109)
47.) (Post 10/12)
48.) (Post 10/190)
49.) (Post 10/16)
50.) (Post 10/12)
51.) (Post 10/34, pt 2 & pt 3)
52.) (Post 30/56)
53.) (Post 30/76)
54.) (Post 10/27, p97)
55.) (Post 6/29)

CHAPTER NINE

1.) (Post 10/131)
2.) (Post 10/59)
3.) (Post 6/30)
4.) (Post 59/40)
5.) Post 10/87, p11)
6.) (Post 10/98)
7.) (Post 114/154)
8.) (Post 6/31)
9.) (Post 10/85)
10.) (Post 35/23, p166)
11.) (Post 6/30)
12.) (Post 10/113)
13.) (Post 10/114)
14.) (Post 10/115)
15.) (Post 10/117)
16.) (Post 10/125)
17.) (Post 30/60)
18.) (Post 10/134)
19.) (Post 10/55)
20.) (Post 10/82)
21.) (Post 10/95)
22.) (Post 10/173)

23.) (Post 10/174)
24.) (Post 10/57)
25.) (Post 5/7, p168)
26.) (Post 30/80B)
27.) (Post 6/34, p294)
28.) (Post 10/121)
29.) (Post 5/7, p175)
30.) (Post 30/74)
31.) (Post 6/34)
32.) Quoted by Robinson
33.) (Post 68/433)
34.) Baines, F.E.

CHAPTER TEN

1.) (Post 96/22, pt. 2 fol.19)

APPENDICES

I

SOURCES

The vast majority of references given in the text are from the records held by the Heritage Trust, Freeling House, unless otherwise stated. The prime series used were:

1	Treasury letter books
2	Receiver General's cash books
3	Accountant General's cash books
4	Accounts of Packet Ship Services
5	Incident Warrant Accounts
6	Incident Bills Account
7	Property and Income Tax Assessments
8	Auditing of Accounts
9	Post Office Accounts
10	Conveyance of mail by road.
11	Conveyance of mail by rail.
12	Conveyance of mail by sea.
13	Inland mail organisation.
14	Minutes, England and Wales.
15	Minutes, Ireland.
16	Packet minutes.
35	Minutes between Secretary and Postmaster General.
40	Postmaster General's Reports Documents 1791-1841.
42	Postmaster General's Reports.
44	Overseas mail.
51	Overseas mail contracts.
58	Appointments.
59	Staff establishment books.
61	Uniforms and discipline.
68	Rules and instructions.
91	Buildings, furniture and fittings.
96	Palmer's letters
97	Walsingham's letters
103	Receiver General's notebook

107   Notices
111   Newspaper cuttings
114   Acts and warrants

II

MAIL COACH OFFICE STAFF 1786

On 19 December 1786 Palmer sent a memorial to the Postmaster General detailing his staff:

> That Thomas Lloyd, Francis Freeling, Robert White, Samuel Lott and Samuel Woodcock have been employed in carrying into execution the several reforms and improvements of posts under the directions of the said John Palmer during the time and in the several capacities herein after described.

Thomas Lloyd had been intermittently employed as a clerk since 6 January 1783, from 5 April 1785 he worked at a separate office in Lombard Street.

Francis Freeling was first employed as a surveyor on a cross road from Bristol to Portsmouth on 5 April 1785.

Robert White had been employed as clerk since September 1785.

Samuel Lott had been employed as surveyor of the Western District since 10 October 1785.

Samuel Woodcock had been employed as a surveyor of South Wales and the adjacent district since 10 October 1785.

Palmer suggested suitable terms of employment; Lloyd was to be First Clerk to Surveyor and Comptroller General at £80 per annum between 5 January 1784 and 5 April 1785. Freeling was to be made a surveyor at £100 p.a. with a guinea a day travelling expenses as of 5 April 1785. White would be second clerk to Surveyor and Comptroller General £69 p.a., Lott was to take up a position as surveyor of Western District at £100 p.a. and Woodcock would be surveyor of South Wales at £100 p.a.

Bonner, whose appointment as Resident Surveyor and Comptroller General was dated 9 November 1796, had been employed by the Post Office since 5 July 1784. Bonner suggested that arrears should be paid from 5 July 1784 to the date of his appointment.

Palmer reminded them that Christopher Saverland had been appointed by the past Postmaster General, he should be added to the list of surveyors at £100 per annum plus a guinea a day.

On 23 December Mr Rose of the Treasury sought Carteret's verdict on whether the staff was not too large. He replied on 5 January 1797 that he thought the number to be not too big in view of the many duties performed by the new office. He went on to say that one of the causes of bad service was the absence of surveyors and that the new system would increase supervision. A copy of each surveyor's book was to be kept at the controller's office and they were to keep regular journals. The six districts would be surveyed by Mr Hodgson and Mr Wilkinson (the old surveyors), as well as Mr Lott, Mr Woodcock, Mr Saverland and Mr Western (the new surveyors). Freeling would oversee the work of all of them. Carteret proposed either superannuating Arbuthnot and not replacing him or replacing Samuel Potts and Nathan Draper. (Post 1/15)

III

MAIL COACH OFFICE STAFF 1835

A new establishment suggested by His Grace the Duke of Richmond and presented to The Lords of His Majesty's Treasury is in a record dated 9 March 1832. It gives a list of the office staff and their dates of recruitment. Apart from the various suggestions it contains interesting comments of the current practice of the office.
It opens with a description of the Mail Coach Office. Its duty is:

> ...to supervise and regulate the conveyance of the mails by coaches throughout Great Britain and Ireland according to the contracts and time bills.

(p 6)(Further comments are given on page 57.) The description continues:

> It is essentially necessary that the superintendents of Mail Coaches should have a thorough practical knowledge of the circulation of letters and the connection of the posts throughout the country further as he has the management of the contracts for the mail coaches a matter becoming progressively of more and more delicacy and difficulty that he should be a person of the strictest integrity. The present superintendent was chief clerk in the secretary's office when it was necessary to induce him to undertake this situation of labor(sic) and responsibility under these circumstances it would not be just to place him in a worse situation than he formerly was but in the want of a vacancy I conceive a competent person might be found in some branch of the department to whom a salary of £450 per annum, in addition to the usual travelling expenses would form an adequate remuneration I have proposed a reduction in the maximum salary of the first clerk with reference to his duties as compared with those in other branches of the department and further that the Travelling allowances to the inspectors and the assistants shall be reduced from 18s to 15s per diem which I conceive will be amply sufficient – the saving under this latter head estimate at about £250 per annum the immediate diminution of expense in the office may be taken at £300 and the prospective reduction at £340.

> The superintendent has frequently to proceed to various parts of the country on business relating to his department.
>
> The assistant superintendent is employed about three days a week on average in travelling with the coaches for the inspection of the conduct of contractors' guards and coachmen to maintain the necessary regularity in the conveyance of the correspondence.

Surveyor and Superintendent
Surveyor, Charles Johnson, salary £750, appointed 1792.
Senior clerk, Robert Perry, salary £250, appointed 1799.
Second clerk, William Wedderburn, salary £40, appointed 1827.
Junior clerks, William Smart, salary £80, appointed 1824,
and James Newman, salary £80, appointed 1831.

Deputy Superintendent
William Akers (1815), Joseph Wilson (1826) a salary of £100 with 15s per day travelling expenses.

Surveyors

These were selected from the most competent officers of the departments:

> They are required to visit frequently the post offices in their respective districts for the purpose of inspecting the mode in which the Deputy Postmasters perform their business.

They were also responsible for contracting for delivery other than by mail coach. Part of their duties was to 'maintain discipline in the horse and foot posts.' They were:

Anthony Scott, appointed 1791;
George Karstadt, appointed 1802;
George Louis, appointed 1810;
Benjamin Churchill, appointed 1804;
Charles Rideout, appointed 1812;
John H. Fletcher, appointed 1804;
George Neal, appointed 1814.
(All except Neal received £300 plus expenses)

There is a further reference to this position on page 58:

> The situation of surveyor is one of the greatest importance both as regards the accommodation of the public and the interest of the revenue - they are the instructors of all postmasters - they are required from their local knowledge to report upon every proposition for the establishment of alteration of the posts in their respective districts and upon their ability and constant superintendence must in a great measure depend the convenience of the public and the advantage of the revenue.

Messengers

Two principal at £150 each; E.V. Williams and F. Cowper
Two senior at £100 each; T. King and T.R. Hood
Board room; I.H. Francis £110
Six messengers at £90 each; I. Coprvie, J. Addams, J. Howlett, I.S. Holbrew, F. Mortlock and A. Navins.

Six messengers at £80: W. Baker, G. Bailey, I. Hodgson, E. Warmford, G. Jupp and W. Bonham.
Six messengers at £70: W. Long, S. Petill, J. Hayes, W. Hall, J. Scott and J. Wyles
Six messengers at £60: W. Bird, P. Tunswill, J. Reynolds, P. Bain, R. Craddock and W. Holland

Gate Porter: I. Grant

Marine Mail Guards
Date of appointment
31 August 1832　　Joseph Wm Mortleman
31 August 1832　　Henry Hare
3 September 1832　Benjm Ward

5 October 1832   William Wadling
20 August 1833   Godfrey Freeman

The rate of pay was £6 per lunar month.
A copy of the instructions were given to the Marine Mail guards.
Memoranda furnished by the Superintendents of Mail Coaches, 29 November 1833.
Number of miles travelled daily by Mail Coaches: 15,934.
Expenses for forwarding the mail: £55,622.
Number of Mail Guards employed: 247.
Total of their wages: £6,734.
Number of roads on which the coachman acted as guard: 33
Number of roads on which the patent coaches were used: 59
Number of roads on which patent coaches were not used: 49

Ireland
Number of coaches: 32
Number of English miles: 4,604
Total mileage: £19,268
Number of mail guards: 73
Total wages: £2,484

Post 59/37

IV

GUARD INSTRUCTIONS 1812

General Post Office
London 181

Instructions For Mail Guards

The Guard is entrusted with the Care of the Letter Bags, and he is to be answerable at his Peril for the Security, safe Conduct, and Delivery of them sealed.

He is to obey the Surveyor's, Superintendent's and Postmaster's Orders respecting the Bye Bags.

He is not to quit or desert the Mail or Bags of Letters, or suffer any loitering or unnecessary stopping at Public Houses, or other mispending of time upon the road, or neglect to give information of such misconduct on the part of the coachman; if he does, he will be liable to be taken before a Justice of the Peace, and committed to Hard Labour, and Imprisonment for One Month, and he is subject to all other Punishments and Penalties which the Laws (as specified in the several Acts of Parliament relative to the Post Office) have hitherto inflicted upon Post Riders who have neglected their duty.

If in Post Towns he, on any account collects or delivers Letters or Packets, or does so upon the Road (except in some particular Cases where the Postmaster of the District or Superior Officers are authorised to order it) he will be liable to an Information before a Justice of the Peace, and to the Payment of Ten Shillings for every Letter, agreeable to an Act of Parliament passed in the First Year of His Present Majesty, and be dismissed from the Service.

The Guard is to behave with civility to passengers, to assist the Coachman on any Occasions that are consistent with his Situation as Protector of the Mails, and do not take him out of Sight of the Place where they are deposited.

He is on no account whatever to give up his Situation to another Person. He is to take care that his Fire Arms are kept in clean and good Condition; that they are always properly loaded and primed when on Duty, and on no account whatever to be *wantonly discharging his Blunderbuss or Pistols as the Carriage is going along the Road, or through a Town;* for every such Offence he forfeits Two Guineas, agreeable to a late Act of Parliament ; also to draw the Charge of them as soon as he has ended his Journey.

He is to sound his Horn as a signal for Carriages to turn out of the Way upon the Approach of the Mail Coach; also to warn Turnpike-men of its coming, that no unneces-sary delay may be occasioned, and likewise to prepare Postmaster against its arrival, and Horse-keepers to bring out such horses at each of the changing places and also it always as a signal to Passengers when the Time is expired that is allowed in the Time-Bill for their stopping to refresh, and use his utmost exertions to prevent delay in all cases whatever.

It is the Guard's Duty to see the time-bill is justly dated and signed at every Place, and where he cannot obtain The Postmaster's Date and Signature, to do it correctly himself, for which as Space is provided, and to deliver it carefully to the Guard who succeeds him at the End of his Journey, or to the Postmaster at the Place where the Route of the Mail Coach ends.

He must be very careful of the Time Piece and Time Bill, and if either should at any time be broken, torn or lost, immediate notice must be given to the Office, or the Cause communicated to the Postmaster of the nearest Place to where it happens, that he may write up an Account thereof, as it is resolved to show no Favour to Offenders in such Cases.

Forfeits will always be levied, or Guards will be suspended, who neglect to deliver the Bye Bags properly; which for want of better attention, have been frequently carried beyond their distance, and sometimes even brought up to London.

Drunkenness, or disobedience of Official Orders, will disqualify them from serving as Mail Guards upon any Road in the Kingdom.

Only two outside passengers are allowed, whose station must be, one of the Box, and one on the roof. The Pretence of taking up a *Caddie*, or Helper, will never be admitted as an excuse for disregarding this order. If a guard neglects to give immediate Notice of any Violation of this Article, with an Account of the Parties who are accessory to it, it will be considered as a very material Breach of his Duty, and he will be punished accordingly.

It is a very necessary part of his duty to report the earliest Intelligence of all Accidents, Delays or Obstructions, of Inattention or Want of Readiness of Horse-keepers, of Misconduct, in any of the Parties concerned in the Performance of his Duty, and of all Occurrences whatever that has a Tendency to impede the Progress of the Mail Coach, or may in any respect be proper to be communicated. He will, if a Mail Coach breaks down, describe what particular Part broke on his Bill, and the next Day, or as soon as possible, by Letter, give Information how it happened, and what Damage was done.

If the Mail Coach breaks down on its way to London, and it cannot be repaired in Half an Hour, or in such time that the Mail may arrive at the Post-Office by its proper Time, the Guard is to ride on with by Horse or Chaise; The Postmasters and Contractors have Directions to furnish such Chaise of Horse, which the Postmaster-General will pay for the Use of, or the Guard may pay for such Post-Horses, Ostlers, and Drivers and directly send the Bills to the Surveyor and Superintendant of Mails, who will reimburse him. If there are not more than two Passengers, who are willing to come on without Luggage, the Guard may bring them, provided they do not impede the Expedition of the Mail, The Guard must do all his Business at the different Offices, and his Road Business, and take Care that he performs his Journey in the same Time as if the Coach travelled.

If the Mail Coach should fail between Stage and Stage, the Guard is to press one of the Mail Coach horses, and ride on to the next Stage with it.

If, in travelling from London an Accident happens, he is to use all possible Expedition in repairing the Coach, and if it cannot be done in an Hour, or an Hour and a Half, as the circumstances of that particular Road will allow, the Guard must take Chaise to forward the Mail.

Guards are to permit Mail Coach Contractors or Postmasters to examine their Mail Box, and see their Time-Bill.

It is a Guard's Duty to report if Horses are unfit for the service; if the Harness and reins are bad.

It is a Guard's Duty always to have a Bag if Tools complete; and every Week, when they go to receive their Wages, the Postmaster has Orders to examine their Fire Arms, to see if they are perfectly clean—Barrel, Lock, and every Part—that they have a Blunderbuss and Case, a Pair of Pistols and Holsters, a Powder Horn, Bullet Mould, Screw-Driver, Touch Hole Picker, and Lock for the Mail Box—likewise a Wrench, Cord, Chain, and Wheel Clips, Shackle Perch Bolt, Drift Pins, Nails, Worms, and Screws. And also a double or long spreading Bar; and if they do not produce all and every the above Articles clean, and in the most perfect Repair, they will not be paid—and the Postmaster will report such Negligence to this Office.

In case of any Accident that occasions the Coach to be stopped in its Progress, it must be the Guard's Duty to see that the Contractors provide Horses for removing it to its proper Place as soon as possible; or, in case of the Contractor's Refusal, the Guards are to get Horses elsewhere, and send an immediate Account of the same to this Office.

The Mail Box, which in Mr Vidler's Patent Coaches is calculated for the Reception of Letter Bags, and such Things only as relate to the Conveyance of the Mail, must be confined entirely to that Use, and neither Packets, Parcels, Luggage, or any other description of Thing whatever, must be put therein, nor any sort of Luggage, or Incumbrances of any Kind to be placed upon the roof or carried on the outside of the Coach, under any Pretence or Necessity whatever. Nor must any Person, of any Description whatever, be suffered to ride with the Guard upon the Mail Box, unless in order to further some necessary Business belonging to the Service; an Authority to justify the same is issued from this Office, with the Office Seal attached to it.

It is likewise the Guard's Duty constantly to examine the Condition and State of the Mail Coaches, particularly of such spare Coach or Coaches as stand upon any Part of the Ground they work, and to see they are properly cleaned and taken Care of; and to report any Deficiencies or Imperfections in them; and each Guard is to be accountable for whatever Damage the Coaches may sustain that are under his Care, and also for the Loss of all Seats, Lamps, Blinds, Poles, Windows, or articles of any Kind; and the Guards are in all cases to obey such Orders, relating to the said Carriages, as may at any Time be given to them by Mr Vidler, or by any Person he may appoint or employ for that Purpose; and to obey the Superintendant, Deputy Superintendants or Assistants in regulating every Part of the Duty.

If at any time the Coaches are not provided with the Best Lamps and Lights, the guards must report the same.

They must never leave the Mail-Box unlocked when the Mail is therein, or take their Lock off where the Guards are changed, till the succeeding Guard has put his Lock thereon.

By Command of the Postmaster General,

Thomas Hasker
Surveyor and Superintendant of Mails.

I do hereby engage to conform to the foregoing regulations, and all such orders as may hereafter be delivered to me, and faithfully to discharge the duties of Mail Guard, or in all cases of failure submit to such forfeits, and other punishments, as the Surveyor and Superintendant, of his Deputy and Assistants, shall think proper to order. As Witness by this hand day of One Thousand Eight Hundred and...

Witness

THE OATH

I do swear, that I will not wittingly, willingly, or knowingly, open, detain, or delay, or cause, procure, permit, or suffer to be opened, detained or delayed any letter or letters, packet or packets, bag or bags, mail or mails which shall come into my hands, power or custody by reason of my employment as Mail Guard- And that I will not embezzle any letter or letters, packet or packets, bag or bags, mail or mails as aforesaid – and that I will not stop to deliver any letter or letters on the road, except ordered so to do by the Postmaster, or by a superior officer, under the Postmaster General; such letters being given by him or them for that purpose – And I will never take up in any Post – Town, nor on the road, any letter or letters but such as I may and shall put into the next post office I shall pass by- And I do in all points swear truly and faithfully to perform my duty to the best of my ability, according to my instructions signed and directions which may be from time to time given.

Sworn before me on the Day of...181

No Person employed by, or acting under his Majesty's Postmaster General can be duly authorised to act until he has taken the oath required before a Justice of the Peace for the County or place where he resides.

(This oath need not be on stamped paper)

The...is requested to set down underneath the birth place age height complexion and general description of... person whether he is single or married whether he is thin middle sized lusty(?) and if he wears his hair and colour of it.

The above...was born at...
In the parish of...
Is about...years of age,...feet...inches high, inclining to be...
Complexion, He is a...man, by profession a...was recommended by
And commenced Mail Guard the...of...181

(Post 30/9)

There is another version which differs slightly in the detail.

V

INSTRUCTIONS FOR THE MAIL GUARDS 1829

This copy is dated 1829 in ink (Post 10/6)

General Post Office

London
Instructions For Mail Guards

1.) The guard is intrusted (sic) with the care of the Letter Bags, and he is answerable at his Peril for the safety, safe conduct of them sealed.

2.) He is not to quit or desert the Mail or Bags of Letters, or suffer any loitering or unnecessary stopping at Public Houses, or other misspending of time, upon the Road, or neglect to give information of such misconduct on the part of the Coachman; if he does, he will be liable to be taken before a Justice of the Peace, and committed to hard labour and imprisonment for One Month, and he is subject to all other Punishments and Penalties which the laws (as specified in the several Acts of Parliament relative to the Post Office) have hitherto inflicted upon Post Riders who have neglected their Duty.

3.) If in Post Towns, he, on any account, collects or delivers Letters or Packets, or does so upon the Road, (except in some particular cases where the Postmasters of the District or Superior Officers are authorised to order it) he will be liable to an Information before a Justice of the Peace, and to the payment of Ten Shillings for every Letter; agreeable to an Act of Parliament passed in the First Year of the Reign of His Majesty George the Third, and will be dismissed the Service.

4.) The Guard is to behave with civility to Passengers, to assist the Coachman on any occasions that are consistent with his Situation as Protector of the Mails, and do not take him out of sight of the Place where they are deposited.

5.) He is on no account whatever to give up his Station to another Person. He is to take care that his Fire Arms are kept in clean and good Condition: that they are always properly loaded and primed when on duty, and on no account whatever to be wantonly discharging his Blunderbuss or Pistol as the carriage is going along the Road or through a Town; for every such Offence he forfeits Two Guineas, agreeable to an Act of Parliament; he is also to draw the charge of them as soon as he has ended his Journey.

6.) He is to sound his Horn as a Signal for Carriages to turn out of the Way upon the approach of the Mail Coach; also to warn Turnpike-men of its coming, that no unnecessary Delay may be occasioned, and likewise to prepare Postmasters against its coming, and Horse-keepers to bring out their Horses at each of the changing Places; and he is to sound it always as a Signal to Passengers when the time is expired that is allowed in the Time Bill for their stopping to refresh, and to use his utmost Exertions to prevent a Delay in all Cases whatever.

7.) It is the Guard's Duty to see the Time Bill is justly dated and signed at every Place, and where he cannot secure the Postmaster's Date and Signature to do it correctly himself, to insert the number of Passengers travelling by the Coach, for which a space is provided and to deliver it carefully to the Guard who succeeds him at the end of his journey, or to the Postmaster at the Place where the route of the Mail Coach ends.

8.) He must be very careful of the Time Piece and Time Bill, and if either should at any time be broken, torn, or lost immediate notice must be given to the Office or the cause communicated to the Postmaster of the nearest Place that he may report the same.

9.) Guards will be suspended and otherwise punished, who neglect to deliver the Bye Bags properly, which for want of better attention have been frequently carried beyond their Distance, and sometimes even brought up to London.

10.) Drunkenness or Disobedience of Official Orders will be punished with Dismission. The Guard is to prevent if possible any more passengers being conveyed than the Contractor allows and if the Guard neglect to give immediate notice of any violation of the Article, with an Account of the Parties who are accessory to it, it will be considered as a very Material Breach of his Duty, and he will be punished immediately.

11.) It is a very necessary Part of his Duty to report the earliest Intelligence of all Accidents, Delays, or Obstructions, of Inattention or want of readiness in Horse-Keepers, of Misconduct in any of the Parties concerned in the Performance of the Duty, and of all Occurrences whatever, that have a tendency to impede the progress of the Mail Coach, or may in any respect be proper to be communicated. He will, if a Mail Coach breaks down, describe what particular Part broke on his Bill, and the very next day, as soon as possible, by Letter give information how it happened, and what Damage was done.

12.) If the Mail Coach breaks down on its way to London, and it cannot be repaired in Half an Hour, or in such time that the mail may arrive at the Post Office by its proper time, the Guard is to ride on with it by Horse or Chaise; The Postmasters and Contractors have directions to furnish such Chaise or Horse which the Postmaster-General will pay for the use of. The Guards must do all his business at the different offices, and his Road Business, and take Care that he perform his Journey in the same time as if the Coach travelled.

13.) If the Coach should fail between Stage and Stage, the Guard is to press one of the Mail Coach Horses and ride on to the next Stage with it.

14.) If in travelling from London an Accident happens, he is to use all possible Expedition in repairing the Coach and if it cannot be done in an Hour or an Hour and a Half, as the circumstances of that particular Road will show the Guard must take Chaise to forward the Mail.

15.) The Guards are on no account to carry Parcels, whether for private use or for Sale; and are to permit Mail Contractors of Postmasters to examine their Mail box, and see their time Bill.

16.) It is a Guard's Duty to report if Horses are unfit for the Service; if the Harness and Reins are bad.

17.) It is Guard's duty always to have a Bag of Tools complete; and every Week when they go to receive their wages the Postmaster has orders to examine their FireArms, to see if they are perfectly clean – Barrel, Lock, and every part, Mould, Touch-Hole Picker, and Lock for the Mail Box – likewise the several Articles enumerated in the Margin; and also a double or long spreading Bar; and if they do not produce them clean and in the most perfect repair they will not be paid and the Postmaster will report such Negligence to this Office.*

18.) In case of any Accident that occasion the Coach to be stopped in its Progress it must be the Guard's Duty to see that the Contractors provide Horses for removing it to its proper Place as soon as possible; or in case of the Contractors refusal, the Guards are to get Horses elsewhere, and send an immediate Account of the same to this Office.

19.) The Mail Box which in the regular Coaches is calculated for the reception of Letter Bags, and such things only as relate to the Conveyance of the Mail, must be confined entirely to that use, and neither Packets, Parcels, Luggage of any other Description of thing whatever, must be put therein.

20.) No luggage can be allowed on the Roof which interferes with the proper packing and safety of any Sacks of Letters which the mails are obliged to carry there. No luggage to be placed on the Roof till after the Boot is full and then only that which belongs to Passengers. No more than three articles, being Portmanteaus or Carpet Bags, are, on any pretence, to be allowed, whether they be large or small; and the largest portmanteau not to exceed 2 feet 4 inches in length, and 1 foot 6 inches in height (70cm by 45cm). They are never to be placed on each other. By Portmanteau is meant, any article made of or covered with Leather or Hair, and of course all Boxes of other materials, Bundles, Baskets, & c are to be rejected. The Portmanteaus are to be fastened at one end to the seat Irons, and a Staple will be placed on each side of the coach, for one strap to go over and further to secure them.

21.) The Guards are never to allow an Extra Person to be put inside, except with the full consent of all the other Passengers. Nor must any Person, of any description whatever, not being an Inspector of the Mail Coach Department be suffered to ride with the Guard upon the Mail Box, unless, in order to further some necessary business belonging to the Service, an authority to justify the same is issued from this Office with the Office Seal affixed to it.

22.) It is likewise the Guard's Duty constantly to examine the condition and state of the Mail Coaches, particularly of such spare Coach or Coaches as stand upon any part of the Ground they work, and to see that they are properly cleaned and taken care of; and to report any deficiencies or imperfections in them; and each Guard is to be accountable for whatever Damage the Coaches may sustain that are under his care, and also for the loss of all Seats, Lamps Windows, or articles of any kind.

23.) If at any time the coaches are not provided with the best Lamps and Lights, the Guards must report the same.

24.) They must never leave their Mail Box unlocked with the Mails therein, or take their Lock off where the Guards are changed, till the succeeding Guard has put his Lock thereon.

By Command of the Postmaster General

Charles Johnson
Surveyor and Superintendent

Printed by J. Hartnell, Wine Office Court, Fleet Street, for His Majesty's Stationery Office.

2 Trace chains	1 Drift pin	Worms
1 Pole chain	1 Large spike bit	Screws
2 Tug chains	2 Gimlets	Nails
1 Hatchet	1 Main bar	Cord
1 Strong hammer	Shackles	
1 Wrench hammer	Bolts	
1 Small wrench	Clips	
1 Small saw	Nuts	

This list is undated but must be *c.*1835. (Post 10/35)

Necessary qualifications For Mail guards

To ensure the well being of the Service it is essential guards should be able bodied men of robust constitutions capable of undergoing great fatigue and should stand five feet six inches high; it is desirable also that they should be accustomed to horses and carriages.

They must be able to read and write plainly (underlined in ink)

A candidate for the appointment must be under thirty years of age and fully possess the above qualifications, he must be furnished with a satisfactory character from his last employer, if he has been in a situation, otherwise from some respectable person to whom he has been known for the previous year, experience has proved this to be necessary as a party recommending a man for the appointment may have a knowledge only of his general character from others, and consequently in the absence of a particular knowledge an improper man might get into the service

The candidate must obtain two housekeepers to be bound for him, the penalty of the bond is £50

On his appointment and arrival at the office he should be in possession of £5, as there will be an outlay necessary of upwards of £4 for the articles detailed below

Geo. Louis
Superintendent

	£	s	d
Bond	1	18	6
Oath of office		1	0
Box and tools	1	7	0
Locks		2	0
Bars		10	0
Lamp		3	8
	4	2	2

VI

SPECIFICATIONS OF ROYAL MAIL COACHES
FROM GENERAL POST OFFICE STATEMENTS

Relative to Edinburgh correspondence (Post 10/109)

This document is undated and offers no real guidance as to provenance apart from the fact that it is associated with material of the 1830s:

Inside

Lining drab lace with double crimson stripes

Carpet at the bottom of the door to match the cloth

Ceiling to be of panted canvas colour like the cloth

Mahogany Glass frames containing only one square of glass each best crown glass

Lined lace shades for glass frames

Leather straps for hat sling

Best horse hair stuffing, stuffing at the front of edge of fronts of seat cushions

Bottom of the coach oilcloth

Two pockets one on each door

At back do at elbows

Dimensions

Bottom to top of rocker 5in

From top of rocker to top of inside seat without cushions 8 ¾ in

From top of seat to roof with lining in 42 ½ in

Width of front inside seat taken beside from pillar to pillar 41 in

Width leg room between inside seat from ridge to top of each 18 ½ in

To be as ample as Mr Wrights for room under the seat

Width of ditto across at the shoulder 43 ½ in

Length of body inside at top of seat under cushion 54 in

Length of ceiling inside 57 in

Width of glass frame 17 ¾ in

Height of ditto 18 in

Glass 13 ¾ high 14 1/3 wide

Opening when window is down 16 ¾ wide 18 in high

Width of back seat at bottom just above seat 38 in

 Do of do independent of cushions 18 in

 Do of door way at the rabbit 21 in

Do between the rockers inside 34 ⅜ in

Do of rocker from outside to 4 ¾ in

Outside

Front boot

Width of coach seat irons 14 ½ in

Height of do   do   11 ¾ in

Top of cushion to top of rail 5 ½ in

Length of coach seat between the irons 43 ¼ in

Length of foot board 40 in

Width of foot board 19 ¾ in

Width in front 36 ½ in

Mouth of boot 16(?) in

BIBLIOGRAPHY

Anderson, R.C. and J.M., *Quicksilver* (Newton Abbot, 1975)

Anon, *Britain's Postal Heritage* (Bath Postal Museum, 2003)

Anon, *A Collection of the Statutes Relating to the Post Office* (London, 1793)

Anon, *Old Coaching Days and the White Horse Cellar, Piccadilly* (London, nd)

Austen, Brian, *English Provincial Posts* (London, 1978)

Bateman, J., *The General Turnpike Road Act* (London, 1823)

Bates, Allen, *Directory of Stagecoach Services 1836* (David and Charles Newton Abbot, edit 1969)

Beale, Philip, *A History of the Post in England from Romans to Stuarts* (Aldershot, c.1998)

Bird, Anthony, *Roads and Vehicles* (London, 1969)

Blackmore, H.L., *A Dictionary of London Gunmakers 1358-1850* (Oxford, 1986)

Body, Geoffrey and Gallop, Roy, *The Coaching Era* (Fiducia Press, 2003)

Bowles, Carrington, *Post Chaise Companion* (2nd edition 2 vols, 1782)

Boyce, Benjamin, *The Benevolent Man, A life of Ralph Allen of Bath* (Cambridge, Mass., 1967)

Clear, Charles, *John Palmer, Mail Coach Pioneer* (London, 1955)

Copeland, John, *Roads and Their Traffic 1750-1850* (Newton Abbott, 1968)

Corbett, Edward, *An Old Coachman's Chatter with some practical remarks on driving* (London, 1890)

Davis, Sally, *John Palmer and the Mailcoach Era* (Bath, 1964)

Ellis, Kenneth, *The Post Office in the Eighteenth Century* (OUP, London, 1958)

Foxell, J. and Spafford. A., *Monarchs of all they surveyed* (London, 1952)

Hanson, Harry, *The Coaching Life Manchester* (1983)

Harlow, Alvin, *Old Post Bags* (New York and London, 1928)

Harper, C.G., *Stagecoach and Mail Coach days of yore* (2 vols, 1903)

Hartmann, Cyril Hughes, *The Story of the Roads* (London, 1927)

Haworth, Capt. M.E., *Road Scrapings* (London, 1882)

Hindley, Geoffrey, *A History of Roads* (London, 1971)

Hughes, P. and Larkin, J., *Tudor Royal Proclamations* (3 vols, London, 1969)

Jepson, Stanley, *The Coach Horse* (London, 1977)

Joyce, Herbert, *The History of the Post Office from its establishment down to 1836* (Richard Bentley & Son, London, 1893)

Kay, George, *Royal Mail* (Rockliff, London, 1951)

Lane, Charles, *Cooper Henderson on the Open Road* (London, 1984)

Laver, Jane (Ed.), *The Regency Road: The Coaching Prints of James Pollard* (Selway, 1957)

Lewins, William, *Her Majesty's Mail: A History of the Post-Office* (London, 1865)

Malet, Capt., *Annals of the Road* (London, 1876)

Marshall, Dendy, *The British Post Office from its Beginnings to the End of 1925* (London, 1926)

Margetson, Stella, *Journey by Stages* (London, 1967)

McAdam, John Loudon, *Remarks on the Present System of Road Making* (London, 1823)

Mountfield, David, *Stage and Mail Coaches* (Shire Publications Princes Risborough, 2003)

Mountford, David, *The Coaching Age* (London, 1976)

Mogg, Edward, *Patersons Roads* (18th edition. London, 1826)

Nimrod, *The Road* ((Murray's Reading for the Rail) London, 1851)

Parnell, Sir Henry, *A Treastise on Roads* (London, 1838)

Perry, C.R, *The Victorian Post Office, Woodbridge* (1992)

Phillips, Daphne, *The Great Road to Bath* (Newbury, 1983)

Pitt Lennox, Lord William, *Coaching with anecdotes of the road* (London, 1876)

Richardson, Clive, *The Hackney* (London, 1995)

Robertson, Alan W., *Great Britain's Post Roads, Post Towns and Postal Rates 1635-1839* (1961)

Sherrington, C.E.R., *A Hundred Year of Inland Transport* (London, 1934)

Sparkes, Ivan, *Stagecoaches & carriages* (Spurbooks Ltd., Bourne End, 1976)

Strong, L.A., *The Rolling Road* (1956)

Stray, Julian, *Moving the Mail by Road* (London, 2006)

Thrupp, G.A., *The History of Coaches* (Kerby & Endean, London, 1877)

Tombs, R.C., *The King's Post* (Bristol, 1905)

Tombs, R.C., *The Bristol Royal Mail* (Bristol, nd)

Vale, Edmund, *The Mail Coach Men* (London, 1960)

Williams, David *The Rebecca Riots* (Cardiff, 1955)

Wilson, Harold S., *The Travelling Post Offices of Great Britain and Ireland* (Derby, 1996)

Wilson Hyde, J., *The Royal Mail* (London, 1889)

INDEX

Abehurch Lane 144, 146, 156

Accidents 8, 41, 66, 68, 97, 99, 100, 101, 104, 106, 113, 123, 132, 154, 162, 168, 171, 172, 174, 175, 181, 186, 188, 204, 207, 209, 211, 204, 207, 209, 211, 222, 223, 228, 233, 237, 245, 274, 275, 278

Allen, Philip 28, 35, 43

Allen Ralph 9, 22, 23, 24, 25

Bath 6, 23, 24, 25, 26, 27, 29, 30, 34, 35, 37, 38, 43, 54, 65, 67, 68, 70, 75, 119, 127, 137, 162, 159, 165, 172, 173, 175, 178, 203, 210, 226, 240

Birmingham 30, 67, 96, 119, 120, 135, 202, 236, 237, 238, 239, 241

Black Book 42, 78, 153, 239

Blunderbuss 28, 30, 46, 93, 95, 96, 98, 99, 100, 101, 102, 103, 104, 105, 106, 107, 108, 112, 113, 114, 115, 129, 131, 140, 143, 169

Bonnor, Charles 43, 44, 45, 49, 50, 51, 52, 53, 93, 124, 148, 187, 192, 202, 205, 206, 207, 208, 209, 216, 219, 221

Bow Street 59, 150, 173, 191

Bridge 164, 168, 172, 178, 179, 181, 183, 185, 187, 189, 191

Broadrib, William 109, 110, 111, 263

Bullet 116

Bye Post 18, 24, 25, 41, 76, 144, 202, 272, 274, 278

Candles 43, 147, 250

Carey, mapmaker 151, 180, 198, 199

Cases for firearms 95, 96, 112, 113

Chester 14, 17, 54, 30, 38, 57, 61, 69, 71, 73, 75, 82, 103, 131, 136, 137, 158, 164, 165, 168, 174, 243, 258

Coach 6, 8, 9, 23, 24, 26, 27, 28, 30, 34, 35, 36, 37, 38, 42, 43, 44, 46, 53, 55, 60, 61, 63, 64, 65, 66, 67, 68, 70, 71, 74, 75, 77, 78, 81, 82, 83, 84, 87, 88, 89, 92, 95, 100, 104, 106, 113, 114, 117, 118, 121, 122, 124, 125, 127, 130, 131, 136, 137, 139, 140-46, 148-178, 180, 183, 185-249, 251, 254, 257, 258, 259, 260, 263, 264, 266, 270, 271, 272, 274, 275, 277, 278, 279, 280, 281

Coach house 170, 207, 208, 231

Coat-of-arms 237

Deputy Postmasters 7, 17, 18, 25, 26, 42, 43, 45, 49, 51, 71, 75, 77, 86, 87, 96, 104, 123, 131, 141, 150, 154, 159, 164, 165, 167, 192, 193, 194, 196, 257, 272, 276

Dover 16, 17, 18, 38, 39, 47, 65, 69, 82, 89, 107, 117, 120, 160, 210, 221, 223, 243, 258

Drivers 7, 8, 34, 36, 37, 62, 63, 66, 68, 77, 103, 104, 105, 122, 123, 143, 153, 154, 155, 156, 164, 165, 166, 167, 168, 170, 171, 172,

173, 175, 176, 185, 186, 187, 188, 199, 202, 203, 207, 210, 211, 222, 223, 225, 227, 229, 240, 241, 244, 274

Dover 16, 17, 18, 38, 39, 47, 65, 69, 82, 89, 107, 117, 120, 160, 210, 221, 223, 243, 258

Drivers 7, 8, 34, 36, 37, 62, 63, 66, 68, 77, 103, 104, 105, 122, 123, 143, 153, 154, 155, 154, 155, 156, 164, 165, 166, 167, 168, 170, 171, 172, 173, 175, 176, 185, 186, 187, 188, 199, 202, 203, 207, 210, 211, 222, 223, 225, 227, 229, 240, 241, 244, 274

Edinburgh 19, 32, 87, 88, 120, 165, 190, 226, 227, 238, 241, 243, 244, 252

Exeter 14, 19, 24, 30, 39, 67, 74, 79, 82, 87, 96, 118, 120, 121, 168, 172, 174, 175, 233, 232, 240, 243, 249, 250, 258

Fagan guard 156, 157, 158

Fire 48, 80, 145, 147, 168, 218, 235, 237

Firearms 30, 45, 48, 63, 76, 77, 78, 88, 92, 93, 94, 95, 96, 97, 98, 99, 101, 102, 104, 105, 106, 107, 108, 109, 111, 112, 113, 114, 115, 116, 118, 121, 131, 132, 133, 134, 139, 142, 156, 174, 176, 260, 278

Fog 168, 228, 229

Freeling, Francis 8, 9, 42, 43, 50, 51, 53, 54, 61, 67, 68, 71, 73, 79, 80, 81, 88, 94, 96, 97, 100, 103, 106, 107, 111, 125, 132, 133, 134, 135, 136, 138, 139, 142, 144, 149, 150, 154, 161, 163, 166, 170, 172, 175, 176, 185, 191, 197, 199, 209, 210, 212, 224, 231, 244, 258, 270

Gallows 56, 151

Glasgow 161, 162, 226, 232, 242

Guard 7, 9, 28, 29, 30, 34, 35, 36, 37, 38, 41, 42, 45, 46, 48, 60, 63, 64, 65, 66, 67, 68, 69, 70, 72-88, 90-94, 96, 97, 98, 99, 100, 101, 103, 105-118, 121-127, 129, 131, 132, 133, 136, 137, 139, 140-143, 151, 153-164, 166-177, 185-189, 193, 194, 197, 201, 202, 206, 209, 211, 215, 218, 221-223, 225, 227, 229, 230, 232, 236-239, 241-243, 246, 247, 257, 258, 271-274, 276

Harding, gunmaker 97, 102-105, 108, 110,

114, 115, 116, 126, 139, 140, 142, 246, 247, 248, 259

Harness 143, 153, 154, 156, 164, 168, 171, 200, 206, 222, 223, 241, 257, 275, 278

Hasker, Thomas 41, 42, 49, 54, 58, 66, 67, 68, 70, 71, 73, 74, 76, 77, 78, 79, 80, 81, 83, 88, 90, 94, 95, 97, 99, 104-111, 117, 121, 122, 123, 125, 126, 128, 131, 137, 144, 150, 152-162, 164, 166, 167, 168, 170, 171, 175, 184, 188, 194, 198, 199, 201, 204, 211, 215, 216, 218-223, 232, 244, 248, 259, 275

Hats 86, 126, 127, 128, 143, 163, 209, 241, 257

Holsters 95, 98, 106, 112, 113, 114, 132, 133, 135, 141, 142, 143, 275

Horn 17, 69, 94, 95, 96, 97, 106, 107, 113, 121, 122, 123, 124, 129, 142, 146, 155, 161, 162, 170, 172, 175, 186, 187, 277

Horses 8, 13, 14-19, 25, 26, 29, 31, 37, 60, 66, 75, 76, 83, 104, 123, 133, 135, 143, 152, 153, 155, 160, 163, 164, 167-174, 178, 185, 187, 188, 200, 201, 204, 209, 211, 216, 217, 219, 219, 222, 223, 226, 227, 228, 229, 231, 234, 235, 238, 240, 241, 257, 258, 274, 275, 277, 278, 279

Ireland 18, 19, 58, 88, 100, 101, 129, 143, 178, 189, 191, 200, 242, 271, 273

Lad Lane, London 38, 60, 210

Leeds 38, 75, 80, 81, 82, 98, 120, 143, 146, 165, 176, 191, 212

Lincolns Inn Field, London 82

Liverpool 27, 30, 38, 45, 62, 75, 78, 82, 83, 121, 131, 137, 158, 161, 162, 167, 197, 206, 236-239

Lombard Street 16, 22, 44, 49, 52, 53, 61, 93, 137, 144, 147, 148, 149, 151, 152, 153, 156, 157, 158, 160, 166, 177, 196, 250, 257, 260, 270

London 8, 9, 14-18, 20, 22, 24-27, 29-34, 38, 42, 47, 56, 57, 61, 65, 70, 79, 80, 81, 82, 83, 97, 103, 109, 117, 121, 123, 136, 148, 149, 150, 165, 174, 175, 178, 202, 207, 217, 218, 228, 232, 236, 238

Louis, George 75, 82, 87, 100, 101, 103, 170, 171, 183, 223, 224, 231, 237, 241, 257, 272, 280

Manchester 38, 67, 75, 78, 82, 83, 87, 120,
126, 131, 161, 164, 173, 174, 188, 212, 235,
236, 237, 243, 244
Maps 9, 151, 180, 198, 199
Macadam, John 190, 191
Mortimer, gunmakers 93, 95, 96, 97, 102–
105, 108, 114, 126, 139, 246, 248, 250, 251

Newspapers 8, 34, 36, 38, 39, 56, 57, 72, 92,
123, 201, 203
Nobbs, Moses 72, 91, 122, 131, 233, 258

Overturns 68, 104, 117, 122, 123, 168, 170–
174, 185, 203, 204, 207, 212, 216, 222
Oxford 20, 24, 30, 80, 90, 103, 165, 257, 258

Palmer, John 8, 22, 24, 26, 27, 28, 34, 35, 36,
38–54, 62, 63, 64, 68, 80, 83, 85, 86, 87, 88,
92–95, 103, 105, 131, 178, 192, 193, 201,
204, 206–210, 218, 219, 220, 221, 244, 254,
268, 270
Parcels 20, 30, 61, 62, 78, 167, 201, 206, 207,
239, 274
Parker, William 140, 141
Pike, James 111, 112, 129, 158, 174
Pistols 30, 46, 93, 95, 96, 98, 99, 102, 103,
104, 105, 108, 112–117, 128, 129, 132–136,
138–143, 176, 233, 246, 247, 252, 258, 274,
275
Police 59, 64, 91, 140, 158, 243, 263
Portmanteau 61, 142, 150–153, 174, 278, 279
Postmaster General 7, 8, 10, 19, 24, 25, 35,
39–43, 45–53, 58, 60, 64, 66–71, 73, 74,
75, 80, 81, 83–86, 88–90, 94–97, 100, 101,
104–107, 109, 111, 117, 119, 120, 123, 124,
126, 131–139, 143–146, 150, 152, 153, 155,
158–161, 167, 168, 170, 171, 172, 176, 185,
188, 192–195, 197, 198, 206, 208–211, 214,
219, 220, 221, 224, 226, 227, 228, 229,
236, 237, 239, 241, 268, 270, 274, 276, 278
Prisoners of war 175, 189, 212
Procession, coaches 82, 83, 122, 125–128,
257

Railways 9, 65, 78, 89, 90, 91, 99, 119, 126,
128, 177, 180, 191, 197, 199, 228, 229, 230,
234–244, 258

Rebecca Riots 186, 283
Reins 53, 67, 79, 111, 131, 153, 156, 164, 171,
175, 176, 210, 214, 222, 223, 275
Rewards 20, 54, 56, 59, 130, 185
Roads 8, 13, 14, 18, 26, 28, 31, 34, 41, 56,
63, 65, 76, 88, 117, 130, 138, 142, 168, 172,
173, 178, 179, 181, 182, 184–187, 189, 190,
192, 199, 200, 203, 206, 209, 211, 216, 218,
219, 223, 226, 242, 273
Robbery 29, 30, 56, 57, 58, 61, 74, 117, 130,
131, 132, 137, 138, 152, 153, 158, 186, 243
Rose, George 41, 43, 64, 81, 270

Scotland 18, 19, 43, 50, 71, 129, 135, 178,
185, 190, 191, 229, 230, 241
Stagecoach 26, 36, 61, 62, 65, 68, 93, 113,
127, 154, 155, 180, 187, 200, 201, 202, 203,
207, 215, 222, 230, 239, 240
Stephenson, George 235, 236
St Martin's-le-Grand 82, 112, 122, 145, 148,
149, 157, 166, 217, 241, 257
Surveyors 8, 25, 27, 28, 34, 37, 40, 42, 46,
101, 102, 110, 132, 134, 135, 137, 139, 182,
187, 192, 193, 194, 196, 197, 198, 244, 270,
272
Swords 39, 140, 141, 283

Telford, Thomas 46, 190, 191
Tenders 125, 223, 224–227, 229, 240
Tipstaff 116
Todd, Anthony 26, 32, 42, 44, 45, 62, 92,
144, 146, 192, 211, 249
Tolls 30, 33, 146, 159, 184, 185
Trevethick, Richard 234, 235
Truncheons 116
Turnpikes 30, 73, 123, 163, 164, 174, 180,
183, 184, 185, 186, 190, 191, 192, 211, 274,
277

Uniform, guards 42, 67, 82–85, 87, 93, 124,
126, 127, 128, 132, 133, 143, 155, 185, 194,
203, 225, 241, 257, 259, 262, 269

Vidler, coachmaker 50, 82, 83, 95, 153, 203,
205, 208–213, 215, 216, 217, 219, 220, 221,
223, 224, 226, 275

Wade, General 23, 178

Wales 25, 87, 102, 103, 186, 190, 191, 199,
    235, 270

Warrants 14, 40, 43, 47, 48, 52, 83-86, 115,
    118, 270

Wheels 14, 112, 142, 164, 170, 171, 182, 184,
    186, 188, 190, 196, 198, 200, 202, 204, 218,
    222, 228, 230, 234, 235, 242, 266, 274

Whips 131, 156, 210, 257, 258

If you are interested in purchasing other books published by Tempus,
or in case you have difficulty finding any Tempus books in your local bookshop,
you can also place orders directly through our website

www.tempus-publishing.com